THE IMPACT OF INSTITUTIONS AND PROFESSIONS ON LEGAL DEVELOPMENT

Legal professions and legal institutions have a profound influence on the direction and form of legal change, but it is often difficult to identify exactly how and why such influence has been exerted. Even those individuals directly involved in bringing about changes may not realise the full impact of professional and institutional factors, since these factors often form part of the participants' own assumed roles.

This collection of essays casts light on how one particularly important legal category, fault liability, has been shaped by legal professions and institutions between 1850 and 2000. Its unique comparative approach highlights how different legal systems generate very different pressures for change, and how actors' perceptions of their own roles can have a profound effect on how changes take effect.

PAUL MITCHELL is Professor of Laws at University College London. He has published widely on the historical development of the common law of obligations.

COMPARATIVE STUDIES IN THE DEVELOPMENT OF THE LAW OF TORTS IN EUROPE

Series Editors
John Bell and David Ibbetson

THE IMPACT OF INSTITUTIONS AND PROFESSIONS ON LEGAL DEVELOPMENT

VOLUME 8

Edited by

PAUL MITCHELL

CAMBRIDGE
UNIVERSITY PRESS

CAMBRIDGE
UNIVERSITY PRESS

University Printing House, Cambridge CB2 8BS, United Kingdom

Cambridge University Press is part of the University of Cambridge.

It furthers the University's mission by disseminating knowledge in the pursuit of education, learning and research at the highest international levels of excellence.

www.cambridge.org
Information on this title: www.cambridge.org/9781107023116

First published 2012
First paperback edition 2014

A catalogue record for this publication is available from the British Library

Library of Congress Cataloguing in Publication data
The impact of institutions and professions on legal development / Paul Mitchell.
p. cm. – (Comparative studies in the development of the law of torts in Europe ; v. 8)
Includes bibliographical references and index.
ISBN 978-1-107-01900-3 (hardback)
1. Torts–Europe–Interpretation and construction. I. Mitchell, Paul, 1972–
KJC1640.I47 2012
346.403–dc23
2012003082

ISBN 978-1-107-01900-3 Hardback
ISBN 978-1-107-47561-8 Paperback

Hardback only available as
ISBN 978-1-107-02311-6 3-volume set

CONTENTS

List of contributors *page* vii
Series Editors' preface ix
Editor's preface xi

1 Introduction 1
PAUL MITCHELL

2 The impact of institutions and professions on fault liability in England 14
PAUL MITCHELL

3 The impact of institutions and professions on compensation for occupational injury in England 36
PETER BARTRIP

4 The impact of institutions and professions in Scotland 59
ELSPETH REID

5 The impact of institutions and professions in France 89
PAULA GILIKER

6 The impact of institutions and professions in Germany 114
JENS M. SCHERPE

7 The impact of institutions and professions in the Netherlands 142
ESTHER ENGELHARD AND IVO GIESEN

8 The impact of institutions and professions in Spain 169
ISABEL GONZÁLEZ PACANOWSKA AND MARTIN GARCÍA-RIPOLL MONTIJANO

9 The impact of institutions and professions in Sweden 198
MÅRTEN SCHULTZ

Index 231

CONTRIBUTORS

PETER BARTRIP is an Associate Research Fellow at the Centre for Socio-Legal Studies, University of Oxford

ESTHER ENGELHARD is Senior Lecturer in Private Law, Utrecht University

MARTIN GARCÍA-RIPOLL MONTIJANO is Professor of Civil Law at the University of Murcia

IVO GIESEN is Professor of Private Law, Utrecht University

PAULA GILIKER is Professor of Comparative Law, University of Bristol

ISABEL GONZÁLEZ PACANOWSKA is Professor of Civil Law at the University of Murcia

PAUL MITCHELL is Professor of Laws, University College London

ELSPETH REID is Professor of Scottish Private Law at the University of Edinburgh

JENS M. SCHERPE is University Senior Lecturer in Law and Fellow of Gonville and Caius College, University of Cambridge

MÅRTEN SCHULTZ is Professor in Private Law, Stockholm University

SERIES EDITORS' PREFACE

The European Legal Development series has arisen from a project funded by the AHRC from January 2005 until February 2008.

The aim of the project as a whole was to examine the nature of legal development in western Europe since 1850, focussing sharply on liability for fault. Behind this there is a more abstract purpose, to attempt to cast some light on the factors that have influenced the way in which the law has changed over this period. Legal historians have looked at the general question, usually focussing on the rather facile distinction between the English common law and Continental European legal systems. Though rooted in the sources, these works have been marred by a somewhat unsophisticated methodology and an inevitably selective use of evidence. Comparative lawyers have developed far more sophisticated methodologies, but their theoretical perspectives have too often borne little relation to empirical data. Over the last 20 years, tort lawyers have looked at the same types of question; but their analysis has invariably been at a high level of generality and has rarely looked at the historical component. By bringing together experts with different disciplinary backgrounds – comparative lawyers and legal historians, all with an understanding of modern tort law in their own systems – and getting them to work collaboratively, we have aimed to produce a more nuanced comparative legal history, and one that is theoretically better informed.

The topic of legal development is broad and, to make it manageable, we have undertaken a programme of work that has built up from a number of case studies and has moved towards a more general analysis and conclusions. Although we have been concerned with the development of the law, and although many of those involved in the project have been lawyers, we have also been concerned to include and benefit from the insights of historians and scholars in other disciplines.

Liability for fault between 1850 to 2000 has been our major area of study. Around 1850, there were many similarities in approaches to liability for fault across the legal systems of western Europe. But since then, there has been significant divergence. Our method has been first to chart the changes and then to seek the explanations for what happened. Although there have been many changes in tort and delict laws over the period, the idea of liability for fault remains central to private law approaches to the compensation of victims of harms caused by the actions of others.

As a first stage, the project worked on six case studies that illustrate the general theme of liability for fault and its development within the period:

- Product Liability
- Legal Doctrine
- Medical Liability
- Relations between Neighbours
- Technological Change
- Traffic and Railways.

Each of the topics gave rise to a volume published by Cambridge University Press in 2010. This research involved scholars from a range of countries, in particular England and Scotland, Spain, the Netherlands, Germany, France, Sweden, Austria, and Italy. Each working group drew on the expertise of both senior and more junior scholars familiar with different European legal systems, and contained a mixture of comparative lawyers and legal historians.

A second stage has involved further groups examining a number of salient factors in legal development. The topics covered in this stage were:

- Social and Political Ideas
- Institutions and Professions
- The Economy (including the impact of insurance)
- A final strand to the work is an overview book.

This book, edited by Paul Mitchell, is the second of the second-stage reviews of factors that influence legal development. The impact of legal actors, especially legal professions, is often difficult to chart, and the multinational team he assembled undertook research that is not commonly undertaken in their own countries – looking for the connections between the judges and legal scholars and the development of the rules of law. We hope this will serve as a model for future research in those countries.

John Bell
David Ibbetson

EDITOR'S PREFACE

This volume of essays forms part of the fruits of the European Legal Development project, which investigated changes in fault liability in Europe from 1850 to 2000. The essays it contains, which were originally presented as papers in 2007, focus on the influence of legal institutions and the legal profession. Their primary purpose is to trace and analyse historical developments; they do not set out to give a comprehensive account of the current law in any of the jurisdictions that they discuss.

We gratefully acknowledge the help and support that we received from the project's directors, John Bell and David Ibbetson, and from the administrative team they assembled to facilitate the project as a whole. In relation to our part of the project, we would also like to thank Aniceto Masferrer and Ken Oliphant, for their commentaries on papers at the meetings of the group, and Matthew Dyson and Sandy Steele for their organisational and secretarial assistance.

1

Introduction

PAUL MITCHELL

I The scope and broad themes of the project

The chapters in this collection examine the influence of legal institutions and the legal profession on changes in European fault liability between 1850 and 2000. We took 'changes' in fault liability in a broad sense, looking not only at the elaboration of fault liability itself, but also at subtractions from the area of fault liability, particularly the creation of special schemes for workmen's compensation. The focus is on the roles of legislators, judges and legal scholars – we do not, for instance, explore the influence of advocates, legal advisers or lawyers' professional bodies.

Rather than covering each and every European country, we selected a range of jurisdictions that seemed most likely to yield fruitful comparisons. For each of these jurisdictions we addressed four broad questions. First, what were the distinctive traits of legal change in each jurisdiction? In answering this question we had particular regard to different legal traditions: the common law in England; the civil law in France, Germany, Spain and the Netherlands; and the distinct systems of Scotland and Sweden. Second, what methods were used to bring about those changes? Third, did the size of the jurisdiction affect the way in which changes took place? Fourth, why, given such differences of legal culture and size, was the movement towards a special scheme of workmen's compensation virtually simultaneous across Europe?

Answering these questions required an investigation of the legal culture of each jurisdiction. We were particularly interested in where the impetus for legal change came from, how ideas were shaped, and how they ultimately became part of the law. This involved examining the respective roles of legislators, judges, academics and law reform bodies, and how they interacted with each other. The efforts of these different participants in each system were clearly shaped by their understanding of what was appropriate to their role. But different members of the same group might have different understandings. And certainly there was no common understanding across the jurisdictions of what each role required. For instance, Hermann Kantorowicz, the great German scholar, is reported to have intervened in an earnest discussion between English academics about whether academic lawyers should contribute to law reform, to say that 'the whole discussion seemed strange to him. On the Continent it was considered essential …'.[1] Kantorowicz's sense of strangeness, his surprise that the scholar's role could be conceived of so differently, encapsulates the broad themes of our investigation: assumptions about one's role in the legal system are implicit, and often unarticulated; but these implicit assumptions colour and shape each participant's contribution. And it is only through comparative work, bringing out the contrasting cultural assumptions elsewhere, that the full effect of these assumptions can be understood.

II Legislators

The legislative influence on fault liability is, at first sight, straightforward. Since legislators make law, they can change what the law is (including the rules on fault liability) whenever they wish. To borrow Alan Watson's idea of a 'hierarchy of lawmakers', the legislator is at the top, and can do what it likes.[2]

But this straightforward account of legislation is misleading. Although there were significant periods of dictatorship, especially in Germany and Spain, from the 1870s elected Parliaments dominated the legislative process, and introduced a democratic element into it. A democratically elected legislator has to act within two obvious constraints: it has to secure parliamentary approval, and, since it is only elected for a limited period, it must prioritise its legislation. What can be got through the legislative process and what is most important are both questions of delicate political judgment, but one thing is clear: the reform of private law is not, in itself, a priority. Where major legal reforms of private law have taken place it is because they have engaged some wider social or political issue: the new Dutch Civil Code, for instance, was part of the effort to 'rebuild the nation' after the Second World War. A similar question of national pride could also be seen in the Scottish legislation on occupiers' liability, which restored the traditional Scottish approach and displaced an

1 A. McNair, 'Law Teaching and Law Reform' (1934) *Journal of the Society of Public Teachers of Law* 1, 9.

2 A. Watson, *The Evolution of Western Private Law* (Baltimore: Johns Hopkins University Press, 2001), p. 65.

English method that had been imposed judicially by the House of Lords. Sometimes technological novelty could move otherwise mundane matters of personal injury up the legislative agenda: the Prussian legislation on railways (1838) and the Swedish traffic liability scheme (1906, 1916) were anticipating, rather than responding to, a social problem. But such legislative prescience was not universal. The French automobile scheme (1985), by contrast, given the extraordinarily high accident rate in France, seems at least fifty years too late. Legislation on private law that does not engage with wider social or political issues is likely to be sporadic at best, unless there is a flow of politically uncontentious proposals that can be passed without requiring much legislative attention.

The most important instance of legislation engaging with social issues in our study relates to workmen's compensation. In each of our jurisdictions, in about 1900, an elaborate legislative scheme for workmen's compensation was enacted. As one might expect, there were certain motivating factors that were common to each jurisdiction: for instance, it was thought that requiring an injured workman to prove fault was too onerous, and that the injury to the workman should be regarded as part of the costs of the enterprise. In Catholic jurisdictions the idea of Christian duty was powerful. But other reasons were more surprising and highlighted some of the peculiarities of legislative change. In both Germany and the United Kingdom the scheme was introduced by Conservative Governments seeking political advantages: the German Conservatives hoped to confuse and divide their socialist opponents; the English Conservatives hoped to attract working-class voters who, with the Labour Party still in its infancy, had no natural political home. The Netherlands had a strong desire to keep up with its French and German neighbours. But perhaps the most striking motives for reform were to be found in Spain. There industrialisation had come late, and only a very small proportion of the workforce was engaged in industry. Workmen's compensation was not the pressing social problem that it was elsewhere. But the Spanish legislature regarded workmen's compensation legislation as a badge of modernity and forward thinking; it did not matter that only a very small number of people could benefit from it.

III Judges

The judicial contribution to legal change was extensive in each of the jurisdictions studied, although its form differed widely. The most overt approach was found in England and Scotland. There the discursive form of judgments, delivered by identifiable individuals, was an ideal vehicle for legal development. Furthermore, the English system's doctrine of precedent committed future subordinate courts to the same approach once a change had been judicially made. Difficult and finely balanced legal questions (which questions about legal change tend to be) could turn on the ideologies of the judges hearing the case.

The potential for English judges to effect change through their judgments was not entirely uncontroversial, even among the most senior judges themselves. But it was not contrary to any fundamental tenet of the English legal system: the common law was acknowledged to be a source of law, and it was the judges' job to find it. Sometimes judges' claims to have 'discovered' a previously overlooked rule or principle might require some suspension of disbelief on the part of the reader. But so long as lawmaking was presented as law finding there could be no formal objection that unelected judges were encroaching on the role of the elected legislature.

In Continental Europe, however, judicial creativity could not be so easily accommodated within the formal structure of the legal system. The French Civil Code, for instance, forbade judges from deciding cases 'by way of general and regulatory provisions' (art. 5). The spirit of this prohibition was reinforced by the popularity of the *école de l'exégèse*, which asserted that there was no place for judicial creativity in the interpretation of the Code's provisions. In the Netherlands, where the Civil Code had been imposed by the French in 1804, a similar approach flourished in the nineteenth century.

Respect for the formal limitations of the judge's role in the legal system was not, however, necessarily incompatible with judicial creativity in practice. In Germany, for instance, the arrival of the railways prompted several courts to impose strict liability on railway operators whilst simultaneously appearing to apply a test of fault. Thus, in one extreme instance, it was said to amount to fault to operate a locomotive at all. In France the courts maintained their formal position that the Civil Code was the only source of law for fault liability, but they interpreted its provisions so creatively that the Code became a 'mere framework'.[3] In the Netherlands a similar approach went further. The draftsman of the new Civil Code recognised the importance and necessary contribution of judicial lawmaking, and deliberately drafted some of the provisions in a way that facilitated judicial creativity. The result was that, whilst, at a formal level, the Code remained the source of law, its provisions amounted to no more than 'an elastic frame' for judicial elaboration.[4]

[3] P. Giliker, 'The impact of institutions and professions in France', this volume, p. 94.

[4] E. Engelhardt and I. Giesen, 'The impact of institutions and professions in the Netherlands', this volume, p. 143.

Ultimately, then, there was often little difference in result between the approaches of the English judiciary and their Continental counterparts. Paradoxically, it may even have been the case that, despite its formally more receptive attitude to judicial creativity, English legal development in the first half of the twentieth century was slightly more constrained than it was in Continental Europe. But what was, and remained, very different was the form of judgments. The discursive, individualistic approach of the common law was not mirrored in Europe: none of the appellate judges delivered separate judgments, and the courts' reasons tended to be brief, with the French and Spanish courts being especially laconic. This brevity and anonymity had its advantages – it had the potential for greater clarity than the common law system – but it also concealed judicial debates and discussions. As F. H. Lawson once put it, the French style of judgment gives 'only the results of the process' and omits the preparatory work.[5]

This brevity and anonymity of the judgments was often compounded by the absence of a tradition of extra-curial writing by judges, and made it difficult to get a sense of which Continental judges were driving forward the process of change in their jurisdictions. It seems extremely likely that, as in England, individual judges disagreed about such finely balanced questions, but (unlike in England) those disagreements are not articulated in the law reports. Certainly, disagreements between different levels of courts in the same case are frequent, and the existence of multiple chambers of the supreme courts in France, Spain and Germany often led to conflicts requiring resolution. Very occasionally, despite the impersonal nature of the official sources, the roles of key individuals can be identified. In Spain, for instance, the introduction of the French doctrine of abuse of rights seems to have been the handiwork of José Castán Tobeñas, the president of the Supreme Court, and an enthusiast for modernising Spanish law by using ideas from other European jurisdictions. In the Netherlands a major expansion of fault liability was possible only after the retirement of a conservative Chief Justice. These are only isolated examples, but we might suspect that they are only isolated because the style of judgment conceals other instances from view.

Finally, it should not be overlooked that, whilst the most obvious way for judges to effect legal change is through their judgments, judges may also have an influential role in law reform and academic work. In Sweden,

[5] F. H. Lawson, 'Comparative Judicial Style' (1977) 25 *American Journal of Comparative Law* 364, 371.

for instance, there is both a formal process of *remissen*, by which courts are invited to respond to legislative proposals, and also a constitutional body (the Lagråd), composed of members of the senior judiciary, whose role it is to advise on the legal soundness of legislative proposals.[6] Such an official judicial role in law reform is, however, unusual, because it has the potential to blur the separation of powers between the judiciary and the executive. More commonly, judges serve as law reformers. Sweden seems to lead the way, with participation in law reform being recognised as an important part of a judicial career,[7] but it is not unique: judges frequently head law reform commissions in England and France.

Academic judicial work has also been influential. In those jurisdictions where judges are regarded as public figures, the judiciary are often invited to deliver prestigious public lectures (which are then published). At their most revealing, those lectures can articulate a vision of the judge's role in legal development. Furthermore, some judicial figures, often following an earlier academic career, produce academic literature alongside their work in practice. Indeed, so potentially influential is this literature, that concerns have been raised about whether judges should be permitted to write extra-curially to criticise decisions by their colleagues.

IV Academics

The academic contribution to legal change is, of course, different in its nature to that of legislators and judges. Academics do not make law. But they do influence its development by advancing new ideas and criticising old ones. The key question for us is: how much attention is paid to their work?

The most obvious evidence of academic influence is express acknowledgment. The consistent contribution of textbooks to Scottish legal development, for instance, is evidenced by their frequent appearance in judgments. But conventions about what it is appropriate to cite may well disguise academic influences. For instance, Scottish periodical literature is, in sharp contrast to textbooks, hardly ever cited by the courts. That might seem to indicate that it has had no influence. However, significant Scottish judicial innovations have followed shortly after important Scottish periodical literature. There were also suspiciously close

[6] J. Bell, *Judiciaries within Europe* (Cambridge: Cambridge University Press, 2006), pp. 270–272.

[7] *Ibid.*, pp. 275–276.

correlations elsewhere. For instance, the debates of French doctrinal writers over the proper scope of the action for unjust enrichment can be linked to the courts' pronouncements on the same subject. The Swedish Supreme Court's approach to fault was almost certainly influenced by the writings of Jan Hellner. But perhaps the most striking illustration of the role of citation convention was provided by the Netherlands: there the convention is that all academic work is read, but nothing is cited.

Despite the uncertainties inherent in ascertaining academic influence, three general themes can be identified. First, the academic role of criticising existing material and advancing new ideas was most powerful where the formal legal sources were most laconic. The epigrams of the French Civil Code, coupled with the French courts' cursory reasoning, left a gap that academic authors were happy to fill. In England, by contrast, there was the greatest resistance to academic commentary, particularly in relation to recent developments; England, as noted above, had the most argumentative and discursive style of judgment. As one author has put it, 'Leading academics do in France what judges do in England.'[8]

Second, the nature of academic influence varies. Its most obvious influence is when some academic literature persuades a court to decide a point in a particular way. But its influence may also be more subtle, and pervade the legal culture as a whole. For instance, the early-nineteenth-century German pursuit of purity in legal reasoning at least partly explains the peculiarity of later judgments that, whilst clearly prompted by social concerns, make no mention of them. Some commentators still detect a German judicial reluctance to deal with policy factors.[9] Similarly, Ivar Strahl's proposal that Swedish tort law should move away from fault and towards insurance solutions was, as Strahl himself acknowledged, too radical to be implemented in legislation. But he had laid the groundwork for the more limited insurance schemes that we now recognise as characterising the Nordic model of tort law. Academic influence might even consist in suggesting new methods of legal analysis in general, without any particular focus on fault liability. In England, for instance, the gradual recognition of the value of Civilian comparative law as an academic discipline led, ultimately, to the use of Civilian comparative materials in late-twentieth-century judgments relating to all areas of law. Such broader

[8] J. Goutal, 'Characteristics of Judicial Style in France, Britain and the USA' (1976) 24 *American Journal of Comparative Law* 43, 64.

[9] B. Markesinis, 'Judicial Style and Judicial Reasoning in England and Germany' [2000] *CLJ* 294, esp. p. 307: 'the English judgments are, in their style and wording, so much more open ...'.

influences on legal change may well have more powerful, and longer-term, effects than critiques of particular doctrines, but they would never be evidenced by citations.

Third, to assess the contribution of academics *as academics* (i.e. teachers and writers) is only to see part of the picture. Academics across all of the jurisdictions studied here often became law reformers, judges and politicians. By way of illustration, José Castán went from a professorship at Murcia to the Supreme Court; Robert Badinter was a professor at Paris and, at the same time, Minister of Justice, in which latter capacity he implemented proposals for an automobile accident scheme. Percy Winfield and W. T. Stallybrass were, respectively, professors in Cambridge and Oxford, who were specially appointed to the Law Reform Committee for its project on contributory negligence. In Sweden two twentieth-century Chief Justices, who served for a total of forty years, had, between them, given groundbreaking lectures and written the first Swedish textbook on tort. To speak of these scholars, and others like them, as being mere peripheral voices, who could do no more than hope that their views might be heard by legislators and judges, would be to miss the importance of their contribution completely. Their later appointments put them in an excellent position to implement the ideas they had developed in their academic careers.

V Other participants

In addition to legislators, judges and academics, several other kinds of participants in the process of legal development deserve consideration.

The first group are law reformers. Typically legislatures delegate the task of formulating proposals for reforming private law to reform bodies made up of some combination of politicians, judges, academics, legal practitioners and others. As those delegating the task often realise, the composition of a law reform body is likely to have a profound effect on the substantive content of its eventual proposals, and great care is taken in choosing both its structure and personnel. Thus, for instance, the plans for the English Law Reform Committee underwent major changes in form and personnel, during which the involvement of politicians was proposed and rejected, and academics only included at a late stage; aptitude for committee work was expressly identified as a key factor in the appointment of individual committee members. Similarly, proposals for the reform of French private law often emanate from specially appointed commissions (rather than the established Section du Rapport et des Etudes of the Conseil d'Etat, which tends to focus on public law), and are typically chaired by academics or judges. The decision to appoint Professor André Tunc to chair a commission on liability for automobile accidents virtually guaranteed a radical proposal.

Of course, not every law reform proposal becomes law. But many do, and it is striking that the legislature tends to alter very little. The English Law Reform Committee, for example, achieved a 100 per cent success rate with its proposals for the reform of tort liability. In the Netherlands the new Civil Code was prepared by, first, Meijers, then a triumvirate. Whilst the legislature was occasionally consulted, it had little direct involvement. Here we can see academics effectively acting as lawmakers.

One notable exception to this pattern of academic law reform was Tunc's proposal concerning automobile accidents. When, eventually, a scheme was created in 1985 it bore little resemblance to Tunc's original proposal. The reasons for the difference highlighted the role of two further types of participants in the process of legal change: lobbyists and the legal profession itself.

Essentially, Tunc's proposals had called for a system of first-party insurance. This threatened the vested interests of both insurers and lawyers (who would be deprived of a fruitful source of work). The proposals were heavily modified to produce a compromise that was acceptable to these powerful lobbyists, but the result inevitably lacked the analytical coherence of the original proposals.[10] A similar example could be seen in the modification of the German Civil Code in response to lobbying by agricultural interests: the original strict liability for animals now applied (effectively) only to pets. In both cases analytical rigour was sacrificed to political expediency.

VI Features of legal change

As the above outline makes clear, the chapters in this collection demonstrate the powerful effect of legal institutions and professions on legal change. In doing so, they provide further support for the theory of legal change pioneered by Alan Watson, but they also enable us to go further, and to identify certain features of legal change.[11]

The rules of fault liability are viewed very differently by the different participants in the process of legal development. For instance, to the

[10] See further, Chapter 5, pp. 106–113.

[11] See, for example, A. Watson, *The Evolution of Law* (Oxford: Blackwell, 1985), revised and expanded as *The Evolution of Western Private Law*. For a very helpful summary and overview of Watson's ideas see W. Ewald, 'Comparative Jurisprudence (II): The Logic of Legal Transplants' (1995) 43 *American Journal of Comparative Law* 489.

drafters of the German Civil Code, the imposition of strict liability for all animals achieved the internal consistency and logic to which they aspired. To contemporary landowners these rules reflected an unfair and unrealistic burden of liability. Similarly, what judges perceived as an application of the universal fault principle to accidents at work, legislatures often saw as a socially unjustifiable burden on workers (and a way in which less responsible factory owners were able to hide their inefficiency by externalising the costs of injuries). In other words, legal rules were being assessed differently because they were being judged against different criteria. Before legal change takes place, a lawmaker will have to be convinced that the particular criterion against which the legal rule is being judged is the most important or relevant one to look at.

Where legislative reform is concerned the most persuasive criterion is likely to be social justice, as can be seen in the arguments that are presented in Parliament in support of legislation. Furthermore, a minor or marginal failure to meet the standard of social justice will not suffice. Any law reform proposal will have to compete with the myriad other matters that legislatures must deal with. Only a proposal seen as having a major effect is likely to receive legislative attention.

A second criterion with the power to persuade legislatures could be called a 'political' one. The democratically elected Government might see in a proposal to alter fault liability the opportunity to attract or reinforce support from key elements in society and thereby strengthen its electoral mandate. On this view, law reform involves building coalitions around key social agendas, a view reinforced by the corporatist nature of many European states in the mid twentieth century. It is not so much the actual effect of the legislation that matters, rather its apparent or symbolic effect. A different dimension of the political criterion can be seen in the reasons behind the new Dutch Civil Code – there a major law reform proposal that had been mooted for at least a decade was triggered by national pride. A similar motivation could be seen in Turkey's wholesale adoption of the Swiss Civil Code.[12]

The criteria by which judges assess the rules of fault liability with a view to altering them are, at least on the surface, very different. The reports of judgments seem largely preoccupied with formal, analytical questions – the meaning of a particular statutory provision, or correct interpretation of an earlier judicial pronouncement, for example. Judges sometimes make the point that they are not concerned with wider questions of social justice, saying that they cannot change the rules merely because the rules

[12] See further, Watson, *The Evolution of Western Private Law*, pp. 14–16.

seem unjust. But the perception of injustice seems to be a necessary first step, as the English judge Lord Denning expressly acknowledged.[13] It is difficult to explain the elaborate judicial reasoning of, say, the French courts on strict liability for machinery, or the German courts on railway operators, on any other basis. Even the political dimension can be detected in some judicial approaches: the Scottish judge Lord Watson, for instance, seems to have been inspired partly by ideas about Scotland's role in the British Empire.

Once the decision has been made that a particular rule is too out of line with the relevant criterion, a choice has to be made about what to replace it with. The legislator seems to have a free choice, but in fact that choice will be politically circumscribed, or, if not politically contentious, delegated to a law reform body. Such politically uncontentious proposals are where academics are most likely to make their mark, although even on law reform committees political skills and political compromise may come into play.

The judicial choice about a new rule is more obviously constrained. Legislation or convention may require that no new rule is formally articulated. If so, it will be left to the expert reader to piece together what the new rule is, from a judgment advancing an apparently implausible interpretation of an existing statute. Where greater latitude is permitted, a judge must put his faith in a particular form of words that he or she feels will function better. 'Better' here means causing less injustice than the old rule, which, as well as the actual results in cases, should include the rule's clarity and coherence. It is partly an aesthetic choice, and may be informed by the choices made by judges elsewhere.[14]

Legal change can therefore be seen as a product of the competition between criteria advanced by participants in different roles. Effectively, each class of participant operates by using a system of ideas and assumptions about how the law works, what it should achieve, and what their role is in attaining that goal.[15] That system suggests the criteria by which

[13] See also the view of Louis Josserand, discussed in M. Lobban and J. Moses, 'Introduction' in M. Lobban and J. Moses (eds.) *The Impact of Ideas on Legal Development* (Cambridge: Cambridge University Press, 2012), p. 25 and J. Bell, 'Continental European Jurisprudence 1850–2000' in M. Lobban and J. Moses (eds.) *The Imapct of Ideas*, p. 25.

[14] Compare the description of changes in scientific theory given by T. S. Kuhn, *The Structure of Scientific Revolutions*, 3rd edn (Chicago: University of Chicago Press, 1996), esp. in Chapter 12.

[15] My use of a systems-based explanation for legal change was prompted by N. Luhmann, *Law as a Social System* (Oxford: Oxford University Press, 2004), and the review of it by J. Bell in [2006] *CLJ* 721.

legal rules should be evaluated, and, therefore, how the law ought to be changed in order better to perform its function.

Which criterion prevails will be determined by which participants are the most powerful or persuasive. Traditionally, we think of the different categories of participants as belonging to a hierarchical structure of lawmakers. The legislature is at the top: it can initiate change, and reverse change introduced by judges. The judges are next: they can make changes within limits, but only so long as the legislature tolerates those changes, by not reversing them. At the bottom of the hierarchy are the academics, reformers and lobbyists: they just have to make their arguments and hope for the best.

If this hierarchical structure is correct, it offers an obvious way of explaining how the competition between different criteria is resolved. And undoubtedly it is correct, at a formal level. Indeed, it is important that it should be correct, since democratic government rests on the sovereignty of the elected legislature. But the important question for us is whether this formal, structural account can also be taken as a description of how law is actually made. Taken in that way, it is utterly misleading.

As we have seen, the way in which the legal system actually effects legal change – what we might call the 'operating system' of legal change – is very different from what the hierarchical picture might suggest. Legislators do not in fact occupy the dominant role that the formal account would imply. They may be prompted to intervene by a dimension of social justice or political significance. But otherwise the real initiative is with judges and law reformers. Furthermore, we might assume from the formal hierarchy of lawmakers that the classes of legislator, judge, reformer and academic are mutually exclusive. In fact, nothing could be further from the truth. The chapters that follow are full of examples of academics becoming legislators, judges or reformers; judges serving on law reform committees; and reformers and judges going into politics. Indeed, in Sweden it has been argued that there should be a limit to the number of roles that can be occupied simultaneously, since it can place courts in a difficult position when a Supreme Court Justice, who has been party to a decision, writes a case note criticising it. There is, in other words, far greater potential for the interpenetration of ideas than we might, formally, have expected. Indeed, so far as the operating system of legal change is concerned, the division into legislator, judge etc. may be unhelpful: it is more accurate to think of those in a position to accomplish change as belonging to a legal elite, whose members can occupy a variety of roles, sometimes simultaneously.

VII Conclusion

What emerges from our study is that legal change is conditioned by the interaction of the different systems to which the participants in legal change subscribe. Each system views the law, in our case fault liability, from a different perspective, and uses different criteria to evaluate its strengths and weaknesses. What is changed, and how, depends on a competition of criteria. It also emerges that the traditional account of law-making in terms of a hierarchy, whilst it is both formally accurate and an important political norm, gives a wholly misleading picture of how legal change actually happens. The 'operating system' of legal change – what actually goes on – is just as important, but gets far too little attention.

2

The impact of institutions and professions on fault liability in England

PAUL MITCHELL

> The history of judge-made law is largely the history of the judges themselves.
>
> Lord Radcliffe, *The Law and Its Compass*

Between 1850 and 2000 fault liability in England was transformed. In 1850 there was no general duty of care, no liability for psychiatric injury, for statements, or for purely economic loss. Nor was there any elaboration of the breach of duty standard, or principles for assessing damages. By 2000 each of these subjects would be central features of the law of negligence; indeed, any university course on the law of tort could not afford to omit them. This expansion of negligence liability, and the elaboration of many of its defining features, were, however, counterbalanced during the same period by the introduction of various statutory schemes and regulations. These, in effect, removed particular subjects from the law of negligence either by supplying claimants with a cause of action in which fault need not be proved, or by creating a statutory compensation scheme. This chapter explores how institutional and professional factors contributed to the expansion and development of negligence liability; the companion chapter by Peter Bartrip (p. 36) deals with statutory schemes and regulations relating to workmen's compensation.

I Judicial development of fault liability

Throughout the period 1850 to 2000 fault liability has been a predominantly common law subject: its rules and principles are to be found in judgments of either the Court of Appeal[1] or the Appellate Committee of the House of Lords.[2]

A Judicial appointments

The classic route to judicial office was a successful career at the Bar.[3] The average age of newly appointed judges in the period 1832 to 1906 was 53[4], and until 1959 there was no statutory retirement age:[5] Lord Denning, for example, was still presiding in the Court of Appeal at the age of 84. 'The organization of the profession', it has been accurately observed, 'was gerontocratic, as indeed it still is, and promotion depended upon approval by the senior members of the profession'.[6] Nor, within the gerontocracy, was selection exclusively based on merit. Throughout the period of our study, judicial appointments were made by the Lord Chancellor, the Government minister responsible for the legal system. At the start of our period the convention was that such appointments should reflect party loyalties:[7] Lord Campbell LC caused offence when he appointed Blackburn – nowadays regarded as one of the great judges of the nineteenth century[8] – ahead of several better known successful barristers of his own party.[9] By

1 Before the creation of the Court of Appeal in 1875, appellate decisions were made by the Court of King's Bench, the Court of Common Pleas or the Court of Exchequer Chamber.

2 On 1 October 2009 the Appellate Committee of the House of Lords was replaced as the final court of appeal by the Supreme Court. For an analysis of the House of Lords' contributions to the law of tort, see R. Stevens, 'Torts' in L. Blom-Cooper, B. Dickson and G. Drewry (eds.), *The Judicial House of Lords 1876–2009* (Oxford: Oxford University Press, 2009), p. 629.

3 G. Simonds, 'Law' in E. Barker (ed.), *The Character of England* (Oxford: Clarendon Press, 1947), p. 112, 134.

4 H. Laski, 'The Technique of Judicial Appointment' in *Studies in Law and Politics* (London: George Allen & Unwin, 1932), p. 163, 172.

5 Judicial Pensions Act 1959, s. 2; see now Judicial Pensions and Retirement Act 1993, s. 26. The compulsory retirement age did not apply to those judges appointed before the 1959 Act came into force.

6 A. W. B. Simpson, 'The Common Law and Legal Theory' in *Legal Theory and Legal History: Essays on the Common Law* (London and Ronceverte: Hambledon Press, 1987), p. 359, 377.

7 G. Jones, 'Three Very Remarkable Nineteenth-Century Lawyers: Lyndhurst, Denman and Campbell' in K. O'Donovan and G. Rubin (eds.), *Human Rights and Legal History: Essays in Honour of Brian Simpson* (Oxford: Oxford University Press, 2000), p. 172, 173–174.

8 See, for instance, the assessment in C. Fifoot, *Judge and Jurist in the Reign of Queen Victoria* (London: Stevens and Sons, 1959), pp. 16–17, concluding that Blackburn was 'one of the greatest common lawyers of all time'.

9 J. Campbell, *Life of John, Lord Campbell*, ed. M. Hardcastle, 2 vols., Vol. II (London: John Murray, 1881), p. 372.

the start of the twentieth century such overt political favouritism had disappeared – perceived bias in appointments by Lord Halsbury LC provoked widespread criticism[10] – but that was not to say that the political dimension had been eliminated. The tradition continued of rewarding loyal party supporters in Parliament with high judicial office. In 1932, for instance, Harold Laski could point out that 'At the present time … the Chief Justiceship, the Mastership of the Rolls, and the Presidency of the Probate, Divorce and Admiralty Divisions are all held by men who played a great part in politics during the last half-dozen years.'[11] Lord Reid, for example, whose judgments were to have a profound effect on fault liability, reluctantly accepted the post of Law Lord when his parliamentary career in the Conservative Party stalled.[12] Other Law Lords bypassing the traditional route of success at the Bar followed by promotion through the ranks of the judiciary included Viscount Radcliffe, Viscount Dilhorne and Lord Carson. It should also be noted that the Lord Chancellor was entitled to sit as a judge in the House of Lords, where his influence on legal development could be powerful. Lord Hailsham's emphatic refusal to impose a duty on occupiers of land to child trespassers[13] – which became the leading authority on the point for over 40 years[14] – was, perhaps, not entirely surprising given that he was the Conservative Government's Lord Chancellor at the time.[15]

Once appointed, any judge would be unlikely to effect much change whilst acting as a judge of first instance. There are, of course, exceptions – such as the test for breach of duty in a medical context, set out by McNair J in *Bolam* v. *Friern Hospital Management Committee*.[16] But, for the most part, promotion to the Court of Appeal or House of Lords was necessary. As with initial appointment, promotion was in the Government's gift, with the Lord Chancellor advising the Prime Minister who should be preferred. The numbers involved were very small. In the early 1950s, the Court of Appeal was still sitting in three divisions (of three judges

[10] J. H. Baker, *An Introduction to English Legal History*, 4th edn (London: Butterworths, 2002), p. 168.

[11] Laski, 'The Technique of Judicial Appointment', p. 169.

[12] P. Mitchell, 'Lord Reid' in J. Ramsden (ed.), *The Oxford Companion to Twentieth Century British Politics* (Oxford: Oxford University Press, 2002), p. 557.

[13] *Robert Addie & Sons (Collieries) Ltd* v. *Dumbreck* [1929] AC 358.

[14] *British Railways Board* v. *Herrington* [1972] 1 AC 877.

[15] For an account of Hailsham's career see R. Heuston, *Lives of the Lord Chancellors 1885–1940* (Oxford: Clarendon Press, 1964), pp. 451–496.

[16] [1957] 1 WLR 582.

each);[17] by 1961 there were four.[18] Around the same time there were nine Law Lords[19]; each case was heard by a panel of five.

B The sources of judge-made law

The primary source of judge-made law was other judicial decisions, some of which might leave no room for doubt about what the law was. In particular, the court system was hierarchical: the House of Lords' pronouncements on the law were binding on all lower courts, and on the House of Lords itself until 1966.[20] The Court of Appeal was also generally bound to follow its own previous decisions. Such a system of precedent was an obvious obstacle to legal change. As we shall see, it placed a premium on the ability to distinguish previous judicial expositions, and brought to the surface judges' conflicting attitudes to common law development.

Alongside these strict rules about binding precedents, however, there were other sources that could be drawn on as catalysts for change. The Law Lords sat not only as the House of Lords hearing English appeals; they also determined Scottish appeals and appeals from Northern Ireland. Indeed, *Donoghue* v. *Stevenson*, the most important case in the entire law of negligence, was a Scottish appeal to the House of Lords.[21] The Law Lords also sat as the Judicial Committee of the Privy Council, where they heard appeals from the appellate courts of various Commonwealth countries. Decisions in both Irish and Scottish appeals and in Privy Council cases were not technically binding – the law in those countries might be different from English law – but in common law subjects such as fault liability those decisions exercised a powerful persuasive force.[22]

A more shadowy role was played by foreign law and academic writings. So far as foreign law was concerned, the classical education of most nineteenth-century judges would have equipped them to make use of

[17] Lord Justice Cohen, 'Jurisdiction, Practice and Procedure of the Court of Appeal' (1951–1953) 11 *Cambridge Law Journal* 3, 5.

[18] R. Evershed, 'The Judicial Process in Twentieth Century England' (1961) 61 *Columbia Law Review* 761, 767.

[19] Morton, 'Address' (1949) 32 *Yearbook of the Canadian Bar Association* 107, 114.

[20] Practice Statement on Precedent, 26 July 1966 [1966] 1 WLR 1234. See further A. Paterson, *The Law Lords* (London and Basingstoke: Macmillan, 1982), pp. 143–151.

[21] [1932] AC 562.

[22] E.g. Northern Ireland: *Century Insurance Co. Ltd* v. *Northern Ireland Road Transport Board* [1942] AC 509 (vicarious liability); Scotland: *Hughes* v. *Lord Advocate* [1963] AC 837 (remoteness of damage); Australia: *Overseas Tankship (UK) Ltd* v. *Morts Dock and Engineering Co. Ltd (The Wagon Mound)* [1961] AC 388 (remoteness of damage).

Roman law materials in their analyses[23] – and there is evidence that some of them did.[24] Modern Civil law, on the other hand, which might have suggested solutions to the new problems stemming from social change across Europe, seems to have had little influence until the late twentieth century. One reason for this was undoubtedly the lack of comparative law teaching and training: it was not until the 1960s, at the earliest, that comparative law really became established as an English university subject.[25] That recognition, largely the fruit of a campaign by Harold Gutteridge from the late 1920s onwards,[26] came too late to influence most of the people occupying judicial positions in the late twentieth century.[27] A second reason may well have been the perception that a codified system was simply too different from the common law for any comparison to be helpful. Kahn-Freund had pointed out, in the context of fault liability, that this was a misperception,[28] but occasional lone voices like his were not enough to overcome the English common lawyer's traditional dislike of statute.[29] Nevertheless, by the end of the twentieth century some interesting comparative material was beginning to surface in appellate case law, with France and Germany featuring most prominently.[30]

The contribution of academic writing is peculiarly difficult to measure because, from 1850 to at least 1950, there was a convention that the works of living writers could not be cited in court.[31] The judges could only be

[23] Laski, 'The Technique of Judicial Appointment', p. 172 notes that over 70 per cent of judges appointed between 1832 and 1906 had studied at either Oxford or Cambridge.

[24] D. J. Ibbetson, '"The Law of Business Rome": Foundations of the Anglo-American Tort of Negligence' (1999) 52 *Current Legal Problems* 74.

[25] J. A. Jolowicz, 'Comparative Law in Twentieth-Century England' in J. Beatson and R. Zimmermann (eds.), *Jurists Uprooted: German-Speaking Emigré Lawyers in Twentieth-Century Britain* (Oxford: Oxford University Press, 2004), p. 345.

[26] E.g. H. Gutteridge, 'The Value of Comparative Law' 1931 *Journal of the Society of Public Teachers of Law* 26.

[27] Lord Justice Denning once commented that some members of the Court of Appeal, 'never having had the time to become familiar with the results of modern research … keep repeating the fallacies they learnt when they were young' (A. Denning, 'The Universities and Law Reform' (1951) 1 *Journal of the Society of Public Teachers of Law*, new series 258, 261).

[28] O. Kahn-Freund, 'Remoteness of Damage in German Law' (1934) 50 *Law Quarterly Review* 512, 515ff.

[29] M. Amos, 'The Interpretation of Statutes' (1933–1935) 5 *Cambridge Law Journal* 163; D. Hughes Parry, 'Modern Problems and Methods of Law Reform' (1934) *Journal of the Society of Public Teachers of Law* 10, 12.

[30] E.g. *White* v. *Jones* [1995] 2 AC 207; *Greatorex* v. *Greatorex* [2000] 1 WLR 1970; *D* v. *East Berkshire Community Health NHS Trust* [2005] 2 AC 373.

[31] N. Duxbury, *Jurists and Judges: An Essay on Influence* (Oxford: Hart, 2001), pp. 62–84.

exposed to the ideas or analyses in such works if they were 'adopted' by counsel. Identifying academic influence may often, therefore, be a matter of detective work. But the convention was inconsistently observed, and a lack of case law might even compel judicial analysis in terms of competing academic views. For instance, when a question arose in the early 1920s about the correct test for remoteness of damage in negligence, there was so little authority that the Court of Appeal heard argument in terms of which writer was correct – Beven or Pollock?[32] Beven was dead, but Pollock was not, and nor was Salmond, to whose work counsel also referred.[33] The Court of Appeal chose Beven, to Pollock's understandable disappointment.[34] Pollock's (spiritual[35]) successor as editor of the *Law Quarterly Review*, A. L. Goodhart, then devoted a generous number of its pages to a campaign against the Court of Appeal's decision.[36] Forty years later the campaign succeeded, when the Privy Council, in a judgment heavily indebted to Goodhart, departed from the Court of Appeal's earlier decision.[37]

Even where authority was abundant, sometimes judges welcomed academic contributions. Attitudes varied over the period. Towards the end of the twentieth century, there was a general recognition of the value of academic work, with distinguished judges such as Lord Goff (himself a former academic) describing the roles of judges and academics as 'complementary', and calling for 'inevitable and desirable' co-operation between them.[38] Earlier attitudes to academic work had been more negative.[39] The pioneer in changing those attitudes was Lord Denning, who put a very high value on academic writings and constantly asserted that the convention against citation of living authors was obsolete;[40] Professor A. G. Guest once described him as 'the judicial patron of all

[32] *In re an Arbitration between Polemis and Another and Furness, Withy and Company Limited* [1921] 3 KB 560, 565.

[33] *Ibid.*, 564.

[34] F. Pollock, 'Liability for Consequences' (1922) 38 *Law Quarterly Review* 165.

[35] Pollock's actual successor was A. E. Randall, whose editorial tenure was both short-lived (1920–1925) and undistinguished. A. Denning, '1885–1984' (1984) 100 *Law Quarterly Review* 513 described him as 'only a stop-gap' (513–514).

[36] For details of the campaign see Duxbury, *Jurists and Judges*, pp. 92–98.

[37] *Overseas Tankship (UK) Ltd* v. *Morts Dock and Engineering Co. Ltd (The Wagon Mound)* [1961] AC 388.

[38] R. Goff, 'The Search for Principle' (1983) 69 *Proceedings of the British Academy* 169, 182–187; 'Judge, Jurist and Legislature' [1987] *Denning Law Journal* 79, 94.

[39] Duxbury, *Jurists and Judges*, Chapter 5.

[40] A. Denning, review of P. H. Winfield, *A Text-Book of the Law of Tort* (1947) 63 *Law Quarterly Review* 516.

law teachers in this country'.[41] As counsel, Denning famously used an article by A. L. Goodhart[42] to attack the authority of a Court of Appeal case on a hospital's liability for the negligence of its nurses; the Court of Appeal accepted Denning's submissions, and overruled its earlier decision.[43] Once on the Bench, Denning continued to encourage academic writers – he gave a series of lectures urging academics to contribute to the process of law reform,[44] and drew on those writings he found helpful.[45] It is interesting to note, however, that his enthusiasm for academic writing did not extend to comparative work. As he himself described his methods, he was not content to accept results that were 'not suited to the times … or … work injustice';[46] rather, he would look for some different principle, which would yield a fairer result. It was the search for this alternative principle in which academic writers could assist: he would 'search the old cases and the writers old and new' until he found it.[47] In other words, academic work was to be used to escape from the otherwise inevitable results required by a strict adherence to precedent. Such academic work, to be useful, would have to be primarily concerned with the reinterpretation of English materials.

C *The structure and style of litigation*

The formal structure of litigation had a profound influence on the judicial development of fault liability. The procedural change from trial by jury to trial by judge alone meant that new questions arose for judicial analysis that had previously been left to the jury's discretion.[48] Thus, the test for breach of duty of care, which in the nineteenth century had required the judge simply to ask the jury whether the defendant had taken reasonable care, now had to be fleshed out. What risks might a reasonable

[41] Notes of discussion following Denning's lecture, 'The Way of an Iconoclast' (1959–1960) 5 *Journal of the Society of Public Teachers of Law*, new series 77, 89.

[42] A. Goodhart, 'Hospitals and Trained Nurses' (1938) 54 *Law Quarterly Review* 553.

[43] *Gold* v. *Essex County Council* [1942] 2 KB 293, overruling *Hillyer* v. *Governors of St Bartholomew's Hospital* [1909] 2 KB 820.

[44] A. Denning, 'The Universities and Law Reform' (1951) 1 *Journal of the Society of Public Teachers of Law*, new series 258; 'The Need for a New Equity' (1952) 5 *Current Legal Problems* 1; 'The Way of an Iconoclast'.

[45] E.g. *White* v. *Blackmore* [1972] 3 All ER 158, 167 (referring to academic literature that counsel had not cited).

[46] Denning, 'The Way of an Iconoclast', 89.

[47] *Ibid.*

[48] P. Mitchell, *The Making of the Modern Law of Defamation* (Oxford: Hart, 2005), pp. 56–57.

man be justified in taking?[49] How much trouble and expense should he be expected to go to?[50] Should the defendant's motive matter?[51] Such questions now had to be answered, rationally, by judges, rather than intuitively, by jurors. Similarly, the judicial assessment of damages assumed a mathematical aspect (with associated mathematical controversies),[52] which it had previously lacked. Furthermore, the award of non-pecuniary general damages by judges triggered concerns about consistency and predictability, neither of which had been seen as objections to jury awards.[53] The result was an innovation in the literature – awards of damages were now reported, and a new practitioners' work emerged, which provided comparisons of previous awards;[54] this, in turn, led to the current tariff-based approach to non-pecuniary damages.[55]

The formal structure of the litigation process also had a more subtle influence. At its heart was the importance of oral argument. Perhaps because most judges were (and continue to be) former barristers, they regarded the really crucial part of the case as counsel's oral submissions. Thus, even though written submissions would be made in advance of the hearing, and, indeed, were compulsory in the House of Lords, they were typically not read, or only read in the barest outline before the case was heard.[56] It seemed to be felt that to form a view of the case based on the written submissions was in some way to 'pre-judge' it unfairly; one nineteenth century Master of the Rolls' habit of doing detailed work on the written submissions before the case was heard was almost seen as an eccentricity.[57]

[49] *Bolton* v. *Stone* [1951] AC 850.

[50] *Latimer* v. *AEC Ltd* [1953] AC 643. Cf. the more subjective approach taken in *Goldman* v. *Hargrave* [1967] 1 AC 645; and *Leakey* v. *National Trust for Places of Historic Interest or Natural Beauty* [1980] 1 All ER 17.

[51] *Watt* v. *Hertfordshire County Council* [1954] 1 WLR 835; *King* v. *Sussex Ambulance NHS Trust* [2002] All ER (D) 95 (Jul). See now Compensation Act 2006, s. 1.

[52] *Wells* v. *Wells* [1999] 1 AC 345 (dispute over rate of return to be assumed when damages award invested).

[53] *Bird* v. *Cocking & Son Ltd* [1951] 2 TLR 1260. See generally Mitchell, *The Making of the Modern Law of Defamation*, pp. 56–59.

[54] D. A. M. Kemp and M. S. Kemp, *The Quantum of Damages in Personal Injury Claims* (London: Sweet and Maxwell, 1954). The importance of the book is well brought out by G. Ellenbogen's review in (1955) 18 *Modern Law Review* 642.

[55] See in particular *Ward* v. *James* [1966] 1 QB 273.

[56] Morton, 'Address', 114–115; Paterson, *The Law Lords*, pp. 35–37.

[57] W. Willis, *Sir George Jessel: A Lecture* (London: E. Marlborough, 1893), p. 20; I. Finestein, 'Sir George Jessel 1824–1883' (1958) 18 *Transactions of the Jewish Historical Society of England* 243, 271.

When the oral argument took place, it was not a matter of formal rhetoric. Instead, there was something closer to a dialogue between judges and barristers, in which questions of authority, interpretation, principle and hypothetical examples would be discussed.[58] Law reporting conventions tend either to omit the dialogue altogether,[59] or underplay it dramatically.[60] In the House of Lords under Lord Reid, for instance, great weight was given to counsel's replies to hypothetical related situations put to them by the judges.[61] Appeals could turn on counsel's presentational skills and speed of thought.

The judgments produced at the end of the process of argument are, naturally enough, shaped by the nature of the process itself. In those cases that effect legal change they are, typically, discursive, lengthy and conflicting. The discursiveness and length can be seen to flow from the central theme in English litigation of argument and persuasion. One commentator has even suggested that the English judge 'is led to see his own role as not altogether different in kind from that of the bar': a judge feels the need to engage with, and respond persuasively to, the arguments he has heard.[62] Equally, the inclusion of matter not strictly necessary for the decision – the *obiter dicta* – makes sense given the typical nature of the preceding argument. Such *dicta* can prove surprisingly powerful: they are not formally binding, but exercise persuasive authority. Perhaps the most famous instance of this in fault liability is *Hedley Byrne & Co Ltd* v. *Heller & Partners Ltd*,[63] where the House of Lords created liability for a negligent statement causing purely economic loss, although on the facts the defendant had successfully disclaimed liability, whether it existed or not.[64] Similarly, the lengthy, discursive approach to judicial reasoning enables different individuals to set out their own personal analysis, and gives the English common law its distinctively personal flavour.[65] Whilst

[58] B. Rudden, 'Courts and Codes in England, France and Soviet Russia' (1973–1974) 48 *Tulane Law Review* 1010.

[59] There is no report of counsel's argument in the Weekly Law Reports, the All England Reports or in electronic reports such as the British and Irish Legal Information Institute (www.bailii.org).

[60] Paterson, *The Law Lords*, p. 70 observed 99 judicial interventions in the first day of argument alone in *Cassell & Co. Ltd* v. *Broome*. The Appeal Cases Report, which includes a summary of counsel's argument, reported none of them ([1972] AC 1027, 1033–1041).

[61] Paterson, *The Law Lords*, p. 75.

[62] Rudden, 'Courts and Codes', 1015.

[63] [1964] AC 465.

[64] R. Dias [1963] *Cambridge Law Journal* 220, 221 argued that it would be 'unreal' to treat the House of Lords' creation of liability as a mere dictum.

[65] O. Kahn-Freund, 'Reflections on Legal Education' (1966) 29 *Modern Law Review* 121, esp. 126.

an individual judge might agree with the conclusion of his colleagues, his own personal analysis might have distinctive characteristics, which could be drawn on in later cases. The first judicial recognition of a general duty of care came in only one judgment of a unanimous Court of Appeal.[66] Its most famous exposition – by Lord Atkin in *Donoghue* v. *Stevenson*[67] – was only one of three differently reasoned majority speeches. Occasionally the sheer volume of reasoning could be overwhelming – as when the five differently reasoned speeches of the unanimous House of Lords in *British Railways Board* v. *Herrington*[68] proved so difficult to disentangle that legislation was necessary.[69] But neither such difficulties, nor powerful academic criticism,[70] have deterred the House of Lords from continuing to pursue a discursive, individualistic approach to decision-making. The loss of certainty that results from multiple judgments is, it is felt, more than compensated by the potential for future development that such multiple judgments permit.[71]

Donoghue v. *Stevenson* also illustrates one of the most distinctive features of English judicial lawmaking: namely, the dissenting judgment.[72] Here is the clearest indication of the individualised nature of the process. At its best it enables ideas to be expressed that can then be developed when the question is revisited. For instance, in *Candler* v. *Crane, Christmas & Co*[73] Denning LJ gave a dissenting judgment in which he attempted to deal with the problem of an indeterminate class of claimants in cases of negligent misstatement; those ideas could later be seen in the House of Lords' unanimous decision defining the limits of such liability in *Caparo Industries plc* v. *Dickman*.[74] But dissenting judgments can also introduce a more controversial element into the judicial process. Since the court's decision only needs to be by a majority, a judge in the Court of Appeal need only persuade one of his colleagues, and a Law Lord only two, to effect a change in the law. Whether the law is changed can come down to force of personality. Indeed, in *Donoghue* v. *Stevenson* itself, this seems to be precisely what happened. A year before the case was heard, Lord Atkin had told an audience of students that 'the whole law of tort'

66 *Heaven* v. *Pender* (1883) 11 QBD 503 (Brett MR).

67 [1932] AC 562. 68 [1972] 1 AC 877.

69 Occupiers Liability Act 1984.

70 R. Cross, 'The *Ratio decidendi* and a Plurality of Speeches in the House of Lords' (1977) 93 *Law Quarterly Review* 378.

71 Paterson, *The Law Lords*, pp. 183–185; Goff, 'The Search for Principle', 174–175.

72 See generally, K. Nadelmann, 'The Judicial Dissent: Publication *v.* Secrecy' (1959) 8 *American Journal of Comparative Law* 415.

73 [1951] 2 KB 164. 74 [1990] 2 AC 605.

could be seen in terms of duties to one's neighbour.[75] But this was not a popular view.[76] Atkin, however, was a determined man – he was described (confidentially) as 'Clever. And a good common lawyer. But obstinate if he has taken a view and quite unpersuadable'[77] – and, following the argument in *Donoghue* he set about convincing his colleagues. His efforts succeeded with his two Scottish colleagues, and he even seems to have persuaded Lord Macmillan to rewrite his speech, so as to give greater support to the idea of a general duty of care in English law.[78] As Lord Denning later pithily described it, 'Lord Atkin persuaded two Scotsmen to agree with him ... But two Englishmen dissented. They had been brought up in Chancery.'[79]

Lord Atkin had written himself 'into the history books',[80] but it was not a coup that he was destined to repeat. When a case on a hospital's liability for its nurses' negligence was appealed to the House of Lords, Lord Hailsham, then the Lord Chancellor, was clearly mindful of what had happened in *Donoghue*. He wrote to Lord Sankey, his predecessor as Lord Chancellor, to ask a favour:[81]

> There is in the list for hearing a case called *The County Council of the Parts of Lindsey (Lincolnshire) v Marshall*. I understand from Schuster[82] that it is a pure common law point and that the sort of question involved is as to the liability of the County Council which provides a hospital for the illness of some unhappy woman patient which is alleged to have occurred owing to the negligence of the matron or doctors of the hospital. Roche cannot sit, as he was in the Court of Appeal, and I shall normally therefore be only left with Atkin, who is rather apt to take the opportunity of making the law as it ought to be, instead of administering it as it is. I am really rather anxious, as to what may be formulated as the Common Law doctrine; Atkin is naturally apt to be followed by his fellow Law Lords of the Chancery or Scottish Bar on a Common Law point, and I should really value your assistance in order to elucidate what the Common Law really is. What I should like best would be for you and me both to sit; but

[75] Lord Atkin, 'Law as an Educational Subject' (1932) *Journal of the Society of Public Teachers of Law* 27, 30.

[76] It remains controversial: e.g. Goff, 'The Search for Principle', 178.

[77] Lord Dunedin writing to Lord Hailsham LC in 1935 with his views on the Law Lords. Quoted in Heuston, *Lives of the Lord Chancellors*, p. 481.

[78] A. Rodger, 'Lord Macmillan's Speech in *Donoghue* v. *Stevenson*' (1992) 108 *Law Quarterly Review* 236.

[79] A. Denning, *The Discipline of Law* (London: Butterworths, 1979), p. 230.

[80] Rodger, 'Lord Macmillan's Speech', p. 246.

[81] Heuston, *Lives of the Lord Chancellors*, p. 531.

[82] Sir Claud Schuster, Permanent Secretary at the Lord Chancellor's Office.

> if it were an inducement to you to come I will gladly let you preside and go to the Privy Council.

Lord Sankey did sit, and Lord Atkin did not. Although doubts were expressed about the present state of the law, no change was made to it,[83] as Hailsham had wished. But it was only a short-lived solution: seven years later Denning KC, relying on an article by A. L. Goodhart, was to persuade the Court of Appeal that a hospital was liable for its nurses' negligence, wherever that negligence took place in the hospital.[84]

Careful selection of personnel could, therefore, prevent anticipated legal change. By the same token, careful selection could almost guarantee change. Lord Denning records[85] that, having given a dissenting speech in the Court of Appeal in favour of liability for negligent statements,[86] he was invited to hear a later case on the same point in the House of Lords.[87] He refused. Lord Devlin, who did sit in that House of Lords case, had previously expressed the view – extra-judicially – that there should be such liability.[88] He acted on that view in his speech. Individualised decision-making was all very well, but individuals' behaviour could be predicted, and either curtailed or encouraged.

D *Judicial ideology*

Judicial elaboration of fault liability can thus be seen as shaped by the processes of judicial appointment and selection, and by the litigation process that gives rise to judgments. But the impact of these processes on different individuals at different times has varied. The period from the 1860s to the 1890s has been seen as a golden age of common law development, the early twentieth century as a disappointment and the 1960s onwards as an improvement.[89] That might be right. Undoubtedly, the increase in

[83] *County Council of the Parts of Lindsey, Lincolnshire* v. *Marshall* [1937] AC 97.

[84] *Gold* v. *Essex County Council* [1942] 2 KB 293.

[85] Denning, *The Discipline of Law*, p. 245.

[86] *Candler* v. *Crane, Christmas & Co.* [1951] 2 KB 164.

[87] *Hedley Byrne & Co. Ltd* v. *Heller & Partners Ltd* [1964] AC 465.

[88] P. Devlin, 'Morals and the Quasi-Criminal Law and the Law of Tort' (Presidential Address to the Holdsworth Club, University of Birmingham, 1961), repr. in P. Devlin, *The Enforcement of Morals* (Oxford: Oxford University Press, 1965), p. 26, 41–42). Lord Devlin's central role is explained in P. Mitchell, '*Hedley Byrne & Co. Ltd* v. *Heller & Partners Ltd* (1963)' in C. Mitchell and P. Mitchell (eds.), *Landmark Cases in the Law of Tort* (Oxford: Hart, 2010), p. 171.

[89] K. Diplock, *The Courts as Legislators* (Birmingham: Holdsworth Club, 1965), pp. 20–22; H. Edmund-Davies, 'Judicial Activism' (1975) 28 *Current Legal Problems* 1.

legislative activity in the early twentieth century seems to have made courts generally more apprehensive about their common law functions.[90] But, it is perhaps more useful to view different judicial approaches in terms of the individual's conception of their judicial role.[91] From the mid twentieth century onwards, leading judges started to make their ideas explicit, typically in extra-judicial lectures to academic or foreign audiences.[92] At the most conservative end of the spectrum, Lord Simonds was very uncomfortable with the idea that judges made law at all. He could give no 'satisfactory' explanation for the phenomenon, and expressed anxiety about the risk of an arbitrary or capricious exercise of judicial power.[93] On the other hand, that did not stop him altering the remoteness of damage rule in negligence from directness to foreseeability.[94] At the opposite end of the spectrum, Lord Denning was never concerned to deny that he sought to do justice in the case before him, if necessary by reshaping the relevant principles.[95] An intriguing intermediate position was taken by Lord Radcliffe, who argued that it was essential for social stability that judges should both deny their lawmaking power and surreptitiously exercise it.[96] Perhaps the most thoroughly worked-through position was Lord Reid's. For him, judicial lawmaking was inappropriate in areas of political controversy; it was also inappropriate where parties might have ordered their affairs on the basis of a particular legal rule.[97] But, in his view, negligence liability fell into neither category.[98] For instance, when he led the House of Lords in creating an occupier's duty to trespassers, Lord Reid did not see this as having a significant political dimension, nor as upsetting a legal position on which potential defendants had relied; it was, rather, a

[90] Evershed, 'The Judicial Process in Twentieth Century England' (1961) 61 *Columbia Law Review* 761, 763–764.

[91] The method used to impressive effect in Paterson, *The Law Lords*.

[92] P. S. Atiyah, 'Judges and Policy' (1980) 15 *Israel Law Review* 346 comments on the contrast between the judges' judicial and extra-judicial utterances. See especially pp. 357 and 360.

[93] G. Simonds, 'Law' in E. Barker (ed.), *The Character of England* (Oxford: Clarendon Press, 1947), p. 112, 115–117; Paterson, *The Law Lords*, pp. 132–133.

[94] *Overseas Tankship (UK) Ltd* v. *Morts Dock and Engineering Co. Ltd (The Wagon Mound)* [1961] AC 388.

[95] E.g. Denning, 'The Way of an Iconoclast'.

[96] Lord Radcliffe, *The Law and Its Compass* (London: Faber, 1961), pp. 11, 39.

[97] Lord Reid, 'The Judge as Law Maker' (1972) 22 *Journal of the Society of Public Teachers of Law*, new series 22.

[98] Lord Reid, 'The Law and the Reasonable Man' (1968) 54 *Proceedings of the British Academy* 189, particularly at p. 203: 'no one goes to his lawyer to ask just how negligent he is entitled to be'.

case where (apolitical) public policy called for a remedy.[99] He later commented that 'we just had to take the bit between our teeth, there was nothing else to be done'.[100]

Ultimately, then, it was an interaction between process and individual temperament that determined how and when fault liability was judicially elaborated. First, the judge would have to be in a position to accomplish change. Second, there would have to be a desire to make a change, and an acknowledgement that accomplishing such change was part of the judicial role; without that, nothing could be done. Once the decision to make a change was taken, its form and method were a function of the common law litigation process. That could often mean that it was lengthy, discursive and, although its real content reflected a choice about the future, it would appear to be necessitated by an account of the past.

II Statutory development of fault liability

The statutory development of fault liability has been sporadic. It can be divided broadly into two categories: statutes designed to reverse a particular judicial decision, and statutes effecting wider reforms. Examples of the first category can be found throughout the period of our study – such as the Directors Liability Act 1891,[101] the Employer's Liability (Defective Equipment) Act 1969[102] and the Compensation Act 2006, s. 3.[103] The provisions of such Acts tend to be short, and do little to elaborate fault concepts. Often they involve recourse to legal fictions. The Employer's Liability (Defective Equipment) Act, for instance, was passed in response to a careful judicial analysis showing that there was no negligence on the part of an employer who supplied a tool with a latent defect to his employee, where the tool had been made by a reputable manufacturer and purchased from a reputable seller.[104] The Act simply decreed that the employer in such a situation was to be treated as if he had been negligent.[105] Clearly the statutory provision could not be explained in terms of fault. But – unlike judicial development – no alternative explanation needed to be given to rationalise the change in the law.

99 *British Railways Board* v. *Herrington* [1972] 1 AC 877, 897.

100 Paterson, *The Law Lords*, p. 155.

101 Reversing *Derry* v. *Peek* (1889) 14 App Cas 337.

102 Reversing *Davie* v. *New Merton Board Mills Ltd* [1959] AC 604.

103 Reversing *Barker* v. *Corus UK Ltd* [2006] 2 AC 572.

104 *Davie* v. *New Merton Board Mills Ltd* [1959] AC 604.

105 Employer's Liability (Defective Equipment) Act 1969, s. 1: 'the injury shall be deemed to be … attributable to negligence on the part of the employer'.

More systematic efforts to reform the common law (including fault liability) were a twentieth-century phenomenon. The starting point was the Law Revision Committee, appointed by Lord Sankey in 1934 'To consider how far, having regard to the statute law and to judicial decisions, such legal maxims and doctrines as the Lord Chancellor may from time to time refer to the Committee require revision in modern conditions'.[106] Its members included judges, barristers, solicitors and academics. The Committee produced a series of Reports containing recommendations for reform, the majority of which were implemented by the legislature. Several of the Reports related to fault liability, the most important one proposing the introduction of apportionment for cases of contributory negligence. It is, therefore, vital to understand how and why the Committee was created.

The obvious catalyst for the creation of the Committee was a speech about law reform in general, given by Llewellyn-Jones MP in a parliamentary debate in December 1932.[107] However, as the Lord Chancellor's Office file on the subject makes clear, Llewellyn-Jones actually played no real part in the process.[108] Rather, it was Donald Somervell MP, who had made only a short speech in the debate,[109] who started things off by later writing to Sir Claud Schuster, the permanent secretary in the Lord Chancellor's Office. Somervell suggested that law reform proposals formulated by the Lord Chancellor's Office should be considered by 'a committee on which there might be a panel of MPs with legal qualifications from all parties with co-opted Law Lords or Judges and practitioners specially qualified to deal with the matter under discussion'.[110] Schuster replied with a different suggestion:[111]

> my mind has been for a long time running on the same lines as yours in this matter ... But while the lines on which my mind has been running have been parallel with yours, they have not been convergent. I am not greatly in love with your proposal for a panel of legal M.P.s ... What I now propose – and have indeed had it in my mind for a long time – is the constitution by the Lord Chancellor of a Standing Committee comprising

[106] Law Revision Committee, Interim Report Cmd 4540 (1934), p. 3.

[107] J. Farrar, *Law Reform and the Law Commission* (London: Sweet and Maxwell, 1974), p. 9.

[108] LCO 2/3565, Law Revision Committee, Personnel of Committee and Terms of Reference.

[109] *Hansard's Parliamentary Debates*, Vol. CCLXXIII, cols. 1133–1134 (21 December 1932).

[110] LCO 2/3565, note drafted by Somervell to Schuster, 21 February 1933.

[111] *Ibid.*, Schuster to Somervell, 24 February 1933.

> Judges, members of the Bar and members of the Law Society as well as one or two persons of experience from the outside world.

It should be noted that there was no role for academic lawyers here.

Schuster envisaged that the Committee would be chaired by Lord Hanworth MR; since Hanworth was then occupied with a committee on the business of the courts, Schuster decided to wait. Nine months later, when Hanworth's committee had completed its work, Schuster wrote to him, saying that 'The Lord Chancellor has for some time had it in mind to appoint a Standing Committee … to advise him as to substantive amendments in the law.'[112] He invited Hanworth to be its chairman, and suggested continuing with the personnel of the business of the courts committee. After some delay, Hanworth accepted, but, he added, 'as to the composition of the Committee. I am rather inclined to think that we should need some heavier metal from the point of pure law added to it.'[113] Schuster's reply was revealing:[114]

> I agree that it would be well to strengthen the Committee on the purely legal side. But it is not very easy to find pure lawyers who are also easy to work with and free from crankiness. Among the Oxford men, I have sat on a Committee with Holdsworth and found him impossible. I do not think very highly of Zulueta. Brierly is excellent, but his strength lies rather in international law than in English Common Law. Of all the teachers, professors and leaders whom I have met in recent years, I prefer Gutteridge, McNair and Wade, all of whom are Cambridge men.

Gutteridge and McNair became the first two academic members of the Committee. Further correspondence showed the similar care taken over other personnel – Cyril Asquith (later Lord Asquith), for instance, was appointed on Lord Hanworth's personal recommendation and insistence.[115] Schuster even worried about having a committee of thirteen – 'So many people have odd ideas about that number that I do not like to take a final step without authority.'[116] Hanworth felt that 'the best plan' would be to find an extra person.[117]

Several points should be noted here. First, whilst the Committee was, formally, appointed by the Lord Chancellor, the decision to create it and whom to put on it was entirely left to Schuster, his permanent secretary.

[112] *Ibid.*, Schuster to Hanworth, 31 October 1933.
[113] *Ibid.*, Hanworth to Schuster, 9 December 1933.
[114] *Ibid.*, Schuster to Hanworth, 11 December 1933.
[115] *Ibid.*, Hanworth to Schuster, 17 December 1933; 20 December 1933.
[116] *Ibid.*, Schuster to Hanworth, 22 December 1933.
[117] *Ibid.*, Hanworth to Schuster, 28 December 1933. The fourteenth man was Topham KC.

Undoubtedly Lord Sankey was sympathetic to the idea – that was perhaps due to Harold Laski, who had urged the creation of such a body, praised Sankey's advanced thinking on such matters[118] and sent Sankey a copy of his article, which Sankey enjoyed.[119] But the fact remained that the real choices were being made by someone else. Second, the academic contribution to law reform had been included very late in the day. But, third, and perhaps more importantly, Schuster's assessment of who would be good to work with had resulted in the appointment of England's leading comparative lawyer. If Holdsworth had been less cranky, it would all have been very different.

The Committee's reports achieved an enviable success rate in their conversion to legislation. They also set a high scholarly standard – the contributory negligence report, for instance, dealt confidently with Admiralty law and a range of Civil law jurisdictions.[120] If they suffered from a defect, it was their narrowness of focus: each Report considered one specific, detailed doctrinal question.[121] There was no scope for discussion of wider issues such as the structure of fault liability, or the kind of broader themes that might unite apparently disparate areas of tort law.[122]

It is tempting to blame the Lord Chancellor (or his Office) for this lack of ambition. According to the terms of reference, he decided what to refer to the Committee,[123] and it is certainly true that the Lord Chancellor supplied the first four (narrow) topics for consideration.[124] But appearances were deceptive. It was not the case that the Committee could never suggest topics[125] – contributory negligence was, for instance, put forward by the Committee's then Chairman, Lord Wright.[126] Wright also asked for

118 Laski, 'Justice and the Law' in *Studies in Law and Politics* (London: George Allen & Unwin, 1932), pp. 276, 291–295.

119 Heuston, *Lives of the Lord Chancellors*, p. 511.

120 Law Revision Committee, Eighth Report (Contributory Negligence) Cmd 6032 (1939), 17.

121 For an instance where the Committee's narrowly defined terms of reference were particularly problematic see P. Mitchell, '*Fibrosa Spolka Akcyjna* v. *Fairbairn Lawson Combe Barbour Ltd* (1942)' in C. Mitchell and P. Mitchell (eds.), *Landmark Cases in the Law of Restitution* (Oxford: Hart, 2006) pp. 247, 259–264.

122 E.g. W. Friedmann, 'Modern Trends in the Law of Torts' (1937) 1 *Modern Law Review* 39. On Friedmann generally see J. Bell, 'Wolfgang Friedmann (1907–1972) with an Excursus on Gustav Radbruch (1878–1949)' in Beatson and Zimmermann, *Jurists Uprooted*, p. 517.

123 Hughes Parry, 'Modern Problems and Methods of Law Reform' 11; R. Lee, in discussion following A. McNair, 'Law Teaching and Law Reform' (1934) *Journal of the Society of Public Teachers of Law* 1, 9; and McNair's reply, *ibid.*

124 LCO 2/3565.

125 Farrar, *Law Reform and the Law Commission*, p. 13.

126 LCO 2/1989, Law Revision Committee – Extended Terms of Reference. Wright to Schuster, 2 April 1937.

two extra academic members to deal with the subject – Stallybrass and Winfield.[127] Both requests were granted.

The real explanation is, it is suggested, both more subtle and more revealing. Statutory reform of the common law was not uncontroversial. There was a lawyer's tradition of, if not hostility, at least adopting a 'formal and arm's-length attitude' towards statutes.[128] Statutes were neither read as expositions of principle, nor as illustrations of some broader idea. They were seen as being foreign to the common law, and were often construed in a literal manner that undermined their purpose. Commentators in the 1930s pointed to the cases narrowly interpreting workmen's compensation legislation as exemplifying what happened when an ambitious statute fell into judicial hands.[129] The importance of a more sophisticated approach to statute was a recurring theme in writings on the reform of legal education.[130]

Against this background, the Law Revision Committee's caution was understandable. So, too, was one of its distinctive drafting techniques, namely, the extensive use of common law concepts. This seems to have been an attempt to embed the statutory provision into the common law. Thus, for instance, the Law Reform (Contributory Negligence) Act 1945 provided in s. 1(1) that:

> Where any person suffers damage as the result partly of his own fault and partly of the fault of any other person or persons, a claim in respect of that damage shall not be defeated by reason of the fault of the person suffering the damage, but the damages recoverable in respect thereof shall be reduced to such extent as the court thinks just and equitable having regard to the claimant's share in the responsibility for the damage.

At first sight this was a broad general principle, which sounded rather like the similar provisions to be found in the French and German Civil Codes. But s. 1(1) had to be read in conjunction with the definition section, s. 4:

127 *Ibid.*

128 Amos, 'The Interpretation of Statutes'.

129 Hughes Parry, 'Modern Problems and Methods of Law Reform', 13; Laski, 'Justice and the Law', pp. 281, 286.

130 Amos, 'The Interpretation of Statutes'; L. Gower, 'English Legal Training' (1950) 13 *Modern Law Review* 137, 176–177; G. Gardiner, 'Law Reform and the Teachers of Law' (1966–1967) 9 *Journal of the Society of Public Teachers of Law*, new series 190, 192 (calling for universities to teach parliamentary drafting skills). One of the innovative features of the *Modern Law Review* was its section devoted to recent statutes: C. Glasser, 'Radicals and Refugees: The Foundation of the Modern Law Review and English Legal Scholarship' (1987) 50 *Modern Law Review* 688, 699.

'"fault" means negligence, breach of statutory duty or other act or omission which gives rise to liability in tort or would, apart from this Act, give rise to the defence of contributory negligence'. This section indicated that the Act applied only to situations where contributory negligence had previously been a defence; it was not introducing a broad general principle of apportionment.[131]

The Law Revision Committee delivered its final report in 1939. The Second World War and postwar reconstruction caused a suspension of its duties, but in 1952 it was resurrected, in all but name and personnel.[132] The Law Reform Committee operated much as its predecessor had done: there was a range of legal experts, serving part-time, and dealing with very specific questions. The same cautious drafting techniques were also in evidence: the Occupiers Liability Act 1957, for example, left the meaning of 'occupier' to be determined by common law and 'amalgamated (without redefining)'[133] the common law categories of invitee and licensee, to whom a common duty of care was to be owed. There was still the sense that statutory reform of the common law was an unwanted guest: it should disturb existing arrangements as little as possible, and keep a low profile.

The creation of the Law Commission in 1965 suggested that this traditional attitude to statutory reform would have to change. Now there was a full-time body, with a statutory duty to reform the law, and an obligation to consider comparative materials.[134] There was even talk of codification.[135] But, nothing has come of it, and little use has been made of the duty to consider comparative materials.[136] Indeed, the most noteworthy contributions to fault liability by the Law Commission have either been prompted by judges,[137] or are narrowly focussed.[138]

The statutory elaboration of fault liability has, therefore, been dictated by the need to accommodate itself to the dominant common law approach. As a result, it has been unambitious, and the influence of

[131] *Standard Chartered Bank* v. *Pakistan National Shipping Corpn (Nos. 2 and 4)* [2003] 1 AC 959.

[132] E. Wade, 'The Machinery of Law Reform' (1961) 24 *Modern Law Review* 3.

[133] *Tomlinson* v. *Congleton Borough Council* [2004] 1 AC 46, [6] (per Lord Hoffmann).

[134] Law Commissions Act 1965, s. 3.

[135] L. Scarman, 'Law Reform: Lessons from English Experience' (1968) 3 *Manitoba Law Journal* 47, 52–53.

[136] Jolowicz, 'Comparative Law in Twentieth-Century England', pp. 359–361.

[137] Occupiers Liability Act 1984, prompted by *British Railways Board* v. *Herrington* [1972] 1 AC 877.

[138] E.g. Defective Premises Act 1972.

comparative material has been slight. Statutory intervention has also, occasionally, been counter-productive in terms of legal change: the courts have said that Parliament has defined the legal position, and that it would contradict Parliament's intentions to go further using common law techniques. Thus, the House of Lords, in *Murphy* v. *Brentwood District Council*,[139] refused to find a duty of care owed by a negligent builder to a purchaser of a house *precisely because* Parliament had given a statutory remedy in the Defective Premises Act 1972 (which could not be used by the purchaser on the facts).[140] It should also be noted that, in ascertaining Parliament's intentions, the courts until recently could not look at any preparatory materials; even now, the range of materials they can consider is circumscribed.[141] As a result, cases could turn on what judges were prepared to read into parliamentary silence on a particular point: did it mean that Parliament wanted the law to stay the same, or that Parliament had no view?[142] This was hardly a satisfactory method for developing the law coherently.[143]

III Conclusion

The judicial and statutory elaboration of fault liability in England has been strongly coloured by institutional and professional factors. Judicial elaboration has been a product of the interaction between the methods of appointment, the style of litigation and individual ideology. In particular, the common law approach to judicial decision-making, with its individualised, discursive style, encouraged the exposition and refinement of principles. Often those principles would be coloured by the facts of the case before the court,[144] but there were prominent instances where courts laid down propositions in abstract terms, or embarked on expositions that were unnecessary for the decision. The decision on remoteness of damage in *In re an Arbitration between Polemis and*

139 [1991] AC 398.

140 For a different approach to the relationship between common law and statute in this situation see R. Cooke (later Lord Cooke), 'An Impossible Distinction' (1991) 107 *Law Quarterly Review* 46, 68–69.

141 *Pepper* v. *Hart* [1993] AC 593. The implications of the decision are well brought out in D. Miers, 'Taxing Perks and Interpreting Statutes: *Pepper* v. *Hart*' (1993) 56 *Modern Law Review* 695.

142 *British Railways Board* v. *Herrington* [1972] 1 AC 877, 897 (Lord Reid).

143 See further A. Watson, *The Evolution of Western Private Law* (Baltimore: Johns Hopkins University Press, 2001), pp. 64–74.

144 Goff, 'The Search for Principle', 183.

Another and Furness, Withy and Company Limited[145] is perhaps the best example of the former; the creation of the principle of assumption of responsibility in *Hedley Byrne & Co. Ltd* v. *Heller and Partners Ltd*[146] is the best example of the latter in the period. There was also significant scope for individual innovation. Since England is one of the larger jurisdictions involved in our study, this might seem at first sight to be surprising. However, the explanation lies in the pyramid structure of the court system. Trial judges had little opportunity to innovate, especially given the constraints of the doctrine of precedent. But appellate judges, of whom there were only a very limited number for most of the period of our study, had such opportunities and sat in small numbers (three in the Court of Appeal, five in the House of Lords). A determined judge needed only to convince one or two of his colleagues to support any proposed innovation.

Statutory elaboration has consistently either responded narrowly to judicial decisions, or made minor amendments to existing law; in either form, it has been in the common law's shadow. The reform of fault liability was clearly not a political priority.[147] The creation of the Law Revision Committee in the 1930s might have signalled more active intervention, but, for the most part, reform has been left to the judges. For some important actors in the development of fault liability, this residual role for statutory reform was not inappropriate. Indeed, Lord Diplock once hinted at a very limited role for statutory reform when he commented that every Law Reform Committee Report announced a failure of judicial courage and imagination.[148] Diplock's point was that an appropriately bold judiciary would render statutory reform unnecessary. That, perhaps, overlooked the possibility that Parliament might not welcome boldness.[149] But his comment also suggests a further point, which can be seen in both judicial and statutory developments of fault liability. Courage and imagination are needed to accomplish legal change, but they are neither equally distributed, nor requirements for a successful legal career. It is pretty easy to spot who has these qualities and who does not: one Lord Chancellor even claimed to have a

[145] [1921] 3 KB 560 (discussed in text accompanying n. 32, above).

[146] [1964] AC 465.

[147] Cf. workmen's compensation reforms, discussed in Chapter 3 by P. Bartrip (p. 36), where orthodox fault liability rules were seen as contributing to a social problem.

[148] Diplock, *The Courts as Legislators*, p. 21.

[149] E.g. Compensation Act 2006, s. 3, reversing *Barker* v. *Corus UK Ltd* [2006] 2 AC 572.

deliberate policy of appointing new Law Lords to achieve 'a good mixture' of personalities.[150] It only takes a minor adjustment in the personnel of a court or committee to tip the balance for or against change; whoever makes those choices goes a long way towards conditioning the final outcome.

[150] Paterson, *The Law Lords*, pp. 199–200 (quoting Lord Gardiner LC).

3

The impact of institutions and professions on compensation for occupational injury in England

PETER BARTRIP

I Introduction

Law and practice affecting compensation for occupational injury in England and Wales underwent several transformations between the mid nineteenth century and the end of the twentieth. In 1850 it was virtually impossible for workers to obtain compensation through the courts for injury sustained at work. Over the next 30 years, judicial decisions further restricted the opportunity for injured workers to win damages. The Factory Act 1844 provided a degree of relief but only in narrowly circumscribed circumstances.[1] More significantly, the Employers' Liability Act 1880 curtailed the defence of common employment that had emerged in the preceding decades. Nevertheless, before and after 1880, injured workers who sought compensation from an employer needed to prove negligence on the part of that employer. This could mean unequal contests between parties with wildly disparate economic resources. Consequently, injured workers often had little recourse but to rely on charity, support from a trade union or friendly society, or the publicly funded and generally much reviled Poor Law.

In terms of legal principle and the transfer of resources, the Workmen's Compensation Act 1897 was more important than either the Employers' Liability Act or any factory Act. It established a no-fault system of compensation for certain categories of occupationally injured (though, initially, not occupationally sick) workers. In future, these workers had 'only' to demonstrate that their injuries had arisen 'out of and in the course of employment' in order to recover compensation, either directly from their employer or from the employer's insurer. Contributory

[1] See P. W. J. Bartrip and S. B. Burman, *The Wounded Soldiers of Industry: Industrial Compensation Policy, 1833–1897* (Oxford: Clarendon Press, 1983), Chapter 3.

negligence provided no bar to recovery, though a worker's 'serious and wilful misconduct' could. The new regime was never meant to provide full restitution; rates of compensation, determined by a claimant's previous earnings, were subject to payment ceilings. Nevertheless, champions of workmen's compensation believed that with the passing of the 1897 Act a simple, non-contentious and swift system of compensating injured workers existed for the first time. Injured workers, hitherto underprivileged, had access to benefits unavailable to others similarly incapacitated.

Workmen's compensation, amended and extended as it was over the decades, lasted for almost exactly 50 years before being replaced by the National Insurance (Industrial Injuries) Act 1946 (implemented in July 1948). A significant development in the course of this half century was extension of the legislation to cover not only accidental injury but also a number of occupational diseases. In the course of its existence workmen's compensation benefited millions of workers and their dependants. It provided a measure of economic security to 'the wounded soldiers of industry' that had not existed before. From the first, however, it was a seriously flawed system. Not only did it generate much litigation, it also damaged industrial relations by pitting workers and trade unions against employers and insurers in a battle over money in the stressful circumstances of injury or bereavement. During the Second World War, when national solidarity was of overriding importance, these flaws came to be seen as intolerable.

From 1948 compensation was provided not by employers or private insurers but by the State through national insurance. A private no-fault scheme became a public one. One thing remained unchanged; those injured in the workplace retained a favoured position. They were still entitled to publicly funded benefits unavailable to those who, though similarly impaired, had sustained their impairment outside the workplace. In short, injured workers, who for most of the nineteenth century had been seriously underprivileged, retained a preferential position compared with the rest of the community. The remainder of this chapter explores the factors responsible for the transformations outlined above; it then briefly reviews post-1948 developments.

II Common law developments

By 1850 the law on fault liability for occupational injury was undergoing important developments. In particular, legal judgments were restricting the opportunity for workers to recover damages for injuries sustained at work almost before any such claims arose. The first such judgment was Lord Abinger's in *Priestley* v. *Fowler* (1837), the first reported High Court case of an employee suing his employer for personal injury sustained at work.[2] Briefly, the facts of the case were as follows. Charles Priestley, a butcher's assistant in Lincolnshire who sustained a broken leg and other injuries when a delivery cart overturned, sued his employer, Thomas Fowler, for damages. The plaintiff's action against his master for breach of the common law duty of care succeeded in the Lincolnshire Assizes. However, on appeal the Court of Exchequer overturned this verdict and found for the master. The case has been so frequently reviewed that it is unnecessary to go into further detail here.[3] For our purposes the essential point is that judgment went in favour of Fowler because of a fiction the court created, namely that in accepting employment an employee also accepted the risks, known or obvious, incidental to that employment.

As has been noted elsewhere, the decision in *Priestley* v. *Fowler* did not mark the beginning of the doctrine of common employment.[4] The true source of the doctrine was an 1842 judgment of the Supreme Court of Massachusetts in the case of *Farwell* v. *Boston and Worcester Railroad Corporation* (1842) in which it was held that the carelessness and negligence of those in the same employment constituted part of the ordinary

[2] (1837) 3 M & W 1; LJ 7 Ex 42; 1 Jur 987; 3 Murph & H 305.

[3] See for example R. L. Howells, '*Priestley* v. *Fowler* and the Factory Acts' (1963) 26 *Modern Law Review* 367–395; L. M. Friedman and J. Ladinsky, 'Social Change and the Law of Industrial Accidents' (1967) 67 *Columbia Law Review* 50–82; T. Ingman, 'The Rise and Fall of the Doctrine of Common Employment' (1978) *Juridical Review* 106–125; T. Ingman, 'A History of the Defence of *volenti non fit injuria*' (1981) *Juridical Review* 1–28; H. Smith, 'Judges and the Lagging Law of Compensation for Personal Injuries in the Nineteenth Century' (1981) 2 *Journal of Legal History* 258–275; R. A. Epstein, 'The Historical Origins and Structure of Workmen's Compensation' (1982) 16 *Georgia Law Review* 775–819; Bartrip and Burman, *The Wounded Soldiers of Industry*, pp. 24–25; anon., comment: 'The Creation of a Common Law Rule: The Fellow Servant Rule, 1837–1860' (1984) 132 *University of Pennsylvania Law Review* 579–620; G. W. Schwartz, 'The Character of Early American Tort Law' (1989) 36 *UCLA Law Review* 641–718; W. R. Cornish and G. de N. Clark, *Law and Society in England, 1750–1950* (London: Sweet and Maxwell, 1989), pp. 496–498; R. W. Kostal, *Law and English Railway Capitalism, 1825–1875* (Oxford: Clarendon Press, 1994), pp. 259–270; A. W. B. Simpson, *Leading Cases in the Common Law* (Oxford: Clarendon Press, 1995), Chapter 5; M. A. Stein, '*Priestley* v. *Fowler* (1837) and the Emerging Tort of Negligence' (2003–2004) 44 *Boston College Law Review* 689–731.

[4] Stein, '*Priestley* v. *Fowler* (1837) and the Emerging Tort of Negligence', 689; T. Beven, *Principles of the Law of Negligence* (London: Stephens and Haynes, 1889), p. 375; Bartrip and Burman, *The Wounded Soldiers of Industry*, p. 105; Kostal, *Law and English Railway Capitalism*, p. 271.

risks that an employee accepted when undertaking a job.[5] The *Farwell* and *Priestley* decisions both non-suited the plaintiff, but they did so on different grounds: voluntary assumption of risk in the *Priestley* case, and common employment in the case of *Farwell*. The similarity between the two cases lay in the denial of the opportunity, scarcely before it had arisen, for employees to sue negligent employers with much hope of success.

From 1850, in particular, a succession of legal judgments on both sides of the Atlantic further limited this opportunity. These judgments included *Hutchinson* v. *York, Newcastle and Berwick Railway Company* (1850), which imported the doctrine of common employment to England.[6] Other significant cases include *Wigmore* v. *Jay* (1850),[7] *Wiggett* v. *Fox* (1856),[8] *Degg* v. *Midland Railway Co.* (1857),[9] *Ormond* v. *Holland & Holland* (1858),[10] *Bartonshill Coal Co.* v. *Reid* (1858),[11] *Potts* v. *Port Carlisle Dock Co.* (1860),[12] *Morgan* v. *Vale of Neath Railway Co.* (1864)[13] and *Wilson* v. *Merry and Cunningham* (1868).[14]

In legal theory (and in practice in some instances) employers remained liable in circumstances where they neglected their personal duty of care.[15] However, economic trends involving the creation of larger work units meant that many employers were distant from the point of production. In these circumstances plaintiffs focussed on an employer's duty to provide safe premises, safe machinery and equipment, and a safe system of working. *Paterson* v. *Wallace* recognised an employer's responsibility to provide safe machinery and equipment, but only where work was 'of a dangerous character'.[16] Judgment in *Dynen* v. *Leach* (1857) further restricted liability by excluding cases in which a worker knew of the hazards of a machine but used it anyway.[17] This was tantamount to a denial that employers were liable for providing faulty equipment. *Brydon* v. *Stewart* (1855) 'firmly established … the employer's duty to provide safe premises for his workmen'.[18] However, subsequent case law established that the employer was liable only when the injured worker was unaware

[5] (1842) 38 Am Dec 339. [6] (1850) 5 Ex 343. [7] *Ibid.*, 354.
[8] (1856) 11 Ex 832. [9] (1857) 1 H & N 773.
[10] (1858) EB & E 102. [11] (1858) 3 Macq 300.
[12] (1860) 8 WR 524. [13] (1864) 5 B & S 570.
[14] (1868) LR 1 HL (Scot.) 326.
[15] *Ashworth* v. *Stanwix and Walker* (1861) 3 El & El 701; *Mellows* v. *Shaw & Unwin* (1861) 5 Ex. 343.
[16] (1854) 1 Macq. 748 HL.
[17] (1857) 26 LJ Ex 221.
[18] Bartrip and Burman, *The Wounded Soldiers of Industry*, p. 121; (1855) 25 LT 58 HL.

of the danger.[19] As for the obligation to provide a safe system of working, *Grizzle* v. *Frost* (1863) was 'one of the few instances of an employer being held liable to provide a safe system of working in the first two-thirds of the [nineteenth] century'.[20]

Where breach of an employer's personal duty of care provided the grounds for an action, the defendant could often defeat a claim by resorting to the defence of *volenti non fit injuria* (voluntary assumption of risk).[21] An even surer defence was that of contributory negligence, which dated back to the non-occupational case of *Butterfield* v. *Forrester* (1809), whereby no accident victim who was in any degree responsible for his own injury could bring a successful suit.[22] Proof of contributory negligence on the part of a plaintiff remained an absolute bar to success until the Law Reform (Contributory Negligence) Act 1945.[23] Unlike the defence of common employment, *volenti* and contributory negligence applied outside the workplace but, it has been observed, these defences 'received particular application' in the occupational context.[24]

For much of the mid nineteenth century, the cost of bringing a damages action surely deterred many injured workers from seeking redress through the courts. But financial barriers apart, the fellow-servant rule, along with the defences of *volenti* (at least until it was limited by a decision in 1891) and contributory negligence effectively ruled out most claims.[25] Indeed, because these defences made successful personal injury actions such an unlikely outcome, there was little point in risking scarce personal resources. Judges, of course, did not make injured workers too poor to sue, but the legal fictions that constituted a second line of defence against potential suitors were inventions of the judiciary. So the question arises, why did judges take a hard line against those injured in the workplace?

In the absence of legal precedent, as Lord Abinger made clear, the decision in *Priestley* v. *Fowler* was based on policy, rather than legal, considerations: 'It is admitted that there is no precedent for the present action by a servant against a master. We are, therefore, to decide the question upon general principles, and in doing so we are at liberty to look at the

19 *Brooks* v. *Courtney* (1869) 20 LT 440.

20 (1863) 3 F & F 622; Bartrip and Burman, *The Wounded Soldiers of Industry*, p. 122. See also *Vose* v. *Lancs. and Yorks. Railway Co.* (1858) 27 LJ Ex 249.

21 *Saxton* v. *Hawksworth* (1872) 26 LT 851.

22 (1809) 11 East 60.

23 8 & 9 Geo. VI c. 28. It could then be no more than a partial defence.

24 H. Luntz, D. Hambly and R. A. Hayes, *Torts, Cases and Commentary* (Sydney: Butterworths, 1980), p. 337.

25 *Smith* v. *Baker and Sons* [1891] AC 325.

consequences of a decision the one way or the other.'[26] He went on to reflect that judgment for the plaintiff would encourage carelessness on the part of workers and, hence, more death and injury. Thus, paradoxically, a judgment for the master would actually serve workers', as well as masters', interests. Elsewhere in his judgment, however, Abinger indicated that he was mainly concerned about leaving employers exposed to frivolous claims.[27]

The reluctance of mid-nineteenth-century judges to find for injured workers raises questions about their impartiality. Were their judgments driven by a desire to uphold the interests of the socio-economic class of which they were members? Alternatively, did their decisions reflect, as Atiyah has argued, prevalent free-market beliefs that held that workers were free to accept or reject employment as they saw fit, including on the basis of risk assessment and wage rates?[28]

Before attempting to answer such questions, it is necessary to ascertain whether High Court judges in our period were drawn from the same class and shared a common background. Daniel Duman has studied the social, occupational and educational backgrounds of the 208 High Court judges who held office in England between 1727 and 1875. He has also investigated their incomes and investments. Across the period as a whole he discerns a 'rapid and continuous decline in the contribution of the landed classes to the English judiciary'.[29] In contrast, the number and percentage of judges from professional backgrounds increased from about one-quarter in the mid eighteenth century to over one-half in the second quarter of the nineteenth. Those from a business or merchant/proprietor background increased steadily from the end of the eighteenth century and constituted 31 per cent of the judiciary between 1850 and 1875. Judges of working-class origin were always uncommon; between 1850 and 1875 there were none. Hence, notwithstanding changes in the social origins of the judiciary (based on father's occupation) across the period, one constant was that the bench 'remained an almost exclusively middle and upper class preserve'.[30] In this respect, there was considerable commonality among judges.

[26] (1837) 3 M & W 5. [27] *Ibid.*, 1; LJ 7 Ex 42; 1 Jur 987; 3 M & H 305.

[28] P. S. Atiyah, *The Rise and Fall of Freedom of Contract* (Oxford: Oxford University Press, 1979), Chapter 13.

[29] D. Duman, *The Judicial Bench in England 1727–1875: The Reshaping of a Professional Elite* (London: Royal Historical Society, 1982), pp. 51–52.

[30] *Ibid.*, p. 53. Duman identifies the professions as: barrister, clergyman, military officer, government official/civil servant, doctor, solicitor/conveyancer, teacher, miscellaneous professions.

As for wealth and income, High Court judges 'were among the most affluent professional men in eighteenth- and nineteenth-century England'.[31] James Scarlett (Lord Abinger) earned some £15,000 p.a. when practising as a barrister between 1818 and 1835. Such an income made him one of the highest earners at the Bar.[32] When Chief Baron his salary and emoluments were in the region of £7,000 p.a. However, the evidence is that judges invested little in canals, railways and other 'speculative ventures'.[33] Accordingly, they had little direct personal economic incentive to treat leniently businessmen who came before their courts as defendants in personal injury actions. If Lord Abinger displayed bias in his ruling in *Priestley* v. *Fowler*, it can hardly be said, given the occupations of the adversaries (a provincial butcher with a failing business and his juvenile assistant) that this bias was towards big business and against the industrial worker. If his lordship was concerned about the potential future liabilities of anyone, he appeared most anxious to protect gentlemen from the legal consequences of negligent domestic servants. So the evidence is conflicting. Bartrip and Burman reject the suggestion 'that judges had a particular interest in protecting employers from any extension of liability'.[34] Kostal observes that charges of class bias, conscious or unconscious, are simplistic and unproven. Nevertheless, as he also points out, 'Victorian judges willed that … workers should fail in their personal injury lawsuits and that [railway] passengers should succeed.' He states, furthermore, that this difference owed much to the presence of middle- and upper-class travellers on trains.[35] Consequently, if judicial decisions against workers were not motivated by personal bias, it is plausible that class interest influenced attitudes. At least, it is hard to deny that judicial decisions reflected a laissez-faire outlook that was broadly favourable to the interests of the well-to-do and inimical to those of the worker.

III Employers' Liability Act 1880

The first attempt to alter the law occurred in 1862, when Acton Ayrton, a lawyer and Liberal MP for Tower Hamlets, joined forces with Lord Robert Montagu, Conservative MP for Huntingdonshire, in an effort to improve

31 *Ibid.*, p. 105. 32 *Ibid.*, pp. 106, 109. 33 *Ibid.*, p. 138.

34 Bartrip and Burman, *The Wounded Soldiers of Industry*, p. 124.

35 Kostal, *Law and English Railway Capitalism*, pp. 106–107, 282, 314. See also M. Lobban, *The Common Law and English Jurisprudence, 1760–1850* (Oxford: Clarendon Press, 1991), Chapter 9.

the lot of injured workers and their families by giving them scope to bring damages actions against masters in most circumstances. Both men had something of the maverick about them. Ayrton, well known as a 'staunch reformer', was also renowned for 'independence of character'. A member of the Law Amendment Society, he was apparently moved to action by the demands of working-class constituents. Montagu, known as a 'controversialist', often espoused unpopular causes and adopted radical positions on social questions.[36] Their Bill was a response to the perceived injustice of the fellow-servant rule, which effectively protected employers who had a screen of employees between themselves and an accident victim.[37] The reports of mines and factory inspectors convinced Ayrton that while many industrialists strove to conduct their operations safely, others were careless either because of their pursuit of profit or because they lacked the skill, humanity or means to take proper precautions. A change in the law would benefit 'well-conducted' businesses by forcing their less scrupulous competitors to bear the cost of accidents. The careless would thereby be encouraged to take safety seriously.[38]

The Bill encountered considerable parliamentary opposition, principally from the Attorney-General, who predicted the ruination of business and flight of capital if it became law.[39] The debate was dominated by fear that employers could face liability for injuries they had no power to prevent, enormous bills for compensation and obligations to workers that far exceeded those involving members of the public or their own families. In the face of such opposition Ayrton and Montagu withdrew their Bill and the prospects of reform disappeared for a decade. When the issue came to the fore in the 1870s the political climate had changed substantially. In 1867 the Second Reform Act greatly increased the size of the electorate. The new voters were working-class males who now formed a majority of voters in urban areas. For years, few workers were elected to Parliament, but with the growing importance through the 1870s of the Trades Union Congress (TUC) and the resolution of union-related grievances involving freedom to picket and the right to quit employment (through the Conspiracy and Protection of Property Act and the Employer and

[36] Articles on Acton Ayrton (1816–1886) and Lord Robert Montagu (1825–1902), www.oxforddnb.com.

[37] HC Deb Vol. III clxv col. 1842 (19 March 1862); Bartrip and Burman, *The Wounded Soldiers of Industry*, pp. 111–112.

[38] Bartrip and Burman, *The Wounded Soldiers of Industry*, p. 113; HC Deb Vol. III clxv cols. 1839, 1841 (19 March 1862).

[39] HC Deb. Vol. III clxv cols. 1843–1849 (19 March 1862).

Workmen Act, both 1875), the question of compensation for occupational injury became a priority for organised labour.

In the early 1870s the Home Office and the National Association for the Promotion of Social Science (successor to the Law Amendment Society) took up the issue. Before long the TUC and individual unions were also involved. A TUC Bill, introduced by Alexander Macdonald, one of the first working-class MPs, came before Parliament in 1876. It sought to abolish the defences of *volenti* and common employment. The TUC lobbied Parliament and submitted a petition with 34,000 names in support of the Bill. MPs with mining and railway connections were strongly opposed; so too was Disraeli's Conservative Government. But in contrast with the debate on Ayrton and Montagu's 1862 Bill, no MP defended the principle of common employment as the courts were then interpreting it.

Macdonald's Bill failed but the Government established a select committee of inquiry to investigate the issue. The TUC, which closely monitored the committee's deliberations, was desperately disappointed by recommendations that envisaged few changes to the existing law and stressed the responsibility of workers for accident prevention. Thereafter, Bills came thick and fast (four in 1879 alone). Essentially, these envisaged either radical reform (abolition of common employment) or more modest change (alteration in the definition of a fellow servant to exclude those in authority). By the end of the 1870s none had made progress.[40]

Employers' liability was an issue in the 1880 general election, with the TUC urging voters to shun candidates opposed to Macdonald's proposals. Gladstone's Liberal Government (1880–1885) was quick to bring forward a Bill. As this measure progressed through the House it elicited a number of reactions. Organised labour sought to uphold its principles and extend the range of occupations it covered. Industrialists and employers associations predicted the ruin of British business. Some judges bemoaned legislative interference with the sanctity of the common law.[41]

The Employers' Liability Act 1880 abolished the fellow-servant rule, but only in four circumstances:

1. For accidents caused by a fellow worker exercising the duty of a superintendent.
2. For accidents caused by a worker's obedience to orders or directions issued by a fellow servant in authority.

[40] Bartrip and Burman, *The Wounded Soldiers of Industry*, pp. 145–149.
[41] *Ibid.*, pp. 149–155.

3. For accidents caused by a fellow servant following the rules or instructions of an employer or someone with delegated authority.
4. For accidents caused by a fellow servant in control of a train or railway signal points.

There were other limitations. The Act did not apply to seamen, domestic servants or, with the exception of railway employees, those engaged in non-manual work; litigants could recover in damages no more than three years' wages; the defences of *volenti* and contributory negligence remained; employees could contract out of its terms – as they did in large numbers in some localities; the Act covered only the victims of accidents, not those who contracted an occupational disease or experienced other types of work-related ill health; injured workers still needed to prove fault and therefore fund suits against defendants in possession of greater financial resources.[42]

Notwithstanding these limitations the *Mining Journal* anticipated disaster all round: production would decline, industrial relations would suffer, impecunious or alienated employers would cease contributing to welfare schemes or working-class institutions. The TUC, on the other hand, was jubilant. In practice, the Act was more a minor adjustment to, than a revolution in, liability law. In 1881 County Courts awarded damages in only 26 instances and the average individual award was less than £70. V. Markham Lester has calculated that there were 3,000 County Court claims between 1881 and 1886 with a total of £120,000 awarded as damages.[43] Data provided by the Employers' Liability Insurance Corporation in 1886 indicated that of all the accidents involving injury or death to the employees of policyholders, only 12 per cent resulted in pay-outs. When a speaker at the TUC's 1891 Annual Congress termed the 1880 Act 'a fallacy, and a fraud on the working classes', his audience responded with cheers.[44]

The shortcomings of the new legislation meant that the movement to amend it arose almost immediately it was passed. Most of the Bills drawn up in the 1880s and 1890s originated with the TUC. Most tinkered with the principal Act by abolishing the right to contract out, further limiting the scope of the fellow-servant rule, raising the level of compensation

[42] 43 & 44 Vict. c. 42.

[43] Bartrip and Burman, *The Wounded Soldiers*, p. 173; V. Markham Lester, 'The Employers' Liability/Workmen's Compensation Debate of the 1890s Revisited' (2001) 44 *Historical Journal* 478.

[44] *Proceedings of the TUC Congress* (1891), 64.

paid or extending the categories of eligible worker. Bills failed for different reasons but, essentially, a Parliament that accorded the working man only a limited voice was unwilling to revisit an issue considered to have been resolved in 1880. With particular reference to the 1890s Lester has argued that the key political debate concerned the use of liability law to improve safety at work by imposing the costs of accidents on those best placed to prevent them – employers – or an insurance solution that guaranteed compensation regardless of fault.[45] There is, however, good reason to see the main thrust of reform efforts in the 1880s and 1890s as being both guaranteed compensation for the injured *and* the imposition on employers of financial burdens that reflected the true cost of accidents.

The 1884 Reform Act created around two million additional voters with a potential personal interest in occupational safety and compensation. During the 1886 general election campaign the TUC urged the newly enfranchised to support only candidates who supported reform of employers' liability law. In the event the Liberals fared badly in the election, not least because of the party's commitment to Irish home rule. In opposition the party, albeit with some ambivalence on the part of its leader, the elderly William Gladstone, began to demonstrate more sympathy to working-class concerns.[46] The Newcastle Programme, adopted by the National Liberal Federation in 1891, espoused a forthright radicalism, including a commitment to reform employers' liability. Though the direction the party took in this period was not universally applauded, the Liberals won the 1892 election and Gladstone returned to power at the head of a Government promising action on employers' liability. At its first annual congress after the election the TUC stressed the need for legislation to abolish the doctrine of common employment and meet its other long-standing demands. In 1893, the new Home Secretary, the reforming Herbert Asquith, produced a Bill that embodied most of the TUC's demands, including the abolition of contracting out. As such it can be seen as the Government's 'payment to labour for their support at the election'.[47]

Lester stresses that Asquith's principal objective was to improve workplace safety by introducing the threat of financial penalties, in the form

[45] Markham Lester, 'The Employers' Liability/Workmen's Compensation Debate', 471–495.

[46] G. R. Searle, *A New England: Peace and War, 1886–1918* (Oxford: Oxford University Press, 2004), pp. 208–209.

[47] Bartrip and Burman, *The Wounded Soldiers of Industry*, p. 191.

of damages payments, for employers who failed to prevent accidents.[48] He contrasts this approach with Joseph Chamberlain's position that '… no amendment of the Law relating to Employers' Liability will be final or satisfactory which does not provide compensation for workmen for all injuries sustained in the ordinary course of their employment and not caused by their own acts or default'.[49] Chamberlain's point was that Asquith's proposals promised to penalise employers for accidents they could not prevent, while failing to assist the many victims of occupational accidents whose injuries or deaths could be ascribed to no one. As he later said: 'You cannot induce the employer to take greater precautions by punishing him for accidents over which any precautions he may take will have absolutely no influence whatsoever … And that is all that the Bill does … If you think that you are going to make the workman more careful by punishing his employer you are very much mistaken.[50] He preferred a scheme that compensated all accident victims regardless of fault.

Lester regards Chamberlain's intervention as a stark parting of the ways between those who viewed compensation policy as a form of social insurance (who ultimately triumphed when the Workmen's Compensation Act 1897 was enacted) and those who saw it as a means towards higher standards of occupational safety. But Chamberlain's suggestion for an insurance-based solution was not new. Decades earlier Edwin Chadwick had argued for the automatic compensation of dependants of deceased accident victims provided death had not been caused by the victim's own 'gross and wilful misconduct'.[51] Insurance-based solutions were also discussed in the 1870s.[52] Neither did Chamberlain ignore the need to penalise negligent employers in the interest of improved safety. Though initially vague about how this should be done, he and others came to place their faith in the operation of the insurance market; by adjusting premiums, insurers would reward businesses with good claims records and penalise those with bad.[53] As for Asquith,

[48] Markham Lester, 'The Employers' Liability/Workmen's Compensation Debate' (2001) 44 *Historical Journal* 471, 479.

[49] HC Deb Vol. VIII col. 1961 (20 February 1893).

[50] HC Deb Vol. XX cols. 17–18 (20 December 1893).

[51] Parliamentary Papers (1846) xiii, Select Committee on Railway Labourers, evidence, p. 586.

[52] Bartrip and Burman, *The Wounded Soldiers of Industry*, pp. 139–145.

[53] University of Birmingham, Joseph Chamberlain Papers, Employers' Liability, JC6/3/3/18: confidential printed memorandum on workmen's accidents compensation, 17 February 1897; Parliamentary Papers (1898) xiv, Report of the Chief Inspector of Factories, pp. 20–21.

although his objective was to encourage employers to be more safety-conscious by imposing higher costs on companies whose workers suffered accidents, he too anticipated a significant role for insurance.[54]

IV Workmen's compensation

Asquith's Bill foundered because the House of Lords insisted that contracting out should be allowed. The next four years saw a great deal of parliamentary and extra-parliamentary debate, which led to the passage of the Workmen's Compensation Act 1897. Much of this debate involved the conversion of parties hostile to a no-fault solution. In essence the Act established that: 'If in any employment to which this Act applies personal injury by accident arising out of and in the course of employment is caused to a workmen, his employer shall … be liable to pay compensation' regardless of his fault in causing the accident and, except in cases of gross and wilful misconduct, regardless of the injured or deceased worker's contribution to his own misfortune. The Act applied to railways, factories, mines, quarries and engineering, and some construction work. It did not cover some large occupational groups such as seamen, domestic servants and agricultural workers. Compensation, payable where incapacity lasted for at least two weeks, was based on previous earnings but could not exceed the somewhat niggardly figures of £300 (lump sum) for a fatality or £1 per week for injury. The objective was not to restore injured workers to the position they occupied before they suffered their injury, but to mitigate the loss they suffered.

Why did the Act pass? Credit must be given to Chamberlain, who was the driving force behind its introduction, and also, over the longer term, to 'moral entrepreneurs' such as Edwin Chadwick. Overseas precedent, notably Germany's, also exerted an important influence.[55] What of the role of the major interest groups, without whose support the law would not have been changed? In fact, there was little enthusiasm for the Act on the part of any large organisation. The TUC and individual trade unions had been campaigning for employers' liability reform for years and were responsible in large part for creating a political climate in which it was accepted that 'something had to be done'. But the 1897 Act did not meet

[54] Bartrip and Burman, *The Wounded Soldiers of Industry*, p. 191.

[55] E. P. Hennock, *British Social Reform and German Precedents: The Case of Social Insurance, 1880–1914* (Oxford: Clarendon Press, 1987), pp. 3–4, 63–105; *The Origin of the Welfare State in England and Germany, 1850–1914* (Cambridge: Cambridge University Press, 2007), pp. 106–110.

the demands of organised labour. They objected to the failure to impose on employers the full costs of accidents suffered by their workers. As such, they feared workmen's compensation would do little to promote their main objective: occupational safety. Ultimately, however, organised labour was prepared to accept workmen's compensation as an attainable reform that promised to provide some relief to many workers. The alternative of a restructured employers' liability law that covered all workers with no contracting out, no defences of *volenti*, common employment or contributory negligence and no ceiling on the amount recoverable was, in contrast, a chimera.[56]

Industrialists were also unenthusiastic about the 1897 solution, for they stood to gain a potentially huge liability to pay compensation regardless of fault. Ultimately, they accepted such an outcome as preferable to the alternative of a punitive employers' liability law involving unpredictable, possibly unlimited damages awards. Workmen's compensation at least had the merit of involving relatively small individual payments for which budgetary provision could be made – not least through insurance. Lawyers, who first raised the insurance solution, were prepared to accept it because it did not interfere with the sanctity of the common law, as a revised employers' liability law threatened to do. For the Conservative politicians, who introduced the Bill, workmen's compensation was a means of appealing to working-class voters over the heads of trade union leaders and, in the process, outflanking the Liberals in the contest for working-class votes without alienating traditional supporters. In this respect the Act owed something to the extension of the franchise in the second half of the nineteenth century. It is notable that the Act did not cover agricultural labourers who constituted a substantial proportion of those enfranchised in 1884. However, the Workmen's Compensation Act 1900, which brought agricultural workers within the workmen's compensation scheme, originated with backbench Conservative MPs representing rural constituencies.[57] In summary, therefore, workmen's compensation was a compromise measure or the least bad solution.

Over the years workmen's compensation was extended and altered in several ways. Agricultural workers were covered from 1901. A 1906 Act mitigated the gross and wilful misconduct clause to the effect that it did not apply in cases of death or of serious and permanent disability. Under

[56] *Proceedings of the TUC Congress* (1895), p. 43.

[57] P. W. J. Bartrip, *Workmen's Compensation in Twentieth Century Britain: Law History and Social Policy* (Avebury: Aldershot, 1987), p. 28.

the same Act workers incapacitated by certain industrial diseases could claim. Further diseases became compensable over the years (30 by 1918). From 1918, special provision was made for silicosis and, later, asbestosis sufferers whose incapacity was slow to develop and hence not necessarily attributable to a single employer. Benefit levels were increased on a number of occasions, notably during the First World War when inflation hit the value of awards.[58] Whereas workers were initially expected to bear up to 50 per cent of any financial losses caused by a workplace injury, by 1940 compensation could cover up to 87.5 per cent of losses.[59] The waiting period for compensation was cut from a fortnight to a week in 1906, and to three days in 1923. From 1934 coal-mining companies were obliged to take out workmen's compensation insurance lest injured miners were left without compensation owing to an employer's bankruptcy.[60]

Notwithstanding such changes, the basic principles of the workmen's compensation system remained intact into the 1940s. Workmen's compensation endured for decades not because it gave universal satisfaction; this was far from the case. It was soon recognised as a badly flawed system that failed to promote safety. It also generated masses of litigation, notwithstanding its no-fault basis; conferred modest benefits (often after lengthy delay) that could be lost if an employer went out of business; and soured industrial relations. In addition, insurance company costs could consume a substantial slice of premium income.[61] In 1938, following years of representations from the TUC and the Labour Party, the Government announced the appointment of a Royal Commission to consider the future of the benefit. In July 1940 the Commission was suspended owing to the war. It never reconvened and never reported, but the evidence it had accumulated was turned over to the Beveridge Committee in June 1941.

V From Beveridge to national insurance

The Social Insurance and Allied Services Committee was appointed, under the chairmanship and almost total control of William Beveridge. It was appointed in large part to demonstrate to the trade unions that,

58 *Ibid.*, Chapters 3 and 4.

59 P. Cane, *Atiyah's Accidents, Compensation and the Law*, 7th edn (Cambridge: Cambridge University Press, 2006), p. 329.

60 Bartrip, *Workmen's Compensation*, Chapter 5.

61 Parliamentary Papers (1920) xxvi, pp. 13–16, Departmental Committee on Workmen's Compensation – though commercial insurers handled only a small proportion of workmen's compensation business (about 15 per cent by pay-out).

notwithstanding the suspension of the Royal Commission, compensation for occupational injury remained a Government concern.[62]

Although Beveridge considered that workmen's compensation 'was based on a wrong principle and has been dominated by a wrong outlook', he also viewed it as 'the pioneer system of social security', which had 'conferred great benefits'.[63] On balance, its 'disadvantages constituted a powerful argument for change'.[64] Beveridge favoured complete unification of workmen's compensation with the rest of national insurance provision. The first draft of his report stated that: 'There is no reason for differentiating in the compensation provided for involuntary loss of earnings, by reference to the contingency which brought it about. The cash benefits in unemployment, sickness and accident insurance should be the same.'[65]

Although such an amalgamation of different schemes 'would effect a tremendous simplification', Beveridge accepted that it was impossible to address problems of social insurance 'in a clear field'.[66] Abolition of a provision that had accorded victims of occupational disability preferential treatment for over 40 years would call for great 'sacrifice on the part of the workmen'. It would also impose unfair obligations on safe industries and remove safety incentives. In Beveridge's eyes, there were arguments (all of doubtful validity) for perpetuating the so-called 'industrial preference'. But the real reason for its retention was that organised labour would never agree to its abolition. So, as 'a somewhat illogical compromise', but also as a 'practical solution', Beveridge recommended only partial unification of industrial injuries compensation with his general scheme. A number of issues remained undecided. Among these was the question of alternative remedies – that is, whether to retain employers' liability at common law alongside a social security scheme. The Beveridge Report observed that it was 'obviously desirable as a matter of social policy to remove provision for the consequence of industrial hazards from the arena of litigation and conflict between the parties to production, so far as this can be done without condoning reprehensible carelessness by the employer'. It recommended that employers in hazardous industries (to be identified by future

62 W. Beveridge, *Power and Influence* (London: Hodder and Stoughton, 1953), p. 306; J. Harris, *William Beveridge: A Biography* (Oxford: Clarendon Press, 1997), p. 382.

63 Parliamentary Papers (1942–1943) vi, Report of the Interdepartmental Committee on Social Services and Allied Services, pp. 153–156.

64 Bartrip, *Workmen's Compensation*, p. 182.

65 Beveridge Papers (BP) viii 46, 'Social Insurance: General Considerations', July 1941; BP viii 32, undated and unsigned 'Memorandum on Industrial Accident and Disease'.

66 *Ibid.*, 'Memorandum by Beveridge on "Workmen's Compensation – Present Position"', June 1942; Parliamentary Papers (1942–1943) vi, pp. 156–157.

inquiry) should pay a levy 'in order to give a definite financial incentive for prevention of accident and disease', but the question of whether to perpetuate the alternative remedy should be remitted to a specialist committee.[67]

The Beveridge Report attracted enormous attention when it was published in December 1942. Partly this was a matter of timing, for the report appeared when the tide of war was turning and reconstruction planning began to seem relevant. It also provided 'something solid for the people to hang their own ideas to'.[68] The report was neither particularly innovatory nor well thought out, and many of its proposals were changed before the National Insurance (Industrial Injuries) Scheme was finalised. But the Beveridge Report did provide the basis for subsequent developments; as such it was 'an important landmark'.[69] Over the next 18 months various ideas about how to deal with the compensation of workplace injury were explored. The solution eventually devised was based largely on the Personal Injuries (Civilians) Scheme. This scheme was formulated to encourage people with jobs vital to the war effort to remain in post through a promise of compensation if they were injured. Funded out of general taxation, it provided flat-rate benefits based on loss-of-capacity criteria.[70]

The coalition Government's White Paper on industrial injury insurance, published in September 1944, promised a scheme 'based on the accepted principles of social insurance', which covered everyone under a contract of service regardless of income. It would cover accidents and scheduled diseases that arose 'out of and in the course of employment'. It would be funded by contributions from employers, employees and the State, and administered by a Ministry of Social Insurance. Claims would be handled by administrative tribunals rather than the courts. Industrial casualties would receive benefits higher than those provided to people whose incapacities arose outside the workplace.[71] The press accorded the

67 Parliamentary Papers (1942–1943) vi, pp. 156–157.

68 P. Malcolmson and R. Malcolmson, *A Woman in Wartime London: The Diary of Kathleen Tipper, 1941–1945* (London: London Record Society, 2006), p. 66; R. Mackay, *Half the Battle: Civilian Morale in Britain during the Second World War* (Manchester: Manchester University Press, 2002), pp. 231–240.

69 Harris, *William Beveridge*, p. 449.

70 The National Archives (TNA), CAB 46/3, ARP 39, Report V(II) on Provision of Personnel, 8 July 1925. PIN 8/17, E. Hale to R. Bannatyne; author's interview with David Caldwell, 21 June 1982.

71 Parliamentary Papers (1943–1944) viii, workmen's compensation: proposals for an industrial insurance scheme, pp. 538–539.

White Paper a warm reception, though neither the TUC nor Parliament was as enthusiastic.[72]

In August 1945 the newly elected Labour Government introduced an Industrial Injuries Bill as one of its first acts. It received the Royal Assent on 26 July 1946 and came into operation on 5 July 1948. Although, in most respects, it was similar to the White Paper, under pressure from the TUC and backbench Labour MPs certain modifications were introduced. These included more generous benefits, which widened the gap between the industrial injury and other schemes, and relaxation of the 'serious and wilful misconduct' clause, which threatened to disqualify some claimants.[73]

The Act replaced a privately funded and administered benefit with a public one. The attraction of public funding and administration was the prospect of improved industrial relations once workers and unions ceased having to fight employers and the insurers to obtain redress. The privileged position occupied by injured workers for 50 years was maintained and extended largely because politicians deemed it impossible to withdraw a benefit that had existed for so long. In the postwar climate of austerity, workers were accorded high importance as producers and foreign currency earners. It was not expedient to 'penalise' them by terminating a long-standing right. This was an important reason why the so-called industrial preference was retained.

As for the alternative remedy, the introduction of workmen's compensation did not prevent injured workers from suing employers for damages. Initially, actions were quite frequent. In the interwar period, however, they became unusual – mainly because net average awards were little if any better than workmen's compensation benefits.[74] Consequently, the injured worker 'turned from the restricted common law remedy to the wider remedy granted to him. Claims under the Employers' Liability Act and at common law became rare as compared with the claims under the new system.'[75] During the late 1930s and into the 1940s, stimulated by a number of legal decisions and Acts of Parliament, changes in judicial attitudes and, perhaps, the publicity given to road traffic cases in which

[72] See for example *The Times*, *Daily Herald*, *Manchester Guardian*, *Daily Express* and *Glasgow Herald* (all 28 September 1944); HC Deb Vol. V col. 404 (8 November 1944).

[73] 9 & 10 Geo. IV c. 62.

[74] Bartrip, *Workmen's Compensation*, p. 221; P. W. J. Bartrip, 'Beveridge, Workmen's Compensation and the Alternative Remedy' (1985) 14 *Journal of Social Policy* 491–511.

[75] A. Russell-Jones, 'Workmen's Compensation, Common Law Remedies and the Beveridge Report' (1944) 7 *Modern Law Review* 13–25.

substantial damages were awarded, the number of suits rose.[76] As Russell-Jones noted:

> ... every report of an industrial accident is now very closely scrutinised by the workman's legal advisers to see if the facts justify a claim at Common Law, and if there is a fair chance of success such a claim is put forward in preference to a claim for compensation. The reason is obvious ... the workman and his advisors [*sic*] prefer the chances of a successful Common Law action with its financial advantages, to the certainty of compensation.[77]

So the Beveridge Committee faced the question (not only in the context of industrial injuries) of whether the right to sue should remain.

Beyond identifying the issue and laying down some general principles, Beveridge ducked the question on the grounds that it involved matters 'too technical for exhaustive discussion'.[78] In due course it was remitted to a departmental committee chaired by Sir Walter Monckton and dominated by big business, trade unionists and lawyers. In evidence the British Employers Confederation (BEC) stated that if a scheme of State insurance substantially funded by employers was introduced, it would be 'manifestly unfair' that employers 'should, in addition, be liable at common law, for any industrial accident caused by the negligence of the workers'. The Home Office, which had been responsible for administering workmen's compensation, broadly agreed. On the other hand several influential organisations favoured retention of the alternative remedy. These included the TUC, the Haldane Society of Socialist Lawyers, the General Council of the Bar, the Association of Mutual Insurance Companies and the Accident Offices Association (representing commercial insurers). In the interest of safety, the TUC pressed for 'easy access' to a common law shorn of the defences of common employment, contributory negligence and *volenti*.[79]

In March 1946 the Monckton Committee recommended that:

1. The right to sue for damages for personal injury should be retained (though social security benefits should be deducted from any award).

[76] *Lochgelly Iron & Coal Co. Ltd* v. *McMullan* [1934] AC 1; *Wilsons & Clyde Coal Co. Ltd* v. *English* [1938] AC 37; *Metcalfe* v. *London Passenger Transport Board* [1938] 2 All ER 352, [1939] 2 All ER 542; *Radcliffe* v. *Ribble Motor Services Ltd* [1939] AC 215; Law Reform (Miscellaneous Provisions) Act 1934 (24 & 25 Geo. V c. 41); Factory Act 1937 (1 Edw. VIII & Geo. VI c. 41).

[77] A. Russell-Jones, 'Workmen's Compensation', 21.

[78] Parliamentary Papers (1942–1943) vi, p. 219.

[79] TNA, PIN 12/85, evidence to the Departmental Committee on Alternative Remedies.

2. The defence of common employment should be abolished.
3. A defence of having taken all reasonable care (valid in coal-mining cases since 1911) should be available in all breach of statutory duty cases.
4. Actions for damages could be brought notwithstanding receipt of compensation.[80]

With reservations about the deduction of social security benefits and creation of a new defence, the TUC welcomed these proposals. The BEC members of the committee, on the other hand, found it 'almost incredible' that retention of the alternative remedy could be countenanced.[81]

When, in late 1947, the Government introduced its Law Reform (Personal Injuries) Bill, the measure was even more in line with TUC objectives, for it stipulated that in assessing damages the courts should take into account only 50 per cent of any social security benefits received during the five years following the cause of action.[82] At the time and since, this compromise has been criticised as unprincipled and unjustifiable.[83] Plaintiffs were further advantaged by a later amendment that prevented employers from defending themselves by pleading that they had taken all reasonable care. Although some Labour MPs remained dissatisfied, the Law Reform (Personal Injuries) Act, which received the Royal Assent on 30 June 1948, largely met TUC demands.[84] Such an outcome owed much to the fact that a reforming Labour Government was highly receptive to the demands of the TUC, individual trade unions and trade unionists, who supplied most of the Labour Party's finances.

At the end of the twentieth century the Industrial Injuries Scheme remained in place in much the same form that it assumed in 1946. In 1996 some 245,000 disablement pensions were being paid under the scheme (more than 80 per cent of them for accidental injury rather than sickness).[85] It remained the case that people injured at work were 'better

[80] *Final Report of the Departmental Committee on Alternative Remedies* Cmd 6860 (London, 1945–1946), pp. 281–356. A minority report expressed reservations about some recommendations.

[81] *Report of Proceedings at the Seventy-Eighth Annual Congress of the TUC* (London, 1946), 103–105; *Final Report of the Departmental Committee on Alternative Remedies* Cmd 6860, pp. 346–352.

[82] HL Deb Vol. CLII col. 1185 (4 December 1947).

[83] *Ibid.*, cols. 1198–1199 (4 December 1947); A. F. Young, *Industrial Injuries Insurance: An Examination of British Policy* (London: Routledge & Kegan Paul, 1964), p. 161.

[84] 11 & 12 Geo. VI c. 41.

[85] P. Cane, *Atiyah's Accidents, Compensation and the Law*, 6th edn (London: Butterworths, 1999), p. 285.

treated by the social security system than any other group of disabled people'. This continuing 'preference in favour of the industrially injured' has been described as 'simply indefensible'. Outside the social security system people injured at work, along with victims of road traffic accidents, were also 'much more likely to obtain tort compensation than any other group of disabled people'.[86]

From the late 1960s serious misgivings about the tort system as a means of compensating for personal injury and death were voiced by academics such as Terence Ison, Harry Street and Derek Elliot.[87] Concern was not particularly focussed on the workplace. For the press, Parliament and the public the failure of the tort action to provide adequate compensation for victims of thalidomide loomed large in what, during the 1970s, became a vigorous public debate about reform. For many, New Zealand's Accident Compensation Act (1972) which abolished tort actions and provided no-fault benefits regardless of how or where the injury was sustained, pointed the way forward. In December 1972, soon after the report of the Robens Committee on Health and Safety at Work, which criticised the tort system for deflecting unions and management from accident prevention, and at the height of concern about the fate of thalidomide victims, Edward Heath announced the appointment of the Royal Commission on Civil Liability and Compensation for Personal Injuries. Chaired by an elderly former Law Lord, Lord Pearson, the Commission sat for more than five years, in the course of which (April 1974) the New Zealand scheme came into operation. The Commission investigated most facets of compensation, accidents in the home being the one important area of personal injury outside its brief.[88]

When the Pearson Commission reported in 1978 it had three main recommendations. These were for a new, no-fault compensation scheme for road traffic accidents; a reformed industrial injuries scheme; and a new benefit for severely handicapped children. It suggested changes to the tort system, but not its abolition, and strict liability

[86] *Ibid.*, pp. 297–298. See also R. Lewis and G. Latta, 'Compensation for Industrial Injury and Disease' (1975) 4 *Journal of Social Policy* 25–55; A. Walker, 'The Industrial Preference in State Compensation for Industrial Injury and Disease' (1981) 15 *Social Policy and Administration* 54–71.

[87] T. G. Ison, *The Forensic Lottery: A Critique on Tort Liability as a System of Personal Injury Compensation* (London: Staples, 1967); H. Street and D. W. Elliot, *Road Accidents* (London: Allen Lane, 1968).

[88] D. K. Allen, C. J. Bourn and J. Holyoak (eds.), *Accident Compensation after Pearson* (London: Sweet & Maxwell, 1979).

for manufacturers of defective products that caused death or serious injury. The Commission's report elicited little enthusiasm. Concern was expressed about the fragmentary nature of the proposals and the creation of further elite groups rather than a universal scheme. For its part, James Callaghan's Labour administration was concerned about costs. The Prime Minister told Parliament that his Government would study the recommendations with 'care and urgency', but by the time it lost power to Margaret Thatcher's Conservatives in May 1979 it had done nothing.[89]

Essentially, the Royal Commission envisaged major social policy initiatives and an enlarged role for social security. Reform of such a nature did not fit with Government ideology of the 1980s, which emphasised individual responsibility and a reduced role for the State.[90] Few powerful interest groups were dissatisfied by the lack of change. The legal profession, for example, did well out of the tort system and was a powerful influence in favour of inertia. The unions had concerns other than accident compensation reform. Not surprisingly, therefore, the Pearson Committee's proposals produced few changes. By the end of the century pressure to replace the tort system was virtually non-existent, even though it remained costly and inefficient and did little to promote safety.

In a review of the influences on the development of English law relating to the compensation of the industrially injured in the period 1850 to 2000, certain long-term factors are discernible. Judges exerted the dominant influence in 1850 and for years thereafter. Their decisions meant that few injured workers recovered damages through the courts. The balance was redressed somewhat through statute law, especially the Employer's Liability Act 1880 and, more particularly, the Workmen's Compensation Act 1897. These measures owed much to pressure exerted by organised labour, even though neither Act fully met reformers' demands. Competition for the votes of newly enfranchised workers made politicians and political parties responsive to this pressure. In the case of the 1897 Act in particular, lawyers and big business were receptive to the introduction of a no-fault solution. Dissatisfaction with workmen's compensation set in early, but it was the Second World War that gave real point to demands for reform. Beveridge stimulated

[89] *The Times*, 17, 18 March and 22 May 1978.

[90] Cane, *Atiyah's Accidents*, 6th edn, pp. 395–396.

the process of change. Thereafter big business and trade unionists were dominant forces. Following the Labour landslide in the 1945 general election, the voice of the worker proved substantially more influential than that of the employer. Reforms enacted in the 1940s substantially met the demands of the TUC and overlooked the objections of employers' organisations. For all the subsequent misgivings of academic lawyers and others, the solutions adopted in the forties proved remarkably enduring.

4

The impact of institutions and professions in Scotland

ELSPETH REID

I Introduction

The first half of the nineteenth century was a period of rapid transformation of Scots court structures and procedures.[1] The structure of the Court of Session (the highest civil court) was modernised in 1808.[2] Civil procedure was reformed in 1825[3] so as to reduce the use of written pleadings, and then, in 1850, to render written argument incompetent.[4] Civil jury trial was introduced by legislation in 1815,[5] and made permanent in 1819,[6] so that cases raised in the Outer House (first instance court) of the Court of Session involving injuries to the person or property were sent to the Jury Court. Increasingly systematised law reporting was giving a new focus to judicial reasoning as a central part of the Scots common law.[7] At the same time, citation of *ius commune* sources dwindled in the

[1] For a detailed account of this period see N. T. Phillipson, *The Scottish Whigs and the Reform of the Court of Session, 1785–1830* (Edinburgh: Stair Society Vol. 37, 1990); also J. W. Cairns, 'Historical Introduction' in K. Reid and R. Zimmermann (eds.), *A History of Private Law in Scotland*, 2 vols., Vol. I (Oxford: Oxford University Press, 2000), p. 14 (pp. 151–155).

[2] Court of Session Act 1808.

[3] Court of Session Act 1825.

[4] Court of Session Act 1850, s. 14. However, the modern procedure in relation to commercial actions once again provides that the commercial judge may, 'if invited to do so by all parties, direct the action to be determined on the basis of written submissions, or such other material, without any oral hearing' (Rules of the Court of Session, r. 47.12(2)(i), as amended by SI 1994/2310).

[5] Jury Trials (Scotland) Act 1815.

[6] Jury Trials (Scotland) Act 1819 (under the initial supervision of a Scots Chief Commissioner, William Adam, who had also been a member of the English Bar).

[7] The *Faculty Collection* of decisions was succeeded by the much fuller *Faculty Decisions* from 1825, and the annual series of reports, initially edited by Shaw, began in 1821. For more details see K. Reid, 'A Note on Law Reporting' in Reid and Zimmermann, *History*, Vol. I, p. liv.

Scots courts, although prominence was still given to statements of law as found in the Scots Institutional writers (authoritative juristic writings of the seventeenth to the early nineteenth centuries).[8] On the Court of Session bench, the last of the pupils of a distinguished teacher, David Hume, were nearing retirement and a connection to a Continental past receded.[9]

The overview offered by Robert Black in his history of delictual liability was that, by the mid nineteenth century, 'the Scots law of reparation was ... both rational and straightforward. Did the pursuer suffer personal injury, or was the pursuer's relative killed, as a result of the defender's *culpa*? If so, then the pursuer was, *prima facie*, entitled to succeed. *Culpa* ... was the failure to behave as a reasonable man would have done in all the circumstances of the case.'[10] Eighty years later, the 'intellectual superstructure'[11] of the law of delict, and indeed the framework of the intentional delicts, remained distinct from the English law of torts. In the assessment of Lord Dunedin in 1901, the Scots lawyer was still inclined to argue from principle as established in the Institutional writings, and Scots law had not become the 'slave of precedent, as the English law has been'.[12] Nonetheless, by the 1930s there had been substantial convergence with English law in relation to the law of negligence.[13] With the decision of the House of Lords in the Scots case of *Donoghue* v. *Stevenson* – the case of the snail in the ginger beer – duty of care emerged as the controlling device.[14] That duty was encapsulated,

[8] See J. W. Cairns, 'Historical Introduction' in Reid and Zimmermann, *History*, Vol. I (Oxford: Oxford University Press, 2000), p. 14 (pp. 170ff.).

[9] Hume, a nephew of the philosopher of the same name, resigned the Chair of Scots Law at the University of Edinburgh in 1822 on being appointed a Baron of Exchequer. For a listing of some of his most distinguished pupils see D. M. Walker, *The Scottish Jurists* (Edinburgh: W. Green, 1985), p. 319. Hume was referred to as 'our venerable instructor' by Lord Cowan in *Christie* v. *Ruxton* (1862) 24 D 1182 (1186), and in the same case Lord Benholme deferred to the 'weight of authority' and 'strength of principle' contained in Hume's *Lectures* (reprinted as *Baron David Hume's Lectures, 1786–1822*, ed. G. Campbell, 6 vols. (Edinburgh: Stair Society Vols. 5, 13, 15, 17, 18, 19, 1939–1958).

[10] R. Black, 'Delictual Liability in Scotland' (1975) 8 *Comparative and International Law Journal of Southern Africa* 189, 211.

[11] H. L. MacQueen and W. D. H. Sellar, 'Negligence' in Reid and Zimmermann, *History*, Vol. II, p. 517 at p. 547.

[12] At the 1901 meeting of the International Law Association in Glasgow, quoted in J. C. Gardner, *Judicial Precedent in Scots Law* (Edinburgh: W. Green, 1936), p. 32.

[13] MacQueen and Sellar, 'Negligence', p. 546.

[14] 1932 SC (HL) 31; [1932] AC 562. For the factual background to that case, see W. W. McBryde, '*Donoghue* v. *Stevenson*: The Story of the "Snail in the Bottle" Case' in A. J.

for both Scotland and England,[15] in the famous dictum by Lord Atkin that focussed upon the concepts of neighbourhood and reasonable foreseeability.[16]

II 1850–1932: from *culpa* to duty of care. Judicial contribution to convergence

There is of course a difficult debate as to whether English or Scots law was the more influential in the process of convergence during this period, but that is not the immediate concern here.[17] Certainly the language of duty had found its way into the pleadings in Scots reparation cases right from the start – indeed it is suggested by Stair's fundamental division into 'conventional' and 'obediential' obligations.[18] Nevertheless, in relation to negligence (although not in relation to the other fault-based delicts) Scots law had apparently shifted by the 1930s from a broadly Civilian model based on a general concept of fault, or *culpa*, in which duty was a relevant but not dominant factor, to a framework dominated by categories of duty, in which Scots law and common law authorities could be applied more or less interchangeably.[19] The question for present purposes is the nature of the judicial contribution to this process.

Gamble (ed.), *Obligations in Context: Essays in Honour of D. M. Walker* (Edinburgh: Green, 1990), p. 13.

15 Lord Atkin prefaced his judgment with the following, at 43 (SC):

> The case has to be determined in accordance with Scots law, but it has been a matter of agreement between the experienced counsel who argued this case, and it appears to be the basis of the judgments of the learned judges of the Court of Session, that, for the purposes of determining this problem, the laws of Scotland and of England are the same. I speak with little authority on this point, but my own research, such as it is, satisfies me that the principles of the law of Scotland on such a question as the present are identical with those of English law, and I discuss the issue on that footing. The law of both countries appears to be that, in order to support an action for damages for negligence, the complainant has to show that he has been injured by the breach of a duty owed to him in the circumstances by the defendant to take reasonable care to avoid such injury.

16 At 44 (SC).

17 See A. Rodger, 'Lord MacMillan's Speech in *Donoghue* v. *Stevenson*' (1992) 108 LQR 236; and response by R. Evans-Jones, 'Roman Law in Scotland and England and the Development of One Law for Britain' (1999) 115 LQR 605, 618–628.

18 On this point see MacQueen and Sellar, 'Negligence', pp. 536–539. See also *Gardner* v. *Main* (1894) 22 R 100, 104, in which Lord McLaren apparently regarded the English case of *Heaven* v. *Pender* (1883) LR 11 QBD 503 as illustrating the 'principle of obediential obligation', which 'in its generalised form is of very respectable antiquity'.

19 On the broad usage of the term *culpa* see G. MacCormack, '*Culpa* in the Scots Law of Reparation' 1974 *Juridical Review* 13.

One practical consideration may have been the changing profile of reparation actions in the Scots courts in the latter part of the nineteenth century. Admittedly, injuries attributable to incidents of urbanisation and industrialisation were hardly new to the courts even by the 1850s. The first reported modern cases establishing liability for negligently caused injury date from the 1790s.[20] These early reports involved, for example, falls in ditches left open at construction sites,[21] or at inadequately fenced coal pits,[22] as well as losses derived from professional negligence.[23] The 'examples of negligence' featured in the first Scots treatise on reparation, published in 1864,[24] included 'injuries occurring from the insufficiency of machinery'[25] and 'use of dangerous implements',[26] as well as 'reckless driving'[27] and accidents on the railways.[28] These early cases had been resolved using the framework of *culpa*,[29] and by reference to Civilian authority, the Institutional writers, Scots case law and, indeed, 'the universal law of humanity'.[30] As yet they had made little use of English law, although a practical treatise on the English law of negligence published in 1871 by an author professionally qualified in both jurisdictions purported to be based upon 'principles substantially common to all parts of the United

[20] The case generally regarded as the first in which damages were awarded for negligently caused injury was *Gardner* v. *Ferguson* (unreported, 1795), noted by Lord MacMillan in *Stewart* v. *London, Midland & Scottish Railway Co.* 1943 SC (HL) 19, 39. This case and subsequent case-law development are discussed by MacQueen and Sellar, 'Negligence', pp. 526–530.

[21] E.g. *Innes* v. *Mags. of Edinburgh* (1798) Mor 13189 and 13967. Relying on the authorities of D. 42.8.2.24, and D. 9.2.29.7, the pursuer argued that the accident could not have occurred without 'a degree of negligence' on the part of the city's Magistrates. The court held that the Magistrates had an important duty 'to take care that the streets of the city are kept in such a state as to prevent the slightest danger to passengers' (13190).

[22] *Black* v. *Cadell* (1804) Mor 13905; (1812) 5 Pat 567. Also *Hislop* v. *Durham* (1842) 4 D 1168.

[23] See for example *McLean* v. *Grant* (1805) Mor Appendix Reparation, no. 2, on 'the general doctrine of the responsibility of a man of business arising from gross ignorance or wilful negligence'.

[24] J. Guthrie Smith, *A Treatise on the Law of Reparation* (Edinburgh: T. & T. Clark, 1864). (It is of course possible that many cases may have been resolved in the sheriff (local) courts and thus did not normally feature in the formal law reports or textbooks.)

[25] *Ibid.*, p. 71; e.g. *Whitelaw* v. *Moffat* (1849) 12 D 434; (1857) *Haggart* v. *Duncan* 20 D 180.

[26] Guthrie Smith, *A Treatise*, p. 69, e.g. *Laing* v. *Darling* (1850) 12 D 1279.

[27] Guthrie Smith, *A Treatise*, p. 67.

[28] *Ibid.*, p. 70.

[29] Defined, for example, by *ibid.*, p. 8 as encompassing both intentional and non-intentional harm: 'the measure of this *culpa* is found in the answer to the question, – How would a man of ordinary prudence and sagacity have acted in like circumstances ...?'.

[30] *Black* v. *Cadell* (1804) Mor 13905, 13906 (pursuer's pleadings).

Kingdom, and ... all countries whose legal system incorporates the results of Latin civilization'.[31] However, in the early 1850s cases involving negligently caused physical injury were as yet few in comparison with cases involving intentional conduct, for example, injury to reputation and wrongful arrest (both in criminal matters and in relation to non-payment of debt).[32] By 1932, a different picture had emerged. Defamation and wrongful arrest appeared infrequently in the law reports.[33] In contrast, personal injury had come to the fore and injuries to property had become more common with urbanisation – suffered owing to building works or following from construction of reservoirs and channelling of water power. The relative sparsity of native authority in relation to rapidly expanding areas of liability naturally meant that Scots pleaders were likely to look to other jurisdictions where case law was more plentiful.

It was perhaps to be expected that during this period there were instances of House of Lords decisions[34] in Scots cases where English judges mistakenly assumed uniformity of Scots and English law or, more rarely, assumed that any divergence between Scots and English law was the result of underdevelopment on the part of the former. This phenomenon is already well documented.[35] *Robertson* v. *Fleming* is a typical example. In that case the Court of Session had considered it uncontroversial that third parties should be entitled to sue a solicitor whose professional negligence in dealings with clients had caused them loss.[36] However, on appeal to the House of Lords that decision was reversed,[37]

[31] R. Campbell, *The Law of Negligence* (London: Stevens and Haynes, 1871), p. 1.

[32] E.g. the 13th volume of Dunlop's reports, covering cases for the session 1850–1851, contained, under the heading of 'Reparation', 11 cases on injury to reputation, 2 on wrongful arrest and 7 on injuries to property.

[33] See H. McKechnie, 'Delict and Quasi-Delict' in G. C. H. Paton (ed.), *Introduction to Scottish Legal History* (Edinburgh: Stair Society Vol. 20, 1958) p. 265 (p. 279): 'intentional injuries bulk very small in our courts today as opposed to faults of omission, fraud alone being a usual ground of action, breach of promise rare and defamation infrequent' (as compared with in the nineteenth century). Lord Kilbrandon in his survey of the law of privacy in the early 1970s also noted the rarity of defamation actions in Scotland as compared to England ('The Law of Privacy in Scotland' (1971) 2 *Cambrian Law Review* 35, 38).

[34] Although the Court of Session is the highest court in Scotland in civil matters, since the Union of the Scots and English Parliaments in 1707 a final appeal may be taken to the House of Lords, and now the Supreme Court, in London. See A. J. MacLean, 'The 1707 Union: Scots Law and the House of Lords' in A. Kiralfy and H. L. MacQueen (eds.), *New Perspectives in Scottish Legal History* (London: Cass, 1984), p. 50.

[35] For example by A. Dewar Gibb, *Law from over the Border* (Edinburgh: W. Green, 1950).

[36] (1859) 21 D 982.

[37] (1861) 4 Macq 167, a decision roundly criticised by T. B. Smith: see *Short Commentary on the Law of Scotland* (Edinburgh: W. Green, 1962) pp. 682–683.

with Lord Campbell stating that he was 'clearly of the opinion that this is not the law of Scotland, nor of England, and it can hardly be the law of any country where jurisprudence has been cultivated as a science'.[38] In similar vein Lord Wensleydale ventured 'One would suppose, *à priori* [*sic*], that the laws of both countries would be the same.'[39] A further well-known example was the application of the doctrine of common employment to Scotland by means of the House of Lords decision in *Bartonshill Coal Co.* v. *Reid*,[40] which similarly reversed decisions of the First Division and the Lord Ordinary.[41] There are numerous other instances, particularly in the period prior to the passing of the Appellate Jurisdiction Act in 1876[42] (although there are also counter examples in which difference was respected[43]), after which Lords of Appeal from Scotland were appointed and it became customary to have two Scots lawyers in the House.[44]

However, a more intriguing aspect to the development of Scots law in the late nineteenth century is the contribution made by Scots judges themselves, both at home and in the House of Lords, to the process of convergence with English law. As Sir Thomas Smith once reflected, 'The main subverters of Scots law in modern times have been the Scots.'[45] There are several significant examples.

A Lords Dunedin and Shaw and occupiers' liability

Prior to 1929, occupiers' liability in Scotland was based upon the general principle of *culpa* (in relation to the occupier) so that the circumstances

38 (1861) 4 Macq 167, 177.

39 *Ibid.*, p. 199.

40 (1858) 3 Macq 266, in which Lord Cranworth famously asked, at 285: 'if such be the law of England, on what ground can it be argued not to be the law of Scotland?'. For commentary, see P. Simpson, 'Vicarious liability' in Reid and Zimmermann, *History*, Vol. II, p. 584 (pp. 591ff.). On the fate of the doctrine, and its ultimate abolition through the medium of a UK statute, the Law Reform (Personal Injuries) Act 1948, see *ibid.*, pp. 599–600.

41 (1855) 17 D 1017.

42 For a detailed discussion, see Dewar Gibb, *Law from over the Border.*

43 For a later example, see *Glasgow Corporation* v. *Barclay, Curle & Company Ltd* 1923 SC (HL) 78, in which the Earl of Birkenhead refrained from arguing the English law with the comment: 'In a Scotch appeal, raising some matters at least which are peculiar to the practice and law of Scotland, I am not prepared to set myself against so great a weight of authority [as that of the Scots Law Lords]. I do not, therefore, great as is the doubt which I have entertained, record a dissenting opinion.'

44 Lord Gordon was appointed to the House in 1876, although the Lord President, Lord Colonsay, had been sent to the House of Lords to assist with Scottish appeals some years earlier, in 1867.

45 *British Justice: The Scottish Contribution* (London: Stevens, 1961), p. 227.

of those entering the premises was a relevant, but not a decisive, consideration. In particular, the fact that the injured person had been trespassing on the defender's property did not bar recovery.[46] However, the decision of the House of Lords in *Dumbreck* v. *Robert Addie and Sons* replaced the general fault-based framework with the English category-based framework, in which trespassers could recover only for intentional harm.[47] The speeches of the two Scots on the Committee, Lords Dunedin[48] and Shaw,[49] were central in assuring their brethren in the House of Lords that English and Scots law were already at one in this area. They were not.

B *Lord Robertson and* Rylands *v.* Fletcher

Enthusiasm for assimilation can be found with regard to the English *Rylands* v. *Fletcher* doctrine of strict liability. Today it is generally acknowledged that the doctrine did not have a principled basis in Scots law, where liability between neighbours is founded upon *culpa*.[50] The modern Scots courts have rejected it unequivocally.[51] Nonetheless, the Scots judge, Lord Robertson, in an appeal in 1902 – which skewed the subsequent development of neighbour law in the Cape of Good Hope[52] – assured his fellow Privy Councillors that 'not only is the principle of *Rylands* v. *Fletcher* fully accepted in Scotland, but it had formed part of the law of Scotland before *Rylands* v. *Fletcher* was decided, and *Rylands* v.

[46] See *The Laws of Scotland: Stair Memorial Encyclopaedia*, Vol. XV (Edinburgh: Butterworths and Law Society of Scotland, 1996), §313.

[47] 1929 SC (HL) 51. [48] *Ibid*., 59.

[49] *Ibid*., 64: on that point 'I do not find that there is any difference between the laws of England and Scotland.'

[50] See R. Zimmermann and P. Simpson, 'Liability among Neighbours' in Reid and Zimmermann, *History*, Vol. II, p. 612 at pp. 616–629.

[51] *RHM Bakeries* v. *Strathclyde Regional Council* 1985 SC (HL) 17 per Lord Fraser at 41, and see commentary in *The Laws of Scotland: Stair Memorial Encyclopaedia*, N. R. Whitty, 'Nuisance' (Reissue, 2001), §93. The only possible exception is where damage has been caused by altering the natural course of a stream: see *Caledonian Railway Co*. v. *Greenock Corporation* 1917 SC (HL) 56 (analysed in G. D. L. Cameron, 'Strict Liability and the Rule in *Caledonian Railway Co*. v. *Greenock Corporation*' (2000) 5 SLPQ 356; Cameron argues that this decision is more properly understood as resting on *culpa*).

[52] *Eastern and South African Telegraph Co. Ltd* v. *Cape Town Tramways Companies Ltd* [1902] AC 381. In South Africa the rule has been rejected by both purists (e.g. T. W. Price, 'Is the Rule in *Rylands* v. *Fletcher* Part of Roman-Dutch Law?' (1953) *South African Law Journal* 381–386) and pragmatists (e.g. R. G. McKerron, *The Law of Delict*, 7th edn (Cape Town: Juta, 1971), p. 246).

Fletcher has been treated by the Scottish Courts as an authoritative exposition of law common to both countries'.[53]

C *Lord Watson and denial of aemulatio vicini*

Lord Watson, a former Lord Advocate who was appointed a Lord of Appeal in Ordinary in 1880 (succeeding Lord Gordon and Lord Colonsay before him), is well known for his dicta in the English case of *Mayor of Bradford* v. *Pickles*.[54] However, from a Scots perspective, his speech in that case is surprising in its denial of the doctrine of *aemulatio vicini* – a Scots variant of the Civilian doctrine of abuse of rights. Lord Watson's observation that the *aemulatio vicini* doctrine had in effect fallen into desuetude in Scots law and that Scots and English law were 'the same'[55] was one of the premises for the important statement that 'no use of property, which would be legal if due to a proper motive, can become illegal because it is prompted by a motive which is improper or even malicious'.[56]

The decision in *Mayor of Bradford* had lasting impact upon English law in that the principles applied there were carried beyond liability between neighbours,[57] and into the framework of the economic torts.[58] In turn, this influenced the development of the economic delicts in Scotland. One of the most notable Scots cases was *Crofter Handwoven Harris Tweed Co.* v. *Veitch*, in which the Lord Chancellor, Viscount Simon, asserted without challenge that, as far as interference with trade was concerned, there was

[53] *Eastern and South African Telegraph Co. Ltd* v. *Cape Town Tramways Companies Ltd* [1902] AC 381, 394.

[54] [1895] AC 587.

[55] *Ibid.*, 598:

> I am aware that the phrase "in aemulationem vicini" was at one time frequently, and is even now occasionally, very loosely used by Scottish lawyers. But I know of no case in which the act of a proprietor has been found to be illegal, or restrained as being in aemulationem, where it was not attended with offence or injury to the legal rights of his neighbour … The law of Scotland, if it differs in that, is in all other respects the same with the law of England.

[56] *Ibid.*

[57] Where a landowner has deprived a neighbour of an amenity such as water or light or prospect in the absence of a relevant easement, or public law controls – see for example *Stephens* v. *Anglian Water Authority* (1988) 55 P & CR 348.

[58] See *Allen* v. *Flood* [1898] AC 1, 92 per Lord Watson: 'the law of England does not … take into account motive as constituting an element of civil wrong … the existence of a bad motive, in the case of an act which is not in itself illegal, will not convert that act into a civil wrong for which reparation is due'.

no difference between Scots law and the English law of tort.[59] For legal nationalists in Scotland this was a 'particularly insidious method of subverting Civilian principles by Common law Doctrines'.[60]

It is now quite clear that while *aemulatio vicini* was, and perhaps remains, a doctrine of uncertain scope, its denial was much too broadly stated by Lord Watson.[61] There has been reappraisal of its status by writers such as McKechnie,[62] Smith[63] and Whitty,[64] and its continued existence is uncontentious in the modern law.[65]

D *The Court of Session bench and duty of care in negligence*

This enthusiasm for English – and therefore Imperial – law was evident not only on the part of the Scots who found themselves in Westminster, but also to an extent on the Court of Session bench itself. The unforced assimilation of English authority is evident in the latter part of the nineteenth century and in the first part of the twentieth. In the law of negligence, for example, while the language of duty was frequently found alongside the language of *culpa*, the shift to duty as the necessary control device had become apparent some time before *Donoghue* v. *Stevenson* – in cases such as *Kemp and Dougall* v. *Darngavil Coal Co.*[66] and *Clelland* v. *Robb*, in which Lord President Dunedin stated that 'Negligence per se will not make liability unless there is first of all a duty which there has

[59] 1942 SC (HL) 1 (2–3). For analysis see J. M. Thomson, 'An Island Legacy: The Delict of Conspiracy' in D. Carey Miller and D. Meyers (eds.), *Comparative and Historical Essays in Scots Law* (Edinburgh: Butterworths, 1992), p. 137.

[60] T. B. Smith, 'Strange Gods: The Crisis of Scots Law as a Civilian System' in *Studies Critical and Comparative* (Edinburgh: W. Green, 1962), p. 72 (p. 83).

[61] See A. T. Glegg, *The Law of Reparation in Scotland*, 4th edn, ed. J. L. Duncan (Edinburgh: W. Green, 1955), p. 16; W. M. Gordon, *Scottish Land Law*, 2nd edn (Edinburgh: W. Green for Scottish Universities Law Institute, 1999), §26–20; Whitty, 'Nuisance', §34; E. Reid, 'Strange Gods in the Twenty-First Century: The Doctrine of *aemulatio vicini*' in E. Reid and D. L. Carey Miller (eds.), *A Mixed Legal System in Transition* (Edinburgh: Edinburgh University Press, 2005), p. 239.

[62] H. McKechnie, 'Reparation' in *Encyclopaedia of the Laws of Scotland* (1931), Vol. XII, §§1075ff.

[63] Smith, 'Strange Gods', p. 83.

[64] Whitty, 'Nuisance', §34.

[65] *More* v. *Boyle* 1967 *Scots Law Times* (Sh. Ct) 38; *Fothringham* v. *Passmore* 1984 SC (HL) 96; *Canmore Housing Association Ltd* v. *Bairnsfather* 2004 *Scots Law Times* 673.

[66] 1909 SC 1314. See Lord Kinnear, who relied on the English authorities of *Indermaur* v. *Dames* (1866) LR 1 CP 274, affirmed at (1866) LR 2 CP 311; and *Heaven* v. *Pender* (1883) LR 11 QBD 503 in asserting: 'it is necessary for the pursuer in such [a negligence] action to shew there was a duty owed to him by the defenders, because a man cannot be charged with negligence if he has no obligation to exercise diligence' (1319).

been failure to perform through that neglect.'[67] The mantra that the 'cases in our own books … are entirely in accordance with the English cases'[68] is often found during this period, as is reference to leading English cases such as *Heaven* v. *Pender*.[69]

E The law of Empire

The question is: why was the Scottish judiciary so often amenable to accepting, and even advancing, the idea of uniformity of English and Scots law, sometimes in the face of patent pre-existing difference? Lord Watson, for example, was said in an obituary by Lord Stormonth Darling to have been 'too good a lawyer to oppose the assimilation of English and Scottish law where that was desirable, and too patriotic a Scotsman to abandon native rules, where these were well-settled and useful, in deference to English decisions';[70] and similar comments were made of the other Scots who went to London.

A partial explanation may be found in a further comment made by Stormonth Darling – that Lord Watson shared 'the qualities which notoriously make Scotsmen good colonists – especially their readiness and capacity to adapt themselves to new ideas and surroundings'.[71] And above all:

> there was a capacity in which he was even greater than in Scotch or English law. He was an Imperial judge of the very first order. The function of such a judge, sitting in the supreme tribunal of the Empire, is to do more than decide what abstract and familiar legal conceptions should be applied to particular cases. His function is to be a statesman as well as a jurist, to fill in the gaps which Parliament has deliberately left in the skeleton constitutions and laws that it has provided for the British Colonies.[72]

House of Lords judges then (as indeed now) spent much time sitting on Imperial business. The theme of law as a unifying force of Empire was later addressed with considerable passion by another Scots Law Lord, Lord Shaw of Dunfermline, in his address to the Canadian Bar Association in

[67] 1911 SC 253, 256. In the same case Lord Kinnear refers to *Pollock on Torts*, 6th edn (London: Stevens, 1901), p. 420 in stating the same principle. See also *McKinlay* v. *Darngavil Coal Co.* 1922 *Scots Law Times* 528, affirmed 1923 SC (HL) 34.

[68] Per Lord Kinnear once more, in *Johnstone* v. *Mags. of Lochgelly* 1913 SC 1078, 1088.

[69] (1883) 11 QBD 503.

[70] M. T. Stormonth Darling, 'Lord Watson' (1899) 11 *Juridical Review* 272, 276.

[71] *Ibid.*, 273.

[72] R. B. Haldane, 'Lord Watson' (1899) 11 *Juridical Review* 278, 279.

1922.[73] Despite the importance of the Civil law tradition in Scots legal history, Lord Shaw thought that the modern world had: 'never known any contrast so great as between empire and law as we conceive them, and empire and law which are the concepts of what may be called the Roman-German system', but that on the other hand 'law, as a link of empire, comes to be a very sacred thing'.[74]

The aspiration to align Scots law with the law of the British Empire is perhaps unsurprising, even leaving aside the obvious lack of linguistic barriers. As in other small jurisdictions, Scots lawyers have traditionally looked outwards in order to supplement native resources. John Blackie, writing on trends in the assimilation of comparative material, has spoken of the Scots tendency in the sixteenth and seventeenth centuries to cite modern Continental European literature, often in preference to older Scots sources: 'The reason was that the world of the *ius commune* at that period was decidedly forward looking. Accordingly, what mattered was to engage with the latest material.'[75] Blackie identifies a shifting focus towards English material during the eighteenth century to the extent that by the mid nineteenth century, the common law had become the 'new "foreign"'. In explaining this shift, politics is as important as the customary Scots pragmatism:[76]

> If Scots practitioners and judges, having long since given up day-to-day involvement with the Civil law, paid more attention to English authority, then ... this was presumably because many of the problems confronting the Scottish courts arose under common legislation or involved situations on which the old Scottish authorities provided little guidance. But an additional factor shaping the attitude of Scots lawyers would have been a tendency, from the later years of the nineteenth century onwards, to see themselves as part of a larger English-speaking family of lawyers scattered throughout the Empire and the United States of America.

For forward-looking Scots, therefore, the obvious path for the development of the legal system would have been harmonisation with the law of the Empire in which they had so enthusiastically participated as administrators and entrepreneurs as well as lawyers.[77] Indeed, a tentative

[73] Lord Shaw of Dunfermline, 'Law as the Link of Empire', reproduced in *Law of the Kinsmen* (London: Hodder and Stoughton, 1923, repr. 1996), p. 133.

[74] *Ibid.*, pp. 155–156.

[75] J. Blackie, 'History, Historiography and Comparative Law' in L. Farmer and S. Veitch (eds.), *The State of Scots Law* (Edinburgh: Butterworths, 2001) p. 75 (pp. 87ff.).

[76] A. Rodger, 'Thinking about Scots law' (1996) 1 *Edinburgh Law Review* 3, 18.

[77] On the willing participation of the Scots in the codification of commercial law see A. Rodger, 'The Codification of Commercial Law in Victorian Britain' (1992) 108 *Law Quarterly Review* 570.

comparison may be drawn with those who today seek harmonisation with the law of other European jurisdictions, as will be discussed below.

F Connections between academic and judicial spheres

The typical judicial career path, in the nineteenth century as later, would have involved exposure to the academic community as well as the world of practice. In Scotland the interaction between judicial and academic circles has traditionally been closer than south of the border. The training of lawyers has been predominantly in the hands of the universities, and the majority of intrants to the profession have acquired qualifications in the required subjects by means of taking university classes. While in earlier times aspiring Scots lawyers went abroad to study in European universities, long before 1850 the teaching of the professional subjects was well established at the universities of Edinburgh, Glasgow and Aberdeen. The position of the law faculties was further strengthened by the creation of the degree of LL.B. by an Ordinance in 1862, following from the Universities (Scotland) Act 1858.

Academic writing, on the other hand, was not the preserve of full-time academics. Perhaps because delict was a practical subject, much litigated and often turning on questions of fact, the major nineteenth-century treatises were written by practitioners. John Guthrie Smith's *Treatise on the Law of Reparation*, published in 1864 (second edition 1889), was the first textbook dedicated to the subject. Arthur Glegg's *Practical Treatise on the Law of Reparation* appeared in 1892 (the introductory adjective will be noted), and ultimately ran to a fourth edition (edited by J. Lindsay Duncan) in 1956. Both Guthrie Smith and Glegg were sheriffs. The author of the important entries on 'Negligence' and 'Reparation' in the *Encyclopaedia of the Laws of Scotland*, edited by Lord Dunedin and published in 1930 and 1931, was Hector McKechnie, an advocate who ultimately became a sheriff.[78] The more specialist texts were similarly written by advocates – John Borthwick's *Law of Libel and Slander* in 1826; Frank Cooper's *Defamation and Verbal Injury* in 1894, revised in 1906; and James Broun's *Law of Nuisance*, published in 1891. *Glegg on Reparation* was eventually ousted from its position as the leading textbook by the publication of D. M. Walker's *Law of Delict in Scotland* in 1966 (with a second edition in 1981). Walker, then Regius Professor of Law at the University of Glasgow, never held judicial office but had at one time practised at the

[78] In Vols. X and XII respectively.

Scots Bar. Such textbooks were regularly cited and held in regard in the Scots courts of this period.[79]

The use made of periodical literature, on the other hand, was less visible, although there has never been a shortage of legal journals in Scotland, nor any difficulty in persuading both academics and practitioners to write for them.[80] Journals such as the *Journal of Jurisprudence* (founded 1857), the *Scottish Law Review* (founded 1885), the *Juridical Review* (founded 1889) and the *Scots Law Times* (founded 1893) published case notes and commentaries from the nineteenth century onwards. However, these journals did not appear to be cited in pleadings, and references to them certainly did not appear in judgments during this period. The importance of academic writing in more recent times is considered further below.

III 1932–1999: trends in the judicial development of delictual liability

A *The role of academic writing*

As in the previous century, in this period there continued to be a degree of interchange between the academic and professional spheres. In a survey of the careers of 87 Court of Session judges between the years 1900 and 1969 it was noted that 9 had at some point lectured at Edinburgh or Glasgow University, and indeed one had retired from the bench to take up a professorial post.[81] That pattern has remained fairly constant, in that of the present list of 34 Court of Session judges, 6 have held full-time academic posts earlier in their careers, although none progressed directly from the university to the bench. Eight of the current Court of Session bench are the authors of significant academic treatises.[82]

Furthermore, while academics have from time to time moved into practice and ultimately progressed to the bench, the universities have regularly offered academic appointments to practitioners. Indeed, until

[79] See J. Blackie and N. Whitty, 'Scots Law and the New *ius commune*' in H. L. MacQueen (ed.), *Scots Law into the 21st Century* (Edinburgh: W. Green, 1996), p. 65 (p. 79), to the effect that textbooks have traditionally been cited more frequently in Scots cases as compared with English.

[80] See R. Zimmermann, 'Law Journals in Nineteenth-Century Scotland' (2008) 12 *Edinburgh Law Review* 9.

[81] A further two had previously had academic careers in other disciplines: I. D. Willock, 'Scottish Judges Scrutinised' 1969 *Juridical Review* 193, 202.

[82] Information provided on Scottish Judiciary website, www.scotland-judiciary.org.uk/34/0/Senators-of-the-College-of-Justice.

late in the twentieth century a number of the chairs in the Scottish law faculties were in the gift of the professional bodies, including the prestigious Chair of Scots Law at Edinburgh, for example. In many cases those nominated brought further distinction to those Chairs – George Joseph Bell was nominated to the Chair of Scots Law at Edinburgh in 1822, proposed by the Dean of the Faculty of Advocates and seconded by Sir Walter Scott; and much later, in 1948, Sir Thomas Smith, then a struggling advocate, was nominated to the Chair of Law at Aberdeen. Other appointments have not been so happy. In what has become a notorious example, at least with hindsight, F. H. Lawson, Adolf Berger, David Daube, Fritz Pringsheim and Fritz Schulz were all disappointed candidates for the Edinburgh Chair of Civil Law in 1938, when the Faculty of Advocates decided instead to award the post to Matthew Fisher, one of their own number who has left no discernible academic legacy.[83]

Despite this interchange between the worlds of academe and practice, by the twentieth century, Scots academic writing was in decline,[84] and the 'better read when dead' rule was said to prevail in the Scots courts.[85] The works of the Institutional writers continued to figure regularly in Scots pleadings, in reparation as in other types of action, and the standard textbooks continued to be cited.[86] Yet a member of the Scots Bar wrote in the *Scots Law Times* in 1950 that 'No one in his sober senses would say that a professor of law has the ability of a Master of the Rolls, or a Lord Chief Justice.'[87] Even as late as in the 1970s references from the bench to journal articles by academics could be scornful of the author's lack of practical credentials, and practitioners were prone to 'pirate' the research of living authors so as not to

[83] See A. Rodger, 'David Daube, 1909–1999' (2001) 118 *Zeitschrift der Savigny-Stiftung für Rechtsgeschichte: Romanistische Abteilung* xiv, xxi–xxiii.

[84] G. Gretton, 'Scots Law in a Golden Age' in A. J. Kinahan (ed.), *Now and Then* (London: Sweet and Maxwell, 1999) p. 163 (p. 166).

[85] W. A. Wilson, 'Knowing the Law and Other Things' (1982) *Juridical Review* 259, 267 (Wilson argued that the rule was 'of the same order of rationality as trial by ordeal'). See also K. Reid, 'The Third Branch of the Profession' in MacQueen, *Scots Law into the 21st Century*, p. 39 (pp. 46–49); and *Rankin* v. *Young* 1934 SC 499, per the Lord Ordinary, Lord Mackay, at 502: 'Certain text-writers have been invoked. As these are mostly living writers and do not profess (at most) to do more than explore the principles, I do not feel that they really help anything beyond the exploration of counsel ...'.

[86] See Blackie and Whitty, 'Scots Law and the New *ius commune*', p. 79.

[87] C. de B. Murray 1950 *Scots Law Times* 1, 2, a comment all the more remarkable in that these paragons of intelligence are members of the English judiciary, not the Scots. (Cited in Reid, 'The Third Branch of the Profession', p. 47.)

'hazard' the client's case.[88] One particularly stinging rebuke was delivered by Sheriff Substitute Dickson in Hamilton Sheriff Court in 1971, who dismissed an article by a young academic as 'written in arrogant vein, coming as it does from the pen of one who is not (at least yet) qualified to represent another in a Scots court'.[89] The 'arrogant' author in question was Alan Rodger, destined to become, successively, Lord Advocate, Lord President and Lord of Appeal in Ordinary.

Several factors have combined to reverse this trend over the last decades of the twentieth century. There was major change in the Scots Law Faculties in 1960, when the LL.B. ceased to be a postgraduate course taken part-time in combination with training in a law office, and became a full-time undergraduate degree. When the vocational Diploma in Legal Practice was introduced in 1981, the providers were again the Scottish law faculties. This meant that law faculties rapidly increased in strength, and steadily the part-time lecturers, who were often also practitioners, were replaced by full-time legal academics with more time to devote to writing as well as teaching.[90]

Also in 1960, Sir Thomas Smith established the Scottish Universities Law Institute (SULI) to encourage the publication of major treatises.[91] Walker's *The Law of Delict* was the first volume published in that series in 1966, and a second edition appeared in 1981.[92] Like many of the other SULI volumes that have followed,[93] Walker's text is considered as authoritative by the Scots courts, and has been cited extensively.

Twenty years later Smith launched a further major publishing project, *The Laws of Scotland: Stair Memorial Encyclopaedia*, Volume XV of which, on the Law of Obligations, was published in 1996, and similarly is cited by counsel without embarrassment. Thomson's *Delictual Liability*, the leading student textbook, first published in 1994 and now in a fourth

[88] See T. B. Smith, 'Authors and Authority' (1972–1973) 12 *Journal of the Society of Public Teachers of Law* 3, 6–7; Reid, 'The Third Branch of the Profession', p. 47.

[89] *Mercantile Credit Co. Ltd* v. *Townsley* 1971 *Scots Law Times* (Sh. Ct) 37, 39 (the offending article had appeared in 1970 *Scots Law Times* (News) 33).

[90] See Reid, 'The Third Branch of the Profession', pp. 42–43.

[91] On the major contribution made by Smith to the renaissance of Scots academic culture in the late twentieth century, see K. G. C. Reid, 'While One Hundred Remain' in Reid and Carey Miller, *A Mixed Legal System*, p. 1.

[92] The first sections of a new multi-authored SULI title on delict, edited by J. Thomson, have been published in loose-leaf form in 2007.

[93] E.g. W. W. McBryde, *The Law of Contract in Scotland*, now in its third edition (Edinburgh: W. Green, 2007).

edition, has also attracted many citations in terms suggesting that the (living) author is accorded respect.

However, reference to periodical literature such as the *Juridical Review* or the *Edinburgh Law Review* (founded 1996) remains relatively infrequent.[94] This does not necessarily indicate that periodical literature has a correspondingly slight impact. A specific illustration can be found in the law of nuisance.

As mentioned above, the applicability of the English *Rylands* v. *Fletcher* rule was for many years the subject of uncertainty in the Scots law of nuisance. A renewed interest in the concept of *culpa* in general and its applicability to nuisance in particular led to publication of a series of important articles in the *Juridical Review* in the 1950s.[95] That literature was not cited in the 1954 leading case of *Watt* v. *Jamieson*,[96] nor in the subsequent case of *RHM Bakeries* v. *Strathclyde Regional Council* in 1985,[97] in which Lord Fraser dismissed the suggestion that the rule was part of Scots law as a 'heresy which ought to be extirpated'.[98] However, it is unlikely that such a conclusion would have been reached without awareness of the academic literature that had helped shape the modern view of *culpa* in neighbourhood law.

In contrast, when, a decade later, the requirement of *culpa* in nuisance came to be restated definitively in *Kennedy* v. *Glenbelle*,[99] Lord President Hope was frank in acknowledging the contribution made by academic literature, giving full credit to the section of *The Laws of Scotland: Stair Memorial Encyclopaedia* upon which, more or less verbatim, he based his account of the modern law.[100] By the end of the twentieth century, therefore, academic writers might be cited before their obituaries appeared, and not only had this ceased to be detrimental to the client's interests, but

94 But see, for example, reference to A. Stewart, 'Damages for the Birth of a Child' (1995) 40 *Journal of the Law Society of Scotland* 298 in *McFarlane* v. *Tayside Health Board* 2000 SC (HL) 1; S. Middlemiss, 'Civil Remedies for Victims of Sexual Harassment' 1997 *Juridical Review* 241 in *Ward* v. *Scotrail* 1999 SC 255.

95 W. A. Elliott, 'Reparation and the English Tort of Negligence' (1952) 64 *Juridical Review* 1; J. J. Gow, 'Is Culpa Amoral?' (1953) 65 *Juridical Review* 17; W. A. Elliott, 'What Is Culpa?' (1954) 66 *Juridical Review* 6.

96 1954 SC 56.

97 1985 SC (HL) 17.

98 *Ibid.*, 41.

99 1996 SC 95.

100 1996 SC 95, 99, *The Laws of Scotland: Stair Memorial Encyclopaedia*, Vol. XIV, §2087, the section on 'Nuisance' by Whitty, now reissued in 2001, in which this is §87 (Whitty, in turn, made extensive reference to the US Restatement (Second) of Torts in this connection – see for example §89). Lord Hope, both as Lord President and as Lord of Appeal, has been fastidious in acknowledging academic sources.

such citation could sometimes make a positive contribution to doctrinal development.

B The role of comparative law in the courts

Despite the historical importance of Civilian sources, citation of foreign sources in Scottish decisions, other than from England and the Commonwealth, was marginal throughout the twentieth century. In 1999 a census identified only a very slight decrease in English authorities cited to the court over the years between 1920 and 1997 and a correspondingly slight increase in the numbers of EC authorities.[101] A survey published in 2000 noted that the 'foreign' in the Scottish courts was mostly English or Commonwealth law, and that reference to Continental and South African authority was rare.[102] Thus while Walker, in his *Law of Delict*, demonstrated an admirable geographical spread in the sources cited, the courts have been less adventurous. In relation to the difficult question of intention in the delict of assault, for example, the definition of *injuria* by Bankton, the Scots Institutional writer, is Walker's starting point,[103] but numerous English, Canadian and South African cases are cited, as well as Prosser on Torts[104] and the *Restatement (Second) of Torts*, §18 on offensive contact.[105] The Scots cases, on the other hand, have confined themselves largely to Scots and occasionally English authority.[106] When comparative law has been used, it has often appeared to perform an 'ornamental' function,[107] confirming, rather than shaping, the analysis of native sources.[108] Comparative references in leading Scots cases in the House of Lords such as *Smith*

[101] C. McDiarmid, 'Scots Law: The Turning of the Tide' 1999 *Juridical Review* 156, 162.

[102] E. Örücü, 'Comparative Law as a Tool of Construction in Scottish Courts' 2000 *Juridical Review* 27, 33.

[103] *The Law of Delict in Scotland*, 2nd edn (Edinburgh: W. Green, 1981), p. 488, citing *Institute* 1.10.22.

[104] E.g. p. 490 n. 21. See also *Reid* v. *Mitchell* (1885) 12 R 1129, in which Sheriff Guthrie Smith, author of an earlier treatise on reparation, discusses the issues of intention by reference to the Massachusetts case of *Fitzgerald* v. *Cavin* 110 Mass 153, Mass 1872, which he had found in *Underhill on Torts*.

[105] E.g. p. 491 n. 43, 492 n. 79.

[106] See for example *Henderson* v. *Fife Police* 1988 *Scots Law Times* 361, relying *inter alia* on *Lindley* v. *Rutter* [1981] 1 QB 128.

[107] See for example H. L. MacQueen, 'Mixing It? Comparative Law in the Scottish Courts' (2003) 11 *European Review of Private Law* 735, 741.

[108] See for example reference to *Bowden* v. *Rudman* 1964 (4) SA 686 in *McDyer* v. *Celtic Football & Athletic Co. Ltd* 2000 SC 379 per Lord President Rodger at 389.

(Maloco) v. *Littlewoods*[109] and *McFarlane* v. *Tayside Health Board*[110] appear to follow this trend. (In the latter, Lord Steyn offered the prosaic reflection that the purpose of comparative law citation was partly to sharpen 'focus on the weight of competing considerations' and partly to remind us 'that the law is part of the world of competing ideas markedly influenced by cultural differences'.[111]) A later survey, however, has suggested that the pattern in recent years may be beginning to change, as will be considered in the final section below.

C *Judicial development and patterns of recruitment to the judiciary*

The dominant pattern in recruitment to the Scottish judiciary for most of the twentieth century was broadly comparable to that of the English, in that the typical Scots judge, at Court of Session level at least, might be characterised, in the acronym coined by a retired Court of Session judge, as a 'MACER' (i.e. male, affluent, Caucasian, elderly and remote).[112] The typical career progression was elevation to the bench after a successful career at the Bar.[113] The social and educational backgrounds of the judiciary during this period suggest a high degree of homogeneity, in that a majority came from legal families, and were educated at one of a small number of fee-paying or selective schools (with the Edinburgh Academy producing significantly more judges than any other school). A significant minority took degrees in other subjects at Oxford or Cambridge before returning to a Scottish university to take a Scots law degree.[114]

[109] 1987 SC (HL) 37 per Lord Goff at 84.

[110] 2000 SC (HL) 1, in which reference was made to J. G. Fleming, *The American Tort Process* (Oxford: Clarendon Press, 1988); B. S. Markesinis, *The German Law of Obligations*, 2 vols., Vol. II: *The Law of Torts: A Comparative Introduction*, 3rd edn (Oxford: Clarendon Press, 1997); W. van Gerven, J. Lever and P. Larouche, *Common Law of Europe Case Book: 'Torts'* (Oxford: Hart, 1998); W. L. Prosser and W. P. Keeton, *Law of Torts*, 5th edn (St Paul: West Publishing, 1984); and F. A. Trindade and P. Cane, *The Law of Torts in Australia*, 3rd edn (Melbourne: Oxford University Press, 1999).

[111] 2000 SC (HL) 1, 15.

[112] Lord McCluskey, as recorded by S. Styles, 'The Scottish Judiciary' (1988) *Juridical Review* 41, 41. (The macer is the usher who carries the ceremonial mace of judicial authority into the court room ahead of the judge as he or she enters.)

[113] Appointment was made by the Sovereign on the nomination of the Secretary of State for Scotland, after consultation with the Lord Advocate.

[114] See Willock, 'Scottish Judges Scrutinised'; Styles, 'The Scottish Judiciary'. Of the current bench of 34, 7 hold prior degrees from either Oxford or Cambridge (information provided on Scottish Judiciary website).

This relatively conservative social background may be one factor underlying the largely pro-defender judgments in cases where negligence on the part of other middle-class professionals was alleged,[115] in particular the negligence of the medical profession. A well-known example is *Hunter* v. *Hanley*,[116] in which the test of liability for medical negligence was set out. As stated by Lord President Clyde in that case, the standard by which a doctor is judged is, in short, 'whether he has been proved to be guilty of such failure as no doctor of *ordinary* skill would be guilty of if acting with *ordinary* care'.[117] Deviation from 'ordinary professional practice' could not of itself give rise to liability since 'all inducement to progress in medical science would then be destroyed'.[118] The *Hunter* v. *Hanley* test has been referred to in English cases, most notably in *Bolam* v. *Friern Hospital Management Committee*,[119] although in *Bolam*, McNair J rephrased it by measuring the defendant's behaviour against 'a practice accepted as proper by a responsible body of medical men skilled in that particular art'.[120] However, in Scotland at least there is support for the view that under the 'no doctor of ordinary competence' test 'patients cannot succeed unless they show that the course adopted is worse than the worst which fellow professionals are prepared to let pass',[121] and that its

[115] And see, for example, G. Stott, *Lord Advocate's Diary* (Aberdeen: Aberdeen University Press, 1991), p. 42, writing in 1962 of a proof before a judge (as compared with a jury trial) in an action arising out of an industrial accident: 'one of the unfortunate things about having a case tried before a judge is that he is liable to prefer the evidence of some officer or other "responsible person" [to that of the pursuer and his mates]'.

[116] 1955 SC 200. (Hanley was alleged to have been negligent in administering an injection to Hunter, in the course of which the needle broke.) The appeal was heard by a court of five judges – normally appeals to the Inner House of the Court of Session are heard by three judges, but occasionally, if a case is particularly important or difficult, or if it is necessary to overrule a previous binding authority, a larger court is convened.

[117] 1955 SC 200, 204–205 (emphasis added). Admittedly, this focus on *ordinary* competence was nothing new; see for example Guthrie Smith, *A Treatise*, p. 115: 'To recover damages from [a professional person] you must show an act of gross ignorance, such as would not have been committed by any other ordinarily informed member of the profession' (citing as authority *Cooke* v. *Falconer* (1850) 13 D 157).

[118] 1955 SC 200, 206. [119] [1957] 1 WLR 582.

[120] *Ibid.*, 587. For the debate as to whether this rewording meant that the standard applied was significantly different as between Scotland and England see, for example, R. B. M. Howie, 'The Standard of Care in Medical Negligence' (1983) *Juridical Review* 193; K. McK. Norrie, 'Common Practice and the Standard of Care in Medical Negligence' (1985) *Juridical Review* 145; A. Stewart, '"Best Interests": Towards a More Patient-Friendly Law' (2007) *Edinburgh Law Review* 62.

[121] Stewart, 'Best interests', 66. For application of the 'ordinary' competence test see *Moyes* v. *Lothian Health Board* 1990 *Scots Law Times* 444; *Smith* v. *Lothian University Hospitals NHS Trust* [2007] CSOH 08, unreported, 18 January 2007 (Lady Clark).

continued existence entails a lower standard for doctors than is applied to other services[122] (as demonstrated by a relatively infrequent success rate of medical negligence cases). Contemporary accounts of the 'court-room dynamics'[123] in *Hunter* v. *Hanley* are of particular interest. Counsel for the pursuer remarked of the charge to the jury by the trial judge, Lord Patrick,[124] that he made 'sure as far as he could that the pursuer would not succeed: the most one-sided charge I have ever heard'.[125] (Lord Patrick had opened by addressing the jury on the 'perturbation' caused by the recent 'outbreak of cases brought against medical practitioners'.[126]) The appeal court agreed that the trial judge's charge was unsound, and allowed a new trial so that the proper test, as stated by Lord Clyde, might be applied, but, as was perhaps inevitable when this unexacting standard was applied, the pursuer was ultimately unsuccessful.[127]

D The boundaries of judicial lawmaking

Scots judges, like the English, clearly have not usually regarded it as their role to make law by departing from established rules or by establishing new frameworks of liability in areas of complex policy, preferring, even in cases of apparent injustice, to defer to Parliament and Scottish Law Commission proposals.[128] Indeed, in emphasising the need for the courts to play a more active part in law reform, Lord Rodger of Earlsferry has

[122] See *The Laws of Scotland: Stair Memorial Encyclopaedia*, M. Earle and N. R. Whitty, 'Medical Law' (Reissue, 2006), §169.

[123] Stewart, 'Best interests', 67.

[124] Reported at 1954 *Scots Law Times* 303.

[125] G. Stott, *QC's Diary* (Edinburgh: Mercat Press, 1998), p. 20.

[126] 1954 *Scots Law Times* 303, 304.

[127] Stott noted of the retrial that, although 'scrupulously fair', once again the trial judge charged on the defender's side (*QC's Diary*, p. 83). For an assessment of the legacy of *Hunter* v. *Hanley* see Stewart, 'Best interests', pp. 71–80.

[128] See for example *Robertson* v. *Turnbull* 1980 SC 108, 135 (affirmed 1982 SC (HL) 1), in which the 'remedial hand of Parliament' (per Lord Cameron at 133) was called for to establish the right of an injured person's family to claim damages where the injury had not caused death; *M'Kendrick* v. *Sinclair* 1972 SC (HL) 25, 55, in which Lord Reid accepted the need to review the rules as to the categories of person entitled to raise an action of damages for the death of a relative, but held that this was more properly a matter for the Scottish Law Commission. Similar sentiments were expressed by the Court of Session in *Dick* v. *Burgh of Falkirk* 1975 *Scots Law Times* 110, ultimately overruled 1976 SC (HL) 1. (In matters of criminal law, however, still largely governed by the common law rather than statute, Scots judges have shown more inclination to decisions that develop the common law: see for example *Webster* v. *Dominick* 2005 1 JC 65 (shameless indecency); *Lord Advocate's Reference No. 1 of 2001* 2002 *Scots Law Times* 466 (whether force required for rape).)

reflected that 'one of the unfortunate ... side effects of the creation of the Law Commissions was a certain tendency for the view to be taken that it was now for the courts to declare the law and for the Law Commissions and Parliament to reform it'.[129]

Even in *Law Hospital NHS Trust* v. *Lord Advocate*,[130] a case heard by a court of five judges,[131] and which followed closely after the House of Lords decision in the English case *Airedale NHS Trust* v. *Bland*,[132] caution is apparent. The court had been asked to issue a declarator that the withdrawal of nutrition to a patient in a persistent vegetative state would not render medical carers delictually liable to her family. Given that the situation was an intolerable one demanding an immediate response, the court accepted that it had 'to proceed as best it [could] in the absence of ... legislation',[133] and it granted the declarator as requested by the hospital authorities. However, in doing so the court emphasised the concern expressed in the English case regarding the need for legislation to regulate issues of authorisation in such circumstances.[134]

At the same time, there is perhaps less rigid constraint upon the development of the common law in the Scots law of delict as compared with the English law of torts.[135] As Peter Birks once noted, the 'true difference' between English and Scots law is not in regard to the content of particular rules, but in regard to structure. Scots law retains a 'commitment to the institutional scheme or, in other words, to a more systematic approach'.[136] At the same time, it does not have the legacy of the forms of action. In keeping with its Civilian roots, the law of delict is not a remedy-based, but a rights-based, system, and specific categories of delictual liability are underpinned by general principle. There are no structural reasons for fettering judicial discretion with regard to the rights that are to be protected, and the existing list may exceptionally be capable of further development if there are cogent reasons why a particular category should be recognised. As summed up by Lord Dunedin:[137] 'Of course, different

[129] Lord Rodger of Earlsferry, 'The Bell of Law Reform' 1993 *Scots Law Times* (News) 339, 345.

[130] 1996 SC 301. [131] See n. 116 above. [132] [1993] AC 789.

[133] Per Lord Milligan, 1996 SC 301, 329. [134] See Lord Milligan, *ibid.*

[135] Scots judgments do not generally contain dicta such as that of Lord Goff in *Cambridge Water Company* v. *Eastern Counties Leather* as to extending the categories of torts in the absence of legislation (in relation to environmental liability) [1994] 2 AC 264, 305.

[136] Peter Birks, 'More logic and less experience' in D. L. Carey Miller and R. Zimmermann (eds.), *The Civilian Tradition in Scots Law* (Berlin: Duncker & Humblot, 1997), p. 167 (p. 174).

[137] 'The Divergencies and Convergencies of English and Scottish Law', fifth lecture on the David Murray Foundation in the University of Glasgow, 21 May 1935.

actions have different names, but the question in Scotland was never as to the remedy – it was always as to the right. You ask for what you want in your summons … You may not get what you want, but that will be because you failed to show that you had the right to get it.' This feature has important implications for the development of new areas of delictual liability. Thus, for example, in *Micosta SA* v. *Shetland Islands Council*,[138] Lord Ross considered that there was no constraint, even in the absence of specific Scots precedent, upon his recognition of a delict of deliberate misuse of statutory powers by a public body.[139] It may also follow therefore that the factors preventing English judges from developing a common law tort of privacy,[140] and compelling them to 'shoe-horn' privacy into confidentiality,[141] do not so constrain the Scots,[142] although the infrequency of relevant case law means that this reasoning is yet to be fully tested in the Scots courts.

E *The courts and legislative change*

Although the law of delict has developed mainly through the medium of case law, there have also been a number of important legislative developments. The emphasis here will be on those statutes that differed significantly from any English counterpart.[143]

138 1986 *Scots Law Times* 193.

139 *Ibid.*, 198:

> There is no such thing as an exhaustive list of named delicts in the law of Scotland. If the conduct complained of appears to be wrongful, the law of Scotland will afford a remedy even if there has not been any previous instance of a remedy being given in similar circumstances. As Professor Walker [*Law of Delict*, 2nd edn (Edinburgh: W. Green, 1981)] puts it at p. 9: 'The decision to recognise a particular interest, and consequently to grant a remedy for its infringement, is a question of social policy, and the list recognised has grown over the years. In considering whether or not to recognise particular interests the courts have had regard to such factors as the moral obliquity of the defenders' conduct, the capacity of the parties to bear the loss, and the consistency of recognition with what is conceived to be public policy.'

140 E.g. *Wainwright* v. *Home Office* [2004] 2 AC 406.

141 *Douglas* v. *Hello* [2006] QB 125 per Lord Phillips at §53.

142 Although the most positive recent statement recognising a delict of breach of privacy is that of Lord Bonomy in *Martin* v. *McGuiness* 2003 *Scots Law Times* 1424 at para 28: 'Of course it does not follow that, because a specific right to privacy has not so far been recognised, such a right does not fall within existing principles of the law.'

143 The Workmen's Compensation Acts of 1897 onwards and subsequent legislation regarding industrial injuries have applied to England and Wales also, as did, for example, the Employers' Liability (Defective Equipment) Act 1969, and the Manual Handling Operations Regulations 1992, and also legislation providing strict liability for specific hazards such as the Civil Aviation Act 1982 or the Nuclear Installations Act 1965.

Some statutes provided a response to specific procedural issues, such as the Damages (Scotland) Act 1976, which clarified the rights of relatives and executors of the deceased to claim damages following death from personal injuries.[144] Another example of this nature is one of the few statutes on the law of delict as yet passed by the Scottish Parliament (to which most private law matters are now devolved), the Rights of Relatives to Damages (Mesothelioma) (Scotland) Act 2007.[145] This similarly addresses a particular problem regarding the entitlement of relatives to sue for damages, although only after the death of a relative from this particular disease. A further example of legislation on a relatively narrow point, albeit an important substantive issue, was the Damages (Asbestos-related Conditions) (Scotland) Act 2009, providing that those affected by pleural plaques following exposure to asbestos could claim damages for personal injury.

Perhaps of greater interest, however, is the judicial and Law Reform Committee background to the statutes that effectively codified discrete areas of liability. The Occupiers' Liability (Scotland) Act 1960 is an example that is frequently cited in this context (and that differs from its English equivalent). As noted above, in 1929 the House of Lords' decision in *Dumbreck* v. *Robert Addie & Sons (Collieries) Ltd*[146] reversed that of the Inner House of the Court of Session and rejected the traditional approach based upon a general concept of fault. Instead the category-based framework of English law was imported into the Scots law. Nonetheless, in the years that followed, the Scots courts demonstrated reluctance in observing the 'rigid line', as drawn in *Dumbreck*,[147] between the categories of invitee, licensee and trespasser,[148] and a restrictive view was taken as to the types of premises for which the rule was applicable.[149] By the 1950s Lord Justice Clerk Thomson was expressing his regret that the courts 'had no option but to approach the problem on the footing that the pursuer must be either an invitee, a licensee or a trespasser'. He continued: 'It may be that we are within reach of the demise of the doctrine. If this

[144] Now repealed and re-enacted with various amendments in the Damages (Scotland) Act 2011.

[145] Now repealed and re-enacted in the Damages (Scotland) Act 2011, s. 5.

[146] 1929 SC (HL) 51. See above pp. 64–65.

[147] *Dumbreck* v. *Robert Addie & Sons (Collieries) Ltd* 1929 SC (HL) 51 per Lord Dunedin at 59.

[148] See *The Laws of Scotland: Stair Memorial Encyclopaedia*, Vol. XV, §315; also *McPhail* v. *Lanarkshire County Council* 1951 SC 301, remarks of Lord President Cooper at 314.

[149] *Carney* v. *Smith* 1953 SC 19.

is a funeral oration its theme must be burial rather than praise.'[150] So serious were expressions of discontent that occupiers' liability became the subject of the *First Report of the Law Reform Committee for Scotland* in 1957.[151] Although this followed on closely from the *Third Report of the Law Reform Committee for England*,[152] the English and Scots statutes, enacted in 1957 and 1960 respectively, differed in one major respect. The English Occupiers' Liability Act 1957 retained the distinction between trespassers and others entering property, so that trespassers were protected only against intentional harm (a position later qualified by the Occupiers' Liability Act 1984). The Scots statute, on the other hand, dispensed with all specific distinctions between persons entering premises, and recognised no fixed categories of pursuer. The occupier's duty became 'such care as in all the circumstances of the case is reasonable',[153] and the fact that the injured person had entered the premises uninvited simply became one of the 'circumstances of the case'. Scots law had turned 'full circle'[154] by reinstating the general principle of *culpa*, and in following the Law Reform Committee's recommendations Parliament had effectively responded to concerns voiced from the bench.

Another example of legislation attributable to a direct Law Reform Committee initiative is the Animals (Scotland) Act 1987. In creating a strict liability regime for damage inflicted by certain types of animal, these provisions followed from recommendations made by the Law Reform Committee in 1963,[155] as taken up 20 years later by the Committee's successor, the Scottish Law Commission[156] (apparently stirred into action by the suggestion of the Pearson Commission that the Animals Act 1971 should be extended to Scotland[157]).

IV 1999 onwards

For Scotland the last year in the study period is of immense significance, both symbolic and practical, in that 1999 saw the inauguration of the Scottish Parliament. Admittedly private law had already been the subject

[150] *Plank* v. *Mags. of Stirling* 1956 SC 92, 104.

[151] (1957) Cmnd 88. [152] (1954) Cmd 9305. [153] S. 2(1).

[154] T. B. Smith, 'Full Circle: The Law of Occupiers' Liability in Scotland' in *Studies Critical and Comparative* (Edinburgh: W. Green, 1962), p. 163.

[155] *Twelfth Report of the Law Reform Committee for Scotland* (1963) Cmnd 2185.

[156] *Report on Civil Liability in Relation to Animals* (1985) SLC 97.

[157] Royal Commission on Civil Liability and Compensation for Personal Injury, Cmnd 7054 I–III, Vol. I, §1626, as noted at *Report on Civil Liability in Relation to Animals*, §1.1.

of administrative devolution through the Scottish Office, a separate department within the UK Civil Service.[158] Furthermore, the devolution of legislative power in the sphere of delict has so far led to relatively little new legislation in this area.[159] Indeed, it is perhaps surprising that one major item of legislation in the field of delict recommended by the Scottish Law Commission in the post-devolution era, the Reparation for Mental Harm (Scotland) Bill,[160] has not been taken up by the Scottish Parliament. This, and other, omissions may raise more general questions about the role of a law reform body such as the Commission in post-devolution Scotland. However, the relative absence of legislation does not mean that devolution has had no impact upon the development of the law of delict.

A *Judicial recruitment*

An example of considerable potential importance to the future development of the law in Scotland is judicial recruitment. Following an early commitment on this matter by the Scottish Ministers, a Judicial Appointments Board, composed of five lay members and five legal members, came into operation in June 2002, and its procedures are set out in the Judiciary and Courts (Scotland) Act 2008. All appointments to judicial office are now made by an open application overseen by the Board. This reform has made a small but perceptible difference to the profile of those appointed, particularly to the shrieval bench. Of the appointments to the Court of Session bench since 2002, 3 out of 20 have been women. This increases the present complement of women judges to 5 out of 34, the first woman judge – now retired – having been appointed in 1996.[161] Only one woman sits in the Inner House, however. The proportion of female appointments to the shrieval bench (including floating and part-time

[158] The Secretary of Scotland Act 1885 provided for the creation of the Scottish Office and the appointment of the Scottish Secretary.

[159] See the Rights of Relatives to Damages (Mesothelioma) (Scotland) Act 2007; Damages (Asbestos-related Conditions) (Scotland) Act 2009 (discussed further below); Damages (Scotland) Act 2011.

[160] Contained in *Report on Damages for Psychiatric Injury* (2004) SLC 196. Although the English Law Commission had also produced a report on this subject, *Liability for Psychiatric Illness* (1998) LC 249, the Scots Commission proposed different provisions for Scotland.

[161] Information obtained from the website for the Scottish Judiciary (www.scotland-judiciary.org.uk/34/0/Senators-of-the-College-of-Justice).

sheriffs) has been higher, at around 25 per cent, with greater numbers of solicitors and procurators fiscal now represented.[162]

B The judiciary and the legislature: the Scotland Act 1998, s. 29

As part of the devolution package, the Scotland Act 1998, s. 29 provided that legislation of the Scottish Parliament should not be incompatible with the European Convention of Human Rights (ECHR). If a court finds legislation to be incompatible with Convention rights, the provisions in question must be struck down as *ultra vires*[163] (as contrasted with a declaration of incompatibility under the Human Rights Act 1998, s. 4(6)(a), which does not immediately affect the continuing validity of Westminster legislation), and an award of damages may be made to the person who claims to have suffered loss. A number of challenges have been brought under s. 29 in recent years.[164] So far most have involved matters of procedure, and one important case involving legislation on the law of delict was unsuccessful.[165] However, the spectre of judicial challenge remains, causing some to question this alteration in the balance between the Parliament and the judiciary and to caution against the possibility of over-zealous scrutiny.[166]

[162] See Judicial Appointments Board website at www.judicialappointmentsscotland.gov.uk/. Moreover the Lord Advocate (most senior law officer and chief prosecutor) from 2006 until 2011, Elish Angiolini – previously Solicitor General, was not only the first woman to occupy this role, but also the first procurator fiscal and the first solicitor (rather than advocate) to do so.

[163] Although in the event that Scots legislation is ruled incompatible with Convention rights, the Scots courts have the power to limit the retrospective effect of that decision, or suspend its effect to enable the Parliament to remedy the defect; Scotland Act, s. 102.

[164] See for example *Adams* v. *Scottish Ministers* 2003 SC 171; *Anderson* v. *Scottish Ministers* 2002 SC (PC) 63.

[165] *AXA General Insurance Ltd* v. *Lord Advocate* [2011] UKSC 46; [2011] 3 WLR. 871; 2011 *Scots Law Times* 1061, challenging the Damages (Asbestos-related Conditions) (Scotland) Act 2009 on various grounds, including that it was incompatible with the petitioners' rights under the ECHR Protocol 1, art.1 and therefore outside the competence of the Scottish Parliament. An earlier case, *Clancy* v. *Caird* 2000 SC 441, involved the mode of appointment of the temporary judge adjudicating a personal injuries claim.

[166] See in particular B. K. Winetrobe, 'The Judge in the Scottish Parliament Chamber' (2005) *Public Law* 3 (commenting in particular on the decision in *Adams* v. *Scottish Ministers* 2003 SC 171). See also A. O'Neill, 'Judging Democracy: The Devolutionary Settlement and the Scottish Constitution' (2004) 8 *Edinburgh Law Review* 177.

C Use of foreign law in the courts

Post-devolution, the balance as between citation of Scots and English cases in the courts has changed little. However, since 2000, there has been a marked increase in the number of citations of European law,[167] and in particular of judgments of the ECHR – some 18 per cent of all case citations in 2001 and 2002[168] (the ECHR having been given effect in Scots domestic law in 1999 by virtue of the Scotland Act 1998). That figure of course reflects a large number of citations to art. 6 ECHR on matters of criminal procedure. Nonetheless, delictual claims are also represented.[169]

It is important to note the change not merely in frequency of citation, but also in the use made of such sources, which, of necessity, is no longer merely 'ornamental'.[170] A survey conducted in the first years following devolution has found the decisions of the Scots courts to be broadly in line with Strasbourg jurisprudence, in that they have been neither more nor less protective of Convention rights.[171] This in itself suggests an important new factor in the development of the law of delict (notwithstanding the

[167] See *Roy* v. *M. R. Pearlman Ltd* 1999 SC 459, 469, in which Lord Hamilton stated (admittedly in relation to the law of agency rather than delict) that, in interpreting an EC Directive, it is no longer necessary to call expert authority to prove French law, but that a Scots court is 'entitled to have direct regard to sources of foreign law' and that 'assistance towards a harmonised approach may be obtained by having regard to the longer experience of the French courts in applying' the Directive. (Cited in MacQueen, 'Mixing It?, 741.)

[168] *Ibid.*, 739.

[169] In a survey of cases heard in the Scots courts between 1999 and 2002, seven cases were identified in which Convention rights were invoked to support delictual claims: see Peter Greenhill *et al.*, *The Use of Human Rights Legislation in the Scottish Courts* (Edinburgh: Scottish Executive Social Research, 2004), published by the Scottish Executive at www.scotland.gov.uk/Publications/2004/11/20181/45874, §2.32.

[170] See n. 107 above, given the positive obligation to secure respect for Convention rights even in the sphere of the relations of individuals (see for example *von Hannover* v. *Germany* (2005) 40 EHRR 1, judgment of the court at 25, §57).

[171] Greenhill *et al.*, *The Use of Human Rights Legislation in the Scottish Courts*. See for example *Martin* v. *McGuiness* 2003 *Scots Law Times* 1424, where the pursuer claimed damages for allegedly overintrusive surveillance by the defender's agents in preparing the defence for a personal injuries claim. The authorities cited included the standard Scots texts and case law as well as six English cases, four cases from the ECtHR, and a passage from R. Zimmermann, *Law of Obligations* (Cape Town: Juta, 1990; repr. Oxford: Oxford University Press, 1996), 1053–1059. There was little dispute that such conduct was capable of infringing art. 8, but in the interests of striking a fair balance between the parties the evidence gathered thereby was ruled admissible and no damages were awarded.

belief prior to 1999 that the protection provided by the Convention was 'already part of our municipal law'[172]). In a recent case on the corporate right to privacy and confidentiality,[173] for example, the court appeared to accept as axiomatic, and the defenders did not dispute, that such a right existed, by reference to *Hoechst AG* v. *Commission of the European Communities*.[174]

D Convergence or divergence and the 'new modern'

The sense of national identity reinforced by the creation of a separate legislature may cause Scots lawyers once again to reappraise what Blackie termed the 'new foreign'. This may even begin to unsettle the process of 'convergence' in the law of negligence.[175] It appears, for example, that the Scottish Law Commission did not feel obliged to justify proposing legislation on reparation for psychiatric injury (noted above), which differed significantly from that recently put forward by the Law Commission in England.[176] Characteristically, the Scots opted for an approach based on general principle rather than the category-based framework suggested south of the border.

In the Court of Session, *Burnett* v. *Grampian Fire and Rescue Service*[177] offers an interesting recent case study. That case involved the liability of the fire service where it had failed to extinguish a fire completely, thus

172 *Moore* v. *Secretary of State for Scotland* 1985 *Scots Law Times* 38, Opinion of the Court at 41 (in similar vein to Lord Woolf's assurance in an address to the ECtHR, shortly after the Human Rights Act had come into force, that the transition to a Human Rights culture in England had gone 'remarkably smoothly', primarily because 'the values to which the European Convention on Human Rights gives effect are very much the same values that have been recognised by the common law for hundreds of years' ('European Court of Human Rights on the Occasion of the Opening of the Judicial Year' (2003) *European Human Rights Law Review* 257, 258).

173 *Response Handling Ltd* v. *BBC* [2007] CSOH 103; 2008 *Scots Law Times* 51.

174 [1989] ECR 2859; [1991] 4 CMLR 410.

175 See n. 13 above.

176 *Report on Damages for Psychiatric Injury*; *Liability for Psychiatric Illness*. Broadly speaking, the proposed Scots legislation opens by stating the general principle that 'A person who causes mental harm to another person is liable to make reparation in accordance with the provisions of this Act', while the proposed English legislation begins by setting out a list of conditions attached to duty of care in relation to 'recognisable psychiatric illness'. A further Discussion Paper in 2007, *Discussion Paper on Damages for Wrongful Death*, no. 135, places an account of the law in England and Wales in Appendix D on 'comparative research'.

177 2007 *Scots Law Times* 61.

allowing its spread to the pursuer's property. The Lord Ordinary, Lord Macphail, in a lengthy and meticulous judgment, declined to follow the decision of the Court of Appeal in an English case that was directly in point, *Capital and Counties plc* v. *Hampshire County Council*.[178] Instead, he ruled against the fire service, drawing attention to important differences in principle between the English and Scots law on liability for omissions,[179] and finding his main authority in two Scots first instance cases.[180]

Similarly, in *Wright* v. *Stoddard International plc*,[181] some months later, the question arose as to apportionment of damages where more than one employer had been implicated in the asbestos exposure that, allegedly, caused the illness and death of the pursuer's husband. Again, English as well as Scots authority was considered, in particular the recent House of Lords decision in the English case of *Barker* v. *Corus UK Ltd*.[182] However, Lord Uist declined to follow the majority in that case, preferring the reasoning of the single Scots Law Lord, who had dissented: 'the decision of the majority in *Barker*, being an English appeal, is not binding on me and I prefer the view of Lord Rodger of Earlsferry on the question of apportionment. I respectfully adopt his analysis of the law on apportionment.'[183] In a further development following this line of cases on the consequences of asbestos exposure, the Scottish Parliament enacted legislation, the Damages (Asbestos-related Conditions) (Scotland) Act 2009, providing that the House of Lords' decision in the English case of *Johnston* v. *NEI International Combustion Ltd*[184] was not to be followed in Scotland.[185] That case ruled that the formation of pleural plaques on the lungs did not constitute actionable damage in negligence. In Scotland, unlike in England, it is competent for those negligently exposed to asbestos and diagnosed with this condition to recover damages in delict.

178 [1997] QB 1004. 179 2007 *Scots Law Times* 61, §34.

180 *Gibson* v. *Orr* 1999 SC 420, involving the liability of the police for taking control of an emergency, and *obiter dicta* in *Duff* v. *Highland and Islands Fire Board* 1995 *Scots Law Times* 1362.

181 [2007] CSOH 138; 2008 Rep LR 2.

182 [2006] 2 AC 572.

183 [2007] CSOH 138; 2008 Rep LR 2, §149.

184 [2008] 1 AC 281.

185 S. 1(1) provides that 'Asbestos-related pleural plaques are a personal injury which is not negligible.' An announcement at www.scotland.gov.uk/News/Releases/2007/11/29102156 by the Justice Secretary, Kenny MacAskill, reflected that 'The effects of asbestos are a terrible legacy of Scotland's industrial past and we should not turn our backs on those who contributed to our nation's wealth in the past.'

At the very least, such developments suggest that convergence is neither complete nor unopposed. Lord Rodger concluded his pre-devolution article on 'Thinking about Scots Law' with the reflection that 'Today when we go to international dinners, it is to be bored by speeches on the European Court of Justice and on law as the link which binds the European Union, just as once our predecessors had to endure speeches on the Privy Council and on law as the link which bound the Empire.'[186] After-dinner speeches apart, the common law has almost certainly lost its exclusive claim on the Scottish legal imagination as the 'new foreign'. Necessity will always force the Scots to look outwards from their small jurisdiction. England will certainly continue to be the first point within their field of vision, but in the twenty-first century they will also look beyond.

[186] Rodger, 'Thinking about Scots Law', 23.

5

The impact of institutions and professions in France

PAULA GILIKER

I Introduction

Any study of the institutional factors influencing the development of fault-based liability in French law must start by distinguishing between different sources of law. Legislative intervention remains the primary source of law. This may take the form of treaties (*traités*); parliamentary statutes (*lois*), including government ordinances (*ordonnances*); or governmental regulations (*règlements*). Whilst custom remains a minor source of law, case law (*jurisprudence*) and academic commentary (*doctrine*) are not recognised as formal sources of law, although their persuasive character is acknowledged. In more recent times, entry into the European Union has led to European law becoming a formal source of law, supreme to national laws.[1]

Yet this formal depiction of legal sources is misleading in a number of ways. First, it fails accurately to describe administrative law which,

[1] Translations are taken from *Legifrance* or are those of the author herself. See Constitution, art. 55: 'Treaties or agreements duly ratified or approved shall, upon publication, prevail over Acts of Parliament, subject, in regard to each agreement or treaty, to its application by the other party.' See also art. 88–2: 'Subject to reciprocity and in accordance with the terms of the Treaty on European Union signed on 7 February 1992, France agrees to the transfer of powers necessary for the establishment of European economic and monetary union.' See Cass Ch. Mixte, 24 May 1975, *Société des cafés Jacques Vabre*, D. 1975, 497 concl. A. Touffait; JCP 1975. II.18180 concl. A. Touffait; Conseil d'Etat, 20 October 1989, *Nicolo*, Rec. Lebon 190; JCP 1989. II.21371 concl. B. Frydman; D 1990.135 note P. Sabourin; (1989) RFDA 813 concl. B. Frydman, note Genevois. The Constitution (including constitutional principles) nevertheless remains the highest source of law. For the influence of human rights and constitutional law, see F. Terré, *Introduction générale au droit*, 8th edn (Paris: Dalloz, 2009), nos. 287 and 253; P. Malaurie and P. Morvan, *Introduction générale*, 3rd edn (Paris: Defrénois, 2009), nos. 308 and 294.

possessing no overarching substantive code,[2] relies heavily on judge-made law, deriving from the case law of the Conseil d'Etat and the administrative courts. Administrative law has thus developed its own principles of tort law that will apply to public body defendants.[3] Second, legislation requires interpretation and the judicial interpretation of the tort provisions of the Civil Code – in 1804, a mere five short provisions – has played a significant role in the construction of modern principles of fault-based liability. Indeed, there is evidence that the drafters of the Code appreciated from the very start that such brief provisions would need to be construed by the courts.[4] Third, academic commentary has also played a vital role in legal development and many significant changes may be traced back to academic, not judicial, sources. Finally, it would be wrong to confine oneself to 'sources' and ignore institutional 'influences' that have shaped the law: for example, the existence of the growing insurance industry, pressure groups representing both professionals and consumers, changing social and political views on compensation, and external influences, either from Europe or the United States. Such influences are often difficult to identify formally as they are rarely officially acknowledged, but, as will be seen, play an underlying role in shaping legal principle in the nineteenth and, particularly, twentieth century and beyond.

This chapter will address the question in two stages. First, it will examine the official and 'non-official' role of the key legal institutions in France and seek to identify how they have influenced the law of tort during the period of this study. Second, it will examine two of the most significant legal developments over the last 150 years: workmen's compensation, and

[2] Apart from certain codes that consolidate specific principles and rules. There are, of course, numerous statutes that regulate public administration activities.

[3] See J. Rivero and J. Waline, *Droit administratif*, 23rd edn (Paris: Dalloz, 2010); M. Lombard and G. Dumont, *Droit administratif*, 9th edn (Paris: Dalloz, 2011); D. Fairgrieve, *State Liability in Tort: A Comparative Study* (Oxford: Oxford University Press, 2003). This is well illustrated by medical law where a visit to a general practitioner would be seen as a matter for the private law of contract, whilst a claim against a public service hospital (obviously distinct from a private clinic) would be brought under the principles of administrative law.

[4] See J.-E.-M. Portalis, 'Discours préliminaire sur le projet de code civil' in P. A. Fenet (ed.), *Recueil complet des travaux préparatoires du Code civil* (1827), 15 vols., Vol. I (repr. Osnabrück: O. Zeller, 1968), p. 471. Some amendments have nevertheless been made to the delictual provisions of the Civil Code since 1804: in relation to fires (*loi* 7 November 1922), parental responsibility (*loi* no. 70–459 of 4 June 1970 and *loi* no. 2002–305 of 4 March 2002), schoolteachers and craftsmen (*loi* 5 April 1937) and the amended Articles 1386–1–1386–18 (*loi* no. 98–389 of 19 May 1998 and *loi* no. 2004–1343 of 9 December 2004).

compensation for motor vehicle accidents. Both areas of law represent matters of concern to the legislator, courts, academic commentators, professions and the public at large. Questions of compensation, proof of fault and causation arise in both and the responses of the French institutions are revealing. A closer examination of the development of these two forms of liability gives a practical insight into the nature of French tortious development from 1850 onwards.

II The overlapping roles of legal institutions in France

This section will examine the legal institutions and how they have contributed to the development of liability in tort. In so doing, its starting point must be 1804 and the promulgation of the Civil Code.

A The legislature

The primary source of law in France, as in most legal systems, is the legislature.[5] Articles 1382–1386 of the Civil Code set out the five key principles for tortious liability. These provide the primary legislative provision. In the ensuing years, a number of supplementary legislative interventions have been made, either to modify the Code,[6] or to make specific provision for particular problems such as workmen's compensation[7] or motor accidents.[8] Today, the Civil Code contains only about 1,115 articles of the original 2,281. The legislature thus has an active role in ensuring the modernisation and future development of the law and this is ably illustrated by the increase in legislation and codification from the mid twentieth century onwards.[9]

B The courts

The Civil Code appears to give rather conflicting indications of the role of the courts. Article 5 states that '[j]udges are forbidden to decide cases submitted

[5] Custom also remains a subsidiary source of law in private law (not public). See Y. Loussouarn, 'The relative importance of legislation, custom, doctrine and precedent in French law' (1958) 18 *Louisiana Law Review* 235. The constitutionality of statutes is subject before promulgation to control by the Conseil constitutionnel under art. 61 of the 1958 Constitution and, following recent reforms, may now also be challenged in a court of law: art. 61–1, Constitution.

[6] See above, n. 4. [7] *Loi* 9 April 1898.

[8] Badinter Act of 5 July 1985.

[9] P. Malaurie and P. Morvan, *Introduction générale*, 3rd edn (Paris: Defrénoism, 2009), no. 117.

to them by way of general and regulatory provisions',[10] and expresses revolutionary distrust of the regional *Parlements* (high courts) under the *ancien régime* and a desire to enforce a strict separation of powers. In contrast, Article 4 finds that '[a] judge who refuses to give judgment on the pretext of legislation being silent, obscure or insufficient, may be prosecuted for being guilty of a denial of justice'. Every decision must therefore be 'motivated'.[11] There is, however, no conflict if the Civil Code is treated as a comprehensive statement of law, capable of responding to all matters if studied with sufficient care. The courts thus adopted a literal method of interpretation and, where this failed, adopted a process, supported by the *école de l'exégèse* (the exegetical school),[12] whereby one seeks to ascertain the intention of the legislator at the time the legislation was enacted. This approach continued to dominate legal thought until the late nineteenth century.[13]

Dissatisfaction with this method of interpretation became more apparent as the century progressed. In particular, industrial development post-1848 in France signified that a Code written in response to a largely agrarian economy became difficult to apply to new economic structures and rising social problems. The courts responded by adopting a more creative role, which still adhered to the spirit of the Code, but sought to provide more equitable legal responses to novel questions of law.[14] By utilising new methods of interpretation, such as the teleological methodology advocated by Josserand,[15] the historical approach[16] or even the more radical methodology espoused by the *école de la libre recherché scientifique*

[10] See also art. 1351: 'The force of *res judicata* takes place only with respect to what was the subject matter of a judgment. It is necessary that the thing claimed be the same; that the claim be based on the same grounds; that the claim be between the same parties and brought by them and against them in the same capacity.'

[11] New Code of Civil Procedure, art. 455: 'The judgment must describe briefly the respective claims of the parties and their grounds. Such presentation may take the form of a reference to the pleadings of the parties with the indication of their date. Reasons for the judgment must be given.'

[12] See, generally, J. Bonnecase, *L'école de l'exégèse en Droit Civil*, 1st edn (Paris: Euvrard-Pichat, 1919), and 2nd edn (Paris: Euvrard-Pichat, 1924); but note modern reappraisals of this period: P. Rémy, 'Eloge de l'exégèse' (1982) *RRJ* 254, and P. Jestaz and C. Jamin, *La doctrine* (Paris: Dalloz, 2004). Malaurie and Morvan, *Introduction générale* argue at no. 113 that 'in breaking with the pre-revolutionary law, they encouraged the essential qualities which *la doctrine française* has inherited: clarity, unity and harmony'.

[13] Note the work, for example, of Charles Demolombe (described as the 'prince de l'exégèse').

[14] '[C]'est ... par la recherche de l'esprit de la loi que l'interprète justifie pour lui-même la solution des questions que le texte légal ne fournit pas': P. Esmein, 'La jurisprudence et la loi' (1947) *Revue trimestrielle de Droit Civil* (hereafter *RTDciv.*) 17, 23.

[15] See L. Josserand, *De l'esprit des droits et de leur relativité* (Paris: Dalloz, 1927).

[16] Used, notably, in relation to the interpretation of art. 1384(1); see section III below.

(school of free scientific research),[17] the courts sought to maintain the vitality and social legitimacy of the Civil Code.

This new approach would appear to challenge the view that case law is not a source of law in French law.[18] The growth of administrative law, in particular, demonstrates the fragility of this precept where fewer rules are found in legislative texts and one must of necessity consult the decisions of the courts to identify the law. The decisions of the administrative courts play a significant creative role in the formation of legal principle. For example, the use of general principles of law (*principes généraux de droit*), such as the principle of equality before the law, demonstrates the role of legal principle in shaping and framing case analysis without reference to legislative instruments. Nevertheless, the style of case reporting – typically brief, formal, non-discursive – and the non-binding nature of the decisions demonstrates the continued adherence of French courts to the doctrine of separation of powers. To this should be added the anonymity[19] and consensual nature of the judgment itself. Even in courts with more than one judge, there is no sign of dissent, dispute or legal differences. A single judgment is given without any indication of the identity or views of the judges involved. As such, it contrasts distinctly with the common law system of judgments and, indeed, the role of common law judgments in providing a discussion of the relevant issues and an assessment of the relevant legal authorities.[20]

In reality, however, as will be illustrated in Section III, the position is less clear-cut.[21] Reports of decisions of the Cour de cassation date back to 1799 and cases will have persuasive, if not precedential, value, particularly if one can identify a *jurisprudence constante* (settled line of authority)

[17] See, notably, F. Gény, *La méthode d'intérpretation et sources du droit privé français*, 1st edn (Paris: LGDJ, 1899), and 2nd edn (Paris: LGDJ, 1919), advocating that legislative gaps should be filled by drawing on the knowledge of the social sciences to identify contemporary social needs, although it may be questioned to what degree this has actually influenced the courts.

[18] It is a matter of continuing debate in French law whether case law is a source of law, although the majority of modern authors recognise that, in reality, it is a source: see Malaurie and Morvan, *Introduction générale*, nos. 346–347.

[19] Although cases will normally disclose the name of the presiding judge and *rapporteur*.

[20] See B. Rudden, 'Courts and Codes in England, France and Soviet Russia' (1973/1974) 48 *Tulane Law Review* 1010; A. Tunc, 'Methodology of the Civil Law in France' (1976) 50 *Tulane Law Review* 459.

[21] See M. Troper and C. Grzegorczyk, 'Precedent in France' in N. McCormick and R. S. Summers (eds.), *Interpreting Precedents: A Comparative Study* (Aldershot: Ashgate/Dartmouth, 1997), pp. 103–140, and M. Lasser, 'Judicial (self-) portraits: Judicial discourse in the French legal system' (1995) 104 *Yale Law Journal* 1325.

or the decision is of the *Assemblée plénière*[22] or *Chambre mixte*[23] of the French Supreme Court.[24] More recently, procedural rules by which a decision of the *Assemblée plénière* of the Cour de cassation may, on second appeal on a point of law, bind the lower court, signify a strengthening of the decision-making power of the Cour de cassation.[25] In addition, whilst, in the majority of cases, if the Supreme Court decides to quash a decision, the case will be referred back to a court of the same level as the court whose decision has been overturned, the court may quash a judgment without appeal if this action does not imply any further ruling on the merits or because the facts, as definitively ascertained and assessed by the trial court, enable it to apply the appropriate rule of law.[26]

Cases such as the *Boudier* decision of 1892[27] and the *Blieck* decision of 1991[28], which establish, respectively, a principle of unjust enrichment and strict liability for harm caused by persons under your control, demonstrate clearly the creative and socially responsive nature of judicial decision-making in France. In these cases, the courts utilise the framework of the Civil Code to generate radical new principles capable of giving rise to liability far beyond that ever contemplated by the drafters of the Code.

Such ingenuity may have permitted the French legal system to continue to work within a Code of over 200 years of age, but presents a number of challenges to the integrity of the legal system. First, on what basis do the courts choose to interpret the law? Second, what accountability exists if, in accordance with art. 5, any new statements of principle cannot be stated openly owing to the ban on general and regulatory principles of law? Third, where does this leave the separation of powers? The answers to such questions may be found in examining the close relationship between the legislature, the courts and *la doctrine* in French law.

[22] French Supreme Court in plenary session.

[23] Mixed chamber of the French Supreme Court, consisting of judges belonging to at least three different chambers of the court.

[24] Note also in recent years the annual reports of the Cour de cassation and Conseil d'Etat.

[25] See art. L431–4, Code of Judicial Organisation (*Code de l'organisation judiciaire*). Decisions of the Conseil Constitutionnel are, of course, binding on all public authorities: see Constitution of 4 October 1958, art. 62: 'No appeal shall lie from the decisions of the Constitutional Council. They shall be binding on public authorities and on all administrative authorities and all courts.'

[26] Art. L411–3, Code of Judicial Organisation.

[27] Req. 15 June 1892 D. 1892.1.596, S. 1893.1.281 note J.-E. Labbé (also known as the *affaire Patureau-Mirand*), discussed below, pp. 96–99.

[28] Ass. plén. 29 March 1991 D. 1991,324 note C. Larroumet, chr. G. Viney p. 157; JCP 1991. II.21673, concl. H. Dontenwille, note J. Ghestin.

C La doctrine

Legal academics have a number of roles in French law. Beyond the provision of treatises, student manuals, dissertations, articles and other works of reference, two particular activities are worthy of comment: the provision of *notes* following case reports and advisory work on law reform.[29] The significance of the *note d'arrêt* owes something to the deference with which the Civil Code was first treated, as outlined above. In view of the political changes which occured during the early part of the nineteenth century, and the uncertainty which resulted, it is understandable that commentators might be unwilling to challenge directly the literal meaning of the Code.[30] However, in the 1830s, it became more common for the cases reported in leading journals such as the Sirey or Dalloz law reports to have short comments discussing the case. Whilst initially confined to brief editorial comments, the *notes* developed into small essays, at first undertaken by practitioners, but, as the nineteenth century progressed, undertaken by legal academics, and the mixture of academics, lawyers and judges writing *notes* continues to this day.[31] Dawson goes so far as to state that '[d]uring the late decades of the 1800s it was through analytical notes in the law reports that leading law professors began to effect a union of jurisprudence and doctrine.'[32] This marked an increasing role for legal commentary in French legal development, both in explaining the underlying reasoning of the court judgment and in placing it in a critical and doctrinal context. Jestaz and Jamin identify in the mid nineteenth century a generational gap between those dealing with the promulgation of the Code and those to whom the Code already seemed dated in the light of industrial development.[33] They note, from 1856, the arrival of a new generation of professors, of which Joseph-Emile Labbé, one of the greatest of the *arrêtistes*, was part. This marked the start of *la doctrine moderne* whereby the development of legal principles was seen as having

[29] One might also note the importance of the doctoral thesis in France to establishing an academic's reputation in contrast to the position in common law countries.

[30] Napoléon is famously reported to have exclaimed 'Mon code est perdu!' on learning of a commentary on the *Code civil*; E. de Las Cases, *Le Mémorial de Sainte-Hélène* (Paris: Gallimard, 1956), 2 vols., Vol. II, p. 153.

[31] See J. P. Dawson, *Oracles of the Law* (Westport: Greenwood Press, 1968), pp. 397–399.

[32] *Ibid.*, p. 398. Note also the establishment of the *RTDciv.* by Esmein and Saleilles at the start of the twentieth century, the first edition commencing with A. Esmein, 'La jurisprudence et la doctrine' (1902) *RTDciv.* 1 – an influential article that stressed the utility of studying case law.

[33] Jestaz and Jamin, *La doctrine*, p. 95.

an indelible link with modern life. The work of Raymond Saleilles and François Gény at the turn of the century highlighted the increasing confidence of academic writers, who saw their role not only as commentators, but as helping to shape the future development of the law. Further, the work of Edouard Lambert, promoting the study of comparative law, emphasised a need to consider different forms of reasoning at a time of great social and economic change.[34]

Recognition of this role may be found in the use by legislators of academics in assisting in the process of law reform. Law professors are frequently used to head commissions on law reform or to participate in the reform process. A brief glance at developments in the twentieth century may identify Henri Capitant in relation to the 1930 law on insurance; René Rodière in relation to the 1966 reform of maritime law;[35] and Jean Carbonnier in relation to the reform of the law of persons, in particular family law, in the 1960s and 1970s. The role of *la doctrine* should not be underestimated.[36]

Yet, it remains the case that *la doctrine* is not formally treated as a source of law.[37] Its influence is nevertheless undeniable and may be illustrated by a number of case-law examples. The *Boudier* case of 1892 provides a rare example of case law recognising a principle – that of unjust enrichment – based primarily on academic commentary.[38] This did not, however, lead to a satisfactory formulation of principle, which came from the interaction of courts and *la doctrine*, in delineating the doctrine of

[34] See E. Lambert, *La fonction du droit civil comparé* (Paris: V. Giard & E. Brière, 1903).

[35] Rodière chaired a committee to update French maritime law after the Second World War. Tetley comments 'If [Rodière] consulted at all, it was only briefly, and then he single-handedly wrote France's five basic maritime laws, which are modern and valid to this day'; W. Tetley QC, 'Rodière: Le plus vénéré, distingué et difficile professeur de droit maritime de France' available online at www.mcgill.ca/maritimelaw/tetley/rodiere/, last accessed 28 November 2011.

[36] Particular note should be made of the position in administrative law where the judges are often the leading writers of *doctrine* (either as *commissaires du gouvernement* or as commentators and textbook writers), although it has been suggested that they are more concerned with the good administration of the law than to produce academic theory: J. Hardy, 'Le statut doctrinale de la jurisprudence en droit administrative français' (1990) *Revue de droit public* 453, 467.

[37] Note, however, the comments of Jestaz and Jamin, *La doctrine*, p. 7. The authors argue that *la doctrine* now represents an entity in its own right (see also the same authors' 'L'entité doctrinale française' D 1997 chron. 167), although this is subject to dispute. Other authors have suggested that such a claim, even if valid, must be confined to civil law – administrative law, for example, has two forms of *doctrine* – from professors, and from the *conseillers d'Etat* and the *commissaires du gouvernement* themselves – which does not fit within the proposed model.

[38] Req. 15 June 1892, D. 1892.1.596, S. 1893.1.281 note J.-E. Labbé.

unjustified enrichment (*enrichissement sans cause*) and distinguishing it from the law of delict. As Labbé immediately appreciated in his note to the decision, the court had relied on the textbook of Aubry and Rau,[39] and yet omitted the conditions that the authors had set down. Aubry and Rau had proposed that any claim should be subject to two restrictions: that the enrichment be without *cause* and that the claimant have no alternative form of action.[40] By omitting these restrictions, the court ran the risk of introducing a broad principle of equity into the law that could not be contained.[41] This led Marcel Planiol to suggest that the case should in fact be absorbed into the law of delict, relying on the wide delictual regime established in art. 1382 of the Civil Code.[42] Georges Ripert and Raymond Teisseire[43] favoured a modified form of this argument: a modern interpretation of delictual responsibility that would rest on the objective theory of risk.[44] Other authors argued for a subjective basis to the doctrine. By 1930, Ripert[45] had decided that objective risk theory created false scientific certainty, whereas the question rested, in reality, on a question of morality.[46]

39 C. Aubry and C. Rau, *Cours de droit civil français*, 12 vols., Vol. IX, 4th edn (Paris: Marchal et Billard, 1871), §578.

40 *Ibid.*, deriving support from several provisions within the Code, in particular art. 559, which awards compensation for a field overtaken by a river during a flood. See also arts. 555, 565, 566.

41 As Labbé stated (above, n. 39), 'rien n'est plus vague, moins précis, moins déterminé que cette théorie de la Cour' ('nothing is more vague, less precise and less clear than this principle set out by the court'). Labbé argued that the condition 'sans juste cause' ('without just cause') was required as a practical necessity.

42 See *Obligations* VII; (1904) *Revue critique de législation et de jurisprudence* 224. By adopting a bilateral view of the law of obligations, Planiol argued that the common element of compensation for unintentional loss/harm in quasi-delict and unjustified enrichment justified the conclusion that they were founded on the same legal principle: 'ne pas nuire sans droit' ('do not harm another without a legal justification'). The defendant's fault lay in retaining the benefit unjustly acquired, thus causing a direct loss to the claimant.

43 'Essai d'une théorie de l'enrichissement sans cause en droit civil français' (1904) *RTDciv.* 727.

44 On this basis, if a causal link could be established between the act of the claimant and the profit of the beneficiary, the latter would be held responsible. The sole limit on recovery would be the existence of a 'just cause', giving the beneficiary a right to retain his benefit.

45 *La règle morale dans les obligations civiles*, 4th edn (Paris: LGDJ, 1949), nos. 133–147.

46 *Ibid.*, nos. 141–142: 'un faux appareil scientifique, une prétention à la méchanique juridique … Le problème consiste tout simplement à préciser suffisamment le devoir moral pour qu'on puisse lui donner figure d'obligation civile.' H. C. Gutteridge and R. David, 'The Doctrine of Unjustified Enrichment' (1933–1935) 5 *CLJ* 204 equally favoured an explanation based on underlying principles of natural justice.

Yet, neither the delictual nor the morality thesis met full approval.[47] The use by Planiol, Ripert and Teisseire of the simple trigger mechanisms of fault and causation were believed to be unsatisfactory.[48] Faced with such competing theories, *doctrine* ultimately focussed on the key concept of *équité*, first stated in the *Boudier* decision, that 'nul ne peut s'enrichir aux dépens d'autrui' ('no-one should enrich themselves at the expense of another').[49] This general principle permitted a flexible approach, freed from technical analysis or a subjective discussion of the current morality of society. It stated a simple rule of conduct, consistent with the spirit of numerous articles of the Code, but as a principle of equity, remained a remedy of last resort when no other action was available.[50] Such an approach was adopted in subsequent case law. As early as 1903, the Cour de cassation had sought to limit the possible range of the *Boudier* principle,[51] but the *Clayette* case[52] of 1914 marked formal acceptance by the Cour de cassation of the need to adopt the limitations expounded by Aubry and Rau in 1871, in particular the notion of unjustified enrichment as a subsidiary remedy.[53] In all these

[47] The use of delict was criticised for failing to recognise the different characteristics of unjustified enrichment: for example, that damages are awarded on a different basis. Planiol's explanation that damages would be governed by perceived degrees of morality, authorising a higher award according to the increasing level of harm to the community, is hardly satisfactory, and received much criticism from contemporary authors: see G. Ripert and M. Teisseire, 'Essai d'une théorie de l'enrichissement sans cause en droit civil français' (1904) *RTDciv.* 727; F. Gény, 'Risques et responsabilité' (1902) *RTDciv.* 812; G. Ripert (1907) *Rev. crit.* 207.

[48] It was generally questioned whether a simple notion of 'cause' was capable of keeping the principle within reasonable bounds or whether it would lead to liability that was 'excessif et injuste': see E. Naquet, note to Civ. 23 November 1908; and F. Goré, *L'enrichissement aux dépens d'autrui* (Paris: Dalloz, 1949).

[49] Petiton's *rapport* and *notes* of Labbé, Wahl and Naquet were also influential.

[50] For modern attempts to formulate a united concept of *enrichissement sans cause*, see C. Filios, *L'enrichissement sans cause en droit privé français*, thèse de doctorat, Lille (Athens: Sakkoulas; Brussels: Bruylant, 1999), who suggests an approach similar to that adopted in German law; and M. Douchy, *La notion de quasi-contrat en droit positif français* (Paris: Economica, 1997).

[51] Cass. civ. 21 July 1903, S. 1904.1.21. Note also Cass. civ. 18 October 1898, S. 1899.1.165, where the action of the tenant's employees against the landlord for his enrichment deriving from his share of the harvest under the tenancy agreement failed; Req. 23 November 1908, S. 1910.1.425 note E. Naquet: payment for improvements by a sublessee not recovered owing to lack of manifest gain; Req. 8 February 1909, S. 1911.1.313 note Bourcart where the court chose to regard the payor as an agent and refused to allow him to use the action *de in rem verso* to gain priority as a creditor.

[52] Civ. 12 May 1914, S. 1918.1.41 *note* E. Naquet, reproducing the actual words of Aubry and Rau, *Cours de droit civil français*, Vol. IX, §578.

[53] The following year, a similar position was taken in the *Briauhant* case: Civ. 2 March 1915 DP 1920.1.102 (*1re espèce*).

cases, the courts sought to avoid a result that would undermine contract and tort law, threatening a 'true judicial anarchy'.[54] In consequence, it was resolved that any claim for unjustified enrichment would now be subsidiary to a claim in contract or tort.

This example is helpful in a number of ways. It demonstrates that, by the end of the nineteenth century, there was already an active dialogue between *la doctrine* and the courts. While some reference is given to the provisions of the Civil Code in the *Boudier* case, for example art. 1165,[55] the principle of unjustified enrichment is described as deriving from a principle of *équité*, which is then developed, questioned, and analysed by the judiciary and *doctrine*.[56] Second, it shows that there has been a clear move away from the exegetical methodology and recognition that there is a need to seek a coherent principled basis for an evolving law of obligations. It may be compared with the *Teffaine* case,[57] which is discussed below in Section III. Here, art. 1384 was expressly relied upon as the source of liability, but, as the commentaries indicate, in a manner that reinterpreted the literal meaning of the provision and greatly extended its possible application in circumstances where *doctrine* and the judiciary were far from agreement on how the law should develop.

The most obvious signs of this collaboration in the development of the law may be seen in the conclusions of the *ministère public* – the judge whose function is to place before the court his or her conclusions as to the result that most favours the public interest. For the Cour de cassation, the *procureur général* or *avocat-général* must submit his or her conclusions (the *commissaire du gouvernement* in administrative law), which may be published as part of the case report. These give a valuable indication of judicial attitudes and awareness of the doctrinal debate.[58] Indeed, Bell comments, in his recent survey of the French judiciary, that:

> [a] particular importance attaches to the conclusions of the *commissaire du gouvernement* in the development of administrative law. These are not

[54] A. Rouast, 'L'enrichissement sans cause et la jurisprudence civile' (1922) *RTDciv.* 35, 44.

[55] Article 1165: 'Agreements produce effect only between the contracting parties; they do not harm a third party, and they benefit him only in the case provided for in Article 1121.'

[56] See B. Nicholas, 'Unjustified Enrichment in the Civil Law and Louisiana Law' (1962) 36 *Tulane Law Review* 605.

[57] Cass. civ. 16 June 1896, S. 1897.1.17 note A. Esmein; D. 1897.1.433 note R. Saleilles.

[58] Note also the *rapport* by one member of the collegial court that is published on occasion, which also discusses the legal issues, but does not advocate a particular result. As Nicholas comments, publication is tantamount to a breach of the principle of collegiality, but gives an insight into the working of judicial minds: B. Nicholas, *The French Law of Contract*, 2nd edn (Oxford: Clarendon Press, 1992), p. 12.

> just pleadings, but part of an ongoing survey and analysis of the law, arguing that it should develop in particular ways. They are points of reference, just as much as any seminal article of a professor, and much like a leading judgment in the common law.[59]

The conclusions of M. l'Avocat-général Sarrut, for example, in the Teffaine case[60] illustrate the obvious tension between a wider reading of art. 1384(1) and a literal interpretation of the Code and the hesitation of the courts in taking such a step. In the *Jand'heur* case discussed in Section III,[61] the report of the Conseiller Le Marc'hadour and the conclusions of the Procureur général Matter are both published. The report, in particular, would not be unfamiliar to a common lawyer with its description of the decisions of the lower courts, review of the arguments for the appellant and respondent, and survey of recent case law and leading commentary. The conclusions of Matter are more opinionated, strongly advocating a continuation of the more flexible approach evident in recent case law, which he believed would lead to a humane and just result that responded to the needs of the modern age.

D The judiciary

Finally, in assessing the contribution of the judiciary to legal development, it is worth noting the background experience that judges bring to the court. In terms of practical expertise, unlike common law jurisdictions, judges may be relatively inexperienced. In France, judges are career professionals who opt, after their law degree, to study to become a judge.[62] The career path of a private law judge will differ from that of a public law judge, who, at the top level, is likely to move between a variety of postings within government and public administration.[63] Some

[59] J. Bell, *Judiciaries within Europe* (Cambridge: Cambridge University Press, 2006), p. 85, see also Lasser (n. 22 above), pp. 1355–1402.

[60] D. 1897.1.433 note R. Saleilles.

[61] Ch. réun. 13 February 1930, DP 1930.1.57 *note* G Ripert; *rapport* Le Marc'hadour, S. 1930.1.121 note P. Esmein.

[62] A private law judge would follow a course of studies at *Ecole Nationale de la Magistrature* in Bordeaux; a public law judge at the *Ecole Nationale d'Administration* in Strasbourg and Paris. Lay judges continue, however, to be used in the lower courts, notably in employment law, commercial law and juvenile criminal justice cases where practical expertise is regarded as a useful addition to the court. See Bell, *Judiciaries within Europe*, Chapter 2.

[63] See, generally, J. Bell, *French Legal Cultures* (London: Butterworths, 2001), pp. 37–43.

administrative judges are deliberately chosen from the civil service to ensure a cross-fertilisation of ideas. Judges have also traditionally provided the civil servants in the Ministry of Justice, which body determines law reform.[64] Private law judges may also be chosen from practice, academia or the civil service. For example, a small number of professors have reached the Cour de cassation,[65] and three, notably, have become president of the Chamber.[66] Professors will also typically give consultations and thereby influence litigation by arguments presented in cases,[67] as well as by doctrinal writing. By this means, greater experience is brought to the court whilst, at the same time, illustrating the importance of interaction between different interest groups in the operation of the law.

E Conclusion to Section II

French law may be seen as a system based on contradictions – it has a formal system of sources of law, and yet case law and academic commentary form an essential part of its legal development.[68] Cases are reported tersely with reference to the appropriate part of the Civil Code and yet the law has been developed 'beyond the Civil Code' to respond to changing social, economic and political needs.[69] The French are immensely proud of their 1804 Code – one of the earliest modern codes – and yet have found themselves turning to, in particular, German legal thought in the nineteenth century for inspiration. The twentieth century brought with it an increasing understanding of sociological literature and an increasing recognition of European and international sources.

Yet, as will be seen below, legal change also owes much to the ordinary participants drawn into the legal process. When ordinary citizens – be they workers, consumers, pedestrians or passengers – are injured in

64 Note also that the president of the Cour de cassation was *ex officio* a member of the Senate until 1919.

65 Louis Josserand (1868–1941), for example, co-authored the project for the Lebanese Code of Obligations and Contracts, was a leading law professor and was *conseiller* at the Cour de cassation in 1938. A more recent example is that of Jean-Luc Aubert in the 1990s.

66 Pierre Lescot (1942), André Ponsard (1973) and Daniel Tricot (current president of the Commercial Chamber). See also D. Tricot, 'L'élaboration d'un arrêt de la Cour de cassation' 2004 JCP. (G) doctrine I.108.

67 Some also continue to act as *avocats*, for example Professor Aynès, who has acted as an advocate in addition to his position at the University of Paris I.

68 See M. Lasser, *Judicial Deliberations: A Comparative Analysis of Judicial Transparency and Legitimacy* (Oxford: Oxford University Press, 2004).

69 To use the famous phrase of Saleilles.

sufficient numbers to cause concern amongst politicians, trade unions, insurance companies and corporations in general, the result is often legal change and the mechanisms used will be explained below. One of the great challenges of the last 150 years has been to adapt the Civil Code to respond to new methods of causing injury arising from the industrial revolution. Factories and motor vehicles, in particular, raised immediate concerns as to safety, and the responses of the courts, and later the legislature, illustrate clearly the interaction of legislation, the courts, *la doctrine*, the professionals and other interest groups in the development of the law.

III Practical examples

This section will aim to support the above analysis by means of practical examples, focussing primarily on developments in workmen's compensation and compensation for motor vehicle accidents. Both represent examples of liability arising from industrial and technological advances. Mass industrialisation had led to increased employment in the industrial sector, and cheaper and more accessible goods from matches to motor cars, but also to exposure to accidents of greater severity and impact than ever known before. The explosion, for example, at the AZF factory at Toulouse on 21 September 2001, which led to the death of 29 people and thousands of injured parties, demonstrated clearly to the French public the negative side of industrialisation.[70] How French law has dealt with these two sources of accidents is helpful in gaining a better understanding of legal development over the period of the study.

One might start, however, with fault-based liability itself. While art. 1382 of the Civil Code requires fault-based liability, art. 1383 merely states that 'Each one is liable for the damage he causes not only by his own intentional act, but also by his negligent conduct or by his imprudence.' No further guidance is given. As Jean-Louis Halpérin indicates in his paper on French doctrine,[71] a definition of fault became the principal challenge for nineteenth century doctrinal writers and the debate as to the nature of

[70] See *Le Monde*, 25 September 2001: 'Toulouse s'interroge sur les causes et les responsabilités de la catastrophe'. In addition, more than 2,400 were injured, 8,000 suffered minor injuries, and 40,000 people were made homeless for several days. The AZF catastrophe has led the recent body proposing comprehensive reform of the Civil Code to recommend the introduction of a special form of strict liability for abnormally dangerous activities: see art. 1362 of P. Catala (ed.), *Avant-projet de réforme du droit des obligations et du droit de la prescription* (Paris: La documentation française, 2006).

[71] In N. Jansen (ed.), *The Development and Making of Legal Doctrine* (Cambridge: Cambridge University Press, 2010), pp. 77ff.

fault continues to this day.[72] Although technically the Cour de cassation controls its meaning,[73] the evolving interpretation of *faute*, in particular the movement from a subjective to a more objective approach, cannot be divorced from an ongoing doctrinal debate as to its meaning and role in French law.[74]

Such debates highlight the limitations of the Civil Code as a source of law. By its very nature, it requires interpretation, but, as will be seen, the response of the courts has gone beyond interpretation to a radical reappraisal of its application to modern social and economic conditions.

A *Industrial accidents*

The treatment of liability for accidents in the workplace provides a useful example of the interaction of legal actors discussed in Section I. In the early nineteenth century, the position was clear. Tortious liability would be based on fault, as set out in arts. 1382 and 1383. Yet, fault inevitably requires proof of fault and the establishment of a causal link between the harm and the tortious act: the burden of which lies on the claimant to prove. In the face of industrialisation, this position was considered by the end of the nineteenth century to be harsh on victims, and *doctrine* formulated a number of means of circumventing this rule.[75] Certain authors, following the lead from the Belgian courts, favoured a contractual approach – imposing an *obligation de sécurité* in the contract of employment rendering the employer liable on breach. Others favoured an extension of art. 1386 from buildings to all chattels.[76] The third approach involved a more radical departure from the strict interpretation of the Code – applying art. 1384(1), not as an introductory provision, but as a statement of legal principle. This article states that '[a] person is liable not

[72] G. Viney and P. Jourdain, *Les conditions de la responsabilité*, 3rd edn (Paris: LGDJ, 2006), nos. 441–444.

[73] Civ. 15 April 1873, S. 1873.1.174.

[74] See Viney and Jourdain, *Les conditions de la responsabilité*, nos. 440ff.

[75] J.-S. Borghetti, 'The Development of Product Liability in French Law' in S. Whittaker (ed.), *The Development of Product Liability* (Cambridge: Cambridge University Press, 2010), pp. 100–101 speculates as to the extent that political convictions of left-wing lawyers had merged with those of the judiciary or other lawyers' Christian concern for the poor and afflicted so as to create a strong pro-victim trend.

[76] 'The owner of a building is liable for the damage caused by its collapse, where it happens as a result of lack of maintenance or of a defect in its construction.' See C. Demolombe, *Traité des engagements qui se forment sans convention* (Paris: Imprimerie générale, 1882), no. 664 ; and Labbé, S. 1871.1.9.

only for the damages he causes by his own act, but also for that which is caused by the acts of persons for whom he is responsible, or by things which are in his custody'. There is no mention of fault. Labbé, changing his mind,[77] came to favour a view that art. 1384(1) should no longer be seen as an introduction to liability for the acts of animals (art. 1385) and for ruined buildings (art. 1386), but as founding liability for the acts of things for which the custodian (*gardien*) must pay compensation irrespective of proof of fault.

It fell to the Cour de cassation in 1896 to deal with an appeal exactly in point: a mechanic had been killed by an exploding boiler in the workplace, but no fault could be attributed to his employer.[78] The Court of Appeal had relied on the first two options – the employer would be liable under a contractual obligation and, applying art. 1386 by analogy to machines, under the law of tort. In the view of the *avocat-général*, Sarrut, both arguments were flawed. A boiler is not a building to which art. 1386 applies and the case law did not support the implied contractual term. However, neither was he prepared to accept a broad reading of art. 1384(1) and chose to reaffirm the importance of proof of fault.[79]

The Cour de cassation, however, disagreed:

> Whereas the decision appealed finds as a matter of fact that the explosion of the machine in the steam-powered tugboat Marie, which caused the death of Teffaine, is due to a fault in construction; that in terms of art. 1384 c. civ. this finding, which excludes *cas fortuit*[80] and *force majeure*, establishes, in relation to the victim of the accident, the liability of the owner of the tugboat.

Saleilles in his note is predictably pleased by this result, which he saw as supporting his view that liability for professional risks should be borne by

[77] S 1890.4.17. See also François Laurent, *Principes de droit civil français*, 33 vols. (Brussels: Bruylant–Christophe; Paris: A. Durand & Pedone-Lauriel, 1869–1878), Vol. XX, no. 639.

[78] *L'affaire Teffaine*: Civ. 16 June 1896, S. 1897.1.17 note A. Esmein; D. 1897.1.433, concl. Sarrut, note R. Saleilles.

[79] D. 1897.1.433, 440: 'en réalité, le code n'a pas dérogé, en ce qui concerne les choses inanimées, à la règle fondamentale, posée aux arts. 1382 et 1383, que la preuve de la faute du défendeur doit être rapportée.'

[80] There is no easy translation of this term and to use the term 'fortuitous event' does not do the concept justice. The leading French law dictionary defines it as an event responding to the same definition as *force majeure* (unforeseeable, irresistible, exterior to the defendant), which constitutes a ground for exonerating the defendant from liability: see G. Cornu, *Vocabulaire juridique*, 7th edn (Paris: PUF, 2005). The nearest common law equivalent would be the doctrine of inevitable accident.

the employer.[81] Esmein's note, in contrast, favoured a contractual explanation and openly doubted an interpretation of the codal provision that bore little relation to earlier law.

The case illustrates a number of the propositions discussed above. *Doctrine* is clearly influential in this case-law development. This is evident from the notes, but also from the conclusions of the *avocat-général*, which indicate the active debate between contractual and tortious solutions. Saleilles notably refers to the principles adopted by the *Conseil d'Etat* towards workers injured whilst working for the State,[82] and both German and Swiss law.

Yet whilst the case marked an important advance in the development of strict liability for the acts of things,[83] the political dimension should not be neglected. Halpérin in his paper identifies that the idea of liability without fault first came from politicians such as Martin Nadaud in 1880[84] and Félix Faure in 1882, who proposed a law on accidents in the workplace.[85] This provoked a response from jurists, economists, employers and unions.[86] A Bill to impose strict liability on employers was already before Parliament in 1896 – a fact of which the Cour de cassation could not avoid being aware. In 1898 – two years after the Teffaine decision – the Government introduced the Workmen's Compensation Act, which imposed strict liability on the employer in its own right.[87] Although the final Act was a compromise in the face of opposition from businessmen and senators, it nevertheless represented a fundamental step forward in

[81] See also R. Saleilles, *Les accidents du travail et la responsabilité civile: Essai d'une théorie objective de la responsabilité délictuelle* (Paris: Arthur Rousseau, 1897); and L. Josserand, *De la responsabilité du fait des choses inanimées* (Paris: Arthur Rousseau, 1897).

[82] Raising the argument often used by authors advocating that civil law adopt the often more generous legal principles of administrative law: 'Quelle raison y aurait-il donc d'appliquer un régime différent de celui de nos grandes compagnies industrielles ou de nos compagnies de transport?' See CE 21 June 1895, DP 1896.3.65 concl. Romieu; S 1897.3.333 concl. Romieu, note Hauriou, in which Romieu discussed the civil law in France, as well as in Belgium and Luxembourg.

[83] See F. Leduc, *La responsabilité du fait des choses: Réflexions autour d'un centenaire* (Paris: Economica, 1997).

[84] See proposition du député Martin Nadaud 29 May 1880, ann. no. 2660: JO 6 June 1880.

[85] J.-L. Halpérin, 'French Doctrinal Writing' in Jansen (ed.), *The Development and Making of Legal Doctrine*, p. 88.

[86] Outlined by P.-J. Hesse, 'La genèse d'une loi: De la révolution industrielle à la révolution juridique' (1998) *Droit social* 638.

[87] *Loi* 9 April 1898. This statute was limited in scope in that it only applied to industrial enterprises and employees acting under a contract of employment (it was extended in 1906 to the workmen and employees of trade undertakings). It was also all-inclusive save in the case of intentional or inexcusable fault (*faute intentionnelle* or *faute inexcusable*).

employment law.[88] From this moment onwards, workmen's compensation was dealt with by its own legislative framework, which, in 1946,[89] moved decisively away from tortious liability and became part of the general social security provision by the State funded by contributions from employers. This has not discouraged subsequent legislative intervention from promoting accident prevention in the workplace and, of course, the increasing European dimension of workers' protection, which has led to modifications to the Labour Code and the Public Health Code. The aim of prevention is taken as a corollary to the political goal of compensation, as evidenced by the notion of 'la sécurité intégrée' (integrated safety) introduced in the 1976 legislation.[90] The National Fund for Health Insurance (CNAM)[91] acts as a national body to promote accident prevention, centralise statistics, co-ordinate its regional offices and manage funds.[92] The structure is therefore administrative and signifies an internalisation of social risk by employers via the mechanism of the State.

B Motor vehicle accidents

Motor vehicles have been a major cause of accidents for almost 100 years. In 2010,[93] 67,288 accidental injuries, 3,992 deaths within 30 days and 84,461 injuries (of which 30,393 led to hospitalisation) were recorded as resulting from lack of road safety in metropolitan France.[94] The development of the law relating to traffic accidents provides an excellent example

88 'Cent années après, on peut dresser un bilan positif de ce texte fondamental du droit du travail, comme du droit de la protection sociale. Non seulement, il servit de base, en 1919, à la réparation des maladies professionnelles, mais l'architecture générale fut reprise lors de l'adoption de la Sécurité sociale au lendemain de la Seconde Guerre mondiale, sauf en ce qui concerne les organismes gestionnaires': Hesse, 'La genèse d'une loi', 642.

89 *Loi* 30 October 1946.

90 *Loi* 6 December 1976, which seeks to cover all problems from the moment of construction of machinery to its utilisation.

91 *Caisse nationale de l'assurance maladie* (www.ameli.fr).

92 For more detail, see M. Meunier-Boffa, *Droit des relations sociales au travail*, 5th edn (Paris: Litec, 2009).

93 See 'La sécurité routière en France: Bilan de l'année 2010', (www.securiteroutiere.gouv.fr). The figures in previous years were even higher – for example, 8,634 deaths in 1953 at a time where motor vehicles were far less numerous – which highlights the ongoing significance of this category of accidents.

94 In comparison, the number of people killed in road accidents reported to the police in Great Britain in 2010 was 1,850, 17 per cent fewer than in 2009. The number of people seriously injured fell to 22,660, 9 per cent fewer than in 2009. Total casualties in 2010 were 208,648, 6 per cent fewer than in 2009: see 'Road Casualties in Great Britain: 2010', www.dft.gov.uk/statistics (accessed 28 November 2011).

of how tort law has evolved over the last 100 years.[95] Unlike workmen's compensation, tort law was not immediately replaced by legislation regulating the risk of injury. One sees instead a battle between the different interest groups: the public, the corporations and their insurers, the legal professionals anxious to retain their involvement in the legal process, and of course an ongoing debate between *la doctrine* and the courts as to how a tortious remedy could evolve from the five articles of the Civil Code. Whilst the legislature intervened as early as 1936,[96] and there have been a number of significant proposals for reform, it was only in 1985 that reliance on the Civil Code was replaced by a legislative structure, which, as will be seen, in contrast to workmen's compensation, amounted to a compromise between tortious and no-fault principles. The 2005 *Proposals for Reform of the Law of Obligations and the Law of Prescription*[97] highlight problems still existing with the 1985 scheme, and ongoing dissatisfaction as to its treatment of victims and the continuing division between road and railway/tramway accidents.[98]

1 Finding a remedy in tort

The problems facing victims of industrial accidents in proving fault under arts. 1382 and 1383 apply equally to those injured in motor vehicle accidents. To these may be added the problem of identifying the culprit and finding a defendant with sufficient funds to meet the claim. Whilst the Teffaine decision indicated that a broad reading of art. 1384(1) might permit recovery without proof of fault, subsequent legislation dealt exclusively with workplace accidents and thereby removed any need to develop this principle further. In addition, as indicated by Esmein's response above, considerable disagreement still existed as to the status of art. 1384(1) as a general statement of principle. Whilst the decision of the Civil Chamber in 1919[99] supported a general presumption of fault based on art. 1384(1) – which could not be rebutted by proof of absence of fault but could be rebutted by *cas fortuit*, *force majeure* or *cause étrangère*[100] not

[95] See G. Viney and A. Guégan-Lécuyer, 'The Development of Traffic Liability in France' in W. Ernst (ed), *The Development of Traffic Liability* (Cambridge University Press, 2010), pp. 60–69.

[96] *Loi* 30 June 1936.

[97] Catala, *Avant-projet de réforme du droit des obligations*.

[98] See proposed art. 1385 and the Preamble of Professor Viney.

[99] Civ. 21 Jan 1919, DP 1922.1.25 *note* G. Ripert.

[100] This term is again difficult to translate, but is commonly defined as a generic term designating all facts or events that impact on the occurrence of damage that possess the triple characteristics of unforeseeability, irresistibility and exteriority: see Cornu, *Vocabulaire juridique*.

attributable to the defendant[101] – a major obstacle still existed. Liability was founded on the act of a thing that, due to a defect or some other reason, caused an accident injuring the victim. It is extremely artificial to claim that a motor vehicle accident occurs because of the act of the car in hitting the pedestrian – it occurs because the vehicle is driven by a human being. On this basis, it seems difficult to fit road accidents within even the more flexible interpretation of the text. By 1885 the Cour de cassation was prepared to find the custodian of an animal liable without fault (subject to the defences of *cas fortuit* or fault of the victim) under art. 1385,[102] which could extend to horse-drawn vehicles, but a horse with a will of its own is distinct from a mechanical vehicle. Nevertheless, in the Jand'heur case of 1930,[103] the Cour de cassation ruled that liability could be found under art. 1384(1), and that no distinction should be made between the act of a person and the act of the thing.[104] In other words, liability arose from the fact of having custody of the object, not the act of the object itself:

> Whereas the presumption of liability established by [art. 1384(1)] against the person who has in his custody the inanimate object which has caused harm to another can only be rebutted by proof of a *cas fortuit* or *force majeure* or a *cause étrangère* which is not attributable to him ... the law ... does not distinguish depending on whether the thing which has caused the harm was or was not activated by human conduct.

Such an extension – rejected twice by the Court of Appeal and thus requiring a decision of the *Chambres réunies* – can only be interpreted as a deliberate decision by the court to use tort law to minimise and internalise the risks of motor vehicle accidents. As the *rapporteur* stated, 'you have today to pronounce in a definitive manner on this question, still controversial,

[101] The most common being fault by the victim. In sum, liability will be avoided when there is an unforeseeable event that makes the accident unavoidable and that is external to the defendant.

[102] See Civ. 27 October 1885, DP 1886.1.207; S.1886.1.33, also discussed in Viney and Guégan-Lécuyer, 'The Development of Traffic Liability in France', p. 60.

[103] Ch. réun. 13 February 1930, DP 1930.1.57 note G. Ripert; rapport Le Marc'hadour S 1930.1.121 note P. Esmein. For background to the case see E. A. Tomlinson, 'Tort liability in France for the act of things: A study of judicial lawmaking' (1988) 48 *Louisiana Law Review* 1299, 1337–1343.

[104] In any event, such a distinction raises difficulties in practice. For example, if a boiler explodes, is it due to the boiler or the way in which a human being manufactured or serviced it? Furthermore, if a road accident occurs, it produces uncertainty for the victim if his or her remedy will differ according to whether the accident is due to a mechanical fault or the conduct of the driver, or, more confusingly, a mixture of both.

of the application of art. 1384(1) to inanimate things and in particular to motor vehicles'.[105] The Supreme Court took up this challenge.

Yet this did not prevent calls for legislation. Proposals had been laid before Parliament from 1906 onwards to no avail.[106] Despite the Jand'heur case, insurance law expert Maurice Picard from 1931 called for a special statute dealing with motor vehicle accidents.[107] Compulsory insurance was introduced in February 1958,[108] and in 1952 a Compensation Fund was established to compensate for personal injuries caused by uninsured and insolvent drivers. In 1964, the Minister of Justice, Jean Foyer, established a Commission to respond to continued dissatisfaction with the system, chaired by Professor André Tunc. The Commission proposed a system of private insurance, taking motor vehicles out of civil law entirely and replacing private law with a system of first party insurance.[109] Such proposals met, however, with stiff opposition, notably from the Bar and the insurance industry, and academics critical of the challenge to private law principles. As a result, the proposals were dropped. Professor Tunc continued nevertheless to advocate the need for change,[110] and finally a redraft of his proposals in 1981[111] met with a more receptive audience: the new Minister of Justice and professor of law,[112] Robert Badinter, who established a new commission in 1981.[113] In 1985, despite ongoing

105 DP 1930.1.57, 60.

106 Interestingly, this earlier proposal by the *Société d'Etudes législatives* was drafted by Ambroise Colin, who later became a judge in the Cour de cassation and was involved in the *Jand'heur* litigation.

107 'Pour une loi sur la réparation des accidents d'automobile' (1931) *Revue generale des assurances terrestres* 5 and 489. Viney and Guégan-Lécuyer note in 'The Development of Traffic Liability in France' p. 62 that a legislative proposal was indeed conceived, but that it was dropped owing to opposition from professionals.

108 Notably, far later than in England or Germany.

109 The Commission included judges, law professors, insurance company presidents, and representatives from the Bar and social security administration. Its proposals and the tension within the committee are described by A. Tunc in 'Traffic Accident Compensation in France: The Present Law and a Controversial Proposal' (1966) 79 *Harvard Law Review* 1409.

110 See the influential *La sécurité routière: Esquisse d'une loi sur les accidents de la circulation* (Paris: Dalloz, 1966); 'Sur un projet de Loi en matière d'accidents de la circulation' (1967) *RTDciv.* 82; and 'The French Law of Traffic Victims Compensation: The Present and the Possible' (1983) 31 *American Journal of Comparative Law* 489.

111 *Pour une loi sur l'indemnisation des accidents de la circulation* (Paris: Economica, 1981).

112 Badinter was a law professor at the University of Paris I. Foyer was additionally a law professor at the University of Lille.

113 This commission was chaired by Pierre Bellet, a former president of the Cour de cassation, and included again members of the Bar and insurance profession, and Professor Tunc.

opposition, legislation introduced a major reform of motor vehicle accidents, replacing, in most cases, liability under art. 1384(1) with strict liability.

2 Legislative intervention

The so-called *loi Badinter*[114] involves a curious mix of civil law principles and a strict insurance-based system. Chapter 1, art. 1 states that it will cover traffic accidents involving vehicles, excluding railways and tramways. *Force majeure* or the acts of third parties will no longer be available as defences,[115] and victims (other than drivers) will be compensated for personal injuries regardless of their own fault – unless it amounts to inexcusable fault which was the sole cause of the accident[116] – and provided that the victim has not deliberately incurred the harm suffered: for example, by a suicide attempt. In contrast, drivers suffering injuries due to the vehicle accident will have their claim for damages reduced or excluded if at fault.[117] The extent will be decided by the lower court judges. Viney describes them as the *victimes sacrifiées* ('sacrificed victims') of the law, adding 'In truth, there are scarcely any good legal reasons for the discrimination practised towards drivers. The only real reason is economic in nature: to avoid too sensitive a rise in insurance premiums, it has been decided to sacrifice the drivers.'[118] Recovery of damage to property is also limited, art. 5 providing that fault by the victim will limit or exclude compensation.[119] Procedural rules additionally rendered the compensation process faster and more efficient.[120] In 1991, Tunc noted that since the

114 *Loi* no. 85–677 of 5 July 1985: 'Loi tendant à l'amélioration de la situation des victimes d'accidents de la circulation et à l'accélération des procédures d'indemnisation'.

115 Art. 2.

116 Art. 3. *Faute inexcusable* is irrelevant, however, where the victim is aged less than 16 years of age, more than 70 years of age, or recognised to suffer from permanent incapacity or invalidity of at least 80 per cent.

117 Art. 4: 'La faute commise par le conducteur du vehicle terrestre à moteur a pour effet de limiter ou d'exclure l'indemnisation des dommages qu'il a subis.' There is also the problem of drivers injured as a result of their own driving – without a third party to blame, a system of responsibility offers no protection.

118 Viney and Jourdain, *Les conditions de la responsabilité*, no. 1024.

119 Although items that have been medically prescribed are subject to the rules relating to personal injury. Note also art. 6: 'The injury suffered by a third party due to the damage caused to the direct victim of a traffic accident will be redressed whilst taking into account the limitations and exclusions applicable to the compensation for these damages.'

120 See arts. L211–8–L211–25 of the Insurance Code, which sets out the procedures for compensation.

reform, the proportion of accidents before the courts had fallen from 20 per cent to 6 per cent.[121]

3 The influence of the relevant interest groups

The 1985 legislation is usually referred to as a 'compromise' – a step forward for victims, but not necessarily as extensive as many writers thought was necessary.[122] One must still show that someone was responsible for the accident and victims are treated differently according to their status and injury suffered. Where does this uneasy compromise come from?

To understand the background to the 1985 reform, one must return to the Jand'heur case. In finding a presumption of liability on drivers in the absence of proof of *cas fortuit*, *force majeure* or *cause étrangère*, the court laid down a principle of strict liability in response to a common and increasing cause of injury to citizens. Practically, however, such a principle was of little utility if claims could not be met. Without legislation to enforce compulsory insurance (and deal with claims against uninsured and unidentified drivers), such claims risked becoming a lottery, depending on whether the driver was insured. As Viney and Guegan-Lecuyer indicate in their paper,[123] even the advent of compulsory insurance in 1958, did not resolve problems resulting from gaps in insurance cover required by law,[124] and an often generous interpretation of the reasons for excluding liability.[125]

Tunc's radical response in 1964, which owes much to his skills as a comparative lawyer, was, however, greeted by a strong counter-campaign, utilising press and radio to undermine his proposals. This negative response brings into clear focus the interest groups involved in legal reform. The criticism from the Bar and insurance bodies, which included the submission of their own sets of proposals, demonstrates the influence these bodies possess in constructing (and obstructing) law reform. More astonishing still is the reaction of the Cour de cassation, which, in 1982, declared that

[121] A. Tunc, *Jalons: Dits et écrits d'André Tunc* (Paris: Société de législation comparée, 1991) postscript, March 1991.

[122] The literature concerning the 1985 reforms is extensive, but for a useful point of reference, see F. Chabas, *Le droit des accidents de la circulation après la réforme du 5 juillet 1985*, 1st edn (Paris: Dalloz, 1985), and 2nd edn (Paris: Dalloz, 1988).

[123] Guégan-Lécuyer, 'The Development of Traffic Liability in France', p. 64.

[124] Notably failing to require cover for injuries to members of the family of the vehicle owner, although this was later required by the Act of 7 January 1981. Such gaps obviously operated in the insurance industry's favour, which (within the limits of the law) was able to word its policies to its own financial advantage.

[125] See Viney and Jourdain, *Les conditions de la responsabilité*, no. 964.

fault of the victim would no longer exonerate the custodian of liability, provided that it did not amount to *force majeure*.[126] This decision divided *la doctrine* and the courts, and inevitably brought condemnation from the legal profession and insurers. Such a provocative step had the result of giving impetus to Badinter's reforms – it is no coincidence that two years after the promulgation of the 1985 Act, the second Chamber rejected its own decision in Desmares,[127] satisfied, one must assume, that the necessary reforms had at last been undertaken.

The 1985 reform is therefore shaped by a number of actors: a law professor steeped in American law,[128] the legal profession concerned about the possible demise of their role in road accident cases, insurers threatening a step increase in premiums and politicians attempting to improve protection for accident victims, whilst acquiring sufficient consensus to legislate and reach a result popular with the general public. The form, timing and treatment of the legislation owe much to these influences.

C Conclusion to Section III

One may contrast the history of workplace and road accidents in France. Both use a broad interpretation of art. 1384(1) to impose strict liability in tort. Such liability owes much to the collaboration of *la doctrine* and case law, and the willingness of *la doctrine* to respond to social needs and consider ideas from neighbouring countries such as Germany and Belgium[129] to formulate legal principles capable of meeting the needs of accident

[126] (*L'arrêt Desmares*) Civ. (2) 21 July 1982, D. 1982, 449 concl. Charbonnier, *note* C. Larroumet; JCP 1982. II 19861 note F. Chabas. See Bell, *French Legal Cultures*, pp. 68–69, who views the case as the best example of the court using its judicial function to make changes and force the hand of the legislator. See also J.-L. Aubert, 'L'arrêt Desmares, une provocation … à d'autres réformes', D. 1983 chron 1.

[127] Civ. (2) 6 April 1987 6 *arrêts*; JCP 1987. II 20828 *note* F. Chabas.

[128] Professor Tunc worked as legal adviser to the International Monetary Fund between 1947 and 1950, and continued during his academic career in France to maintain links with the United States and the United Kingdom. Notably his works *Le droit des États-Unis d'Amérique: Sources et techniques* (Paris: Dalloz, 1955); *Le droit des États-Unis* (Paris: Presses universitaires de France, 1964) (with S. Tunc); and *Le droit Américain des sociétés anonymes* (Paris: Economica, 1985) brought American law to the attention of a French audience. Tunc was clearly familiar with the American debate as to the role of insurance in this context, notably the 1965 work of American Professors Keeton and O'Connell, which strongly advocated replacing tort law with a form of direct insurance in the context of road accidents (R. Keeton and J. O'Connell, *Basic Protection for the Traffic Victim: A Blueprint for Reforming Automobile Insurance* (Boston: Little, Brown and Co., 1965)).

[129] The rapport to the *Jand'heur* case even refers to an English statute of 14 August 1903.

victims. Yet, whereas workplace accidents were immediately brought within a statutory insurance scheme and later absorbed within the social security system, road traffic accidents were left to the civil courts, despite numerous attempts to suggest reform from academics, various commissions and numerous professional representations. The eventual legislative scheme represents a compromise between articulate and forceful interest groups, and the last 20 years of its implementation has demonstrated that, although widely regarded as an improvement, agreement has yet to be reached on how the law should deal with road accident claims.

IV Conclusion

As this chapter illustrates, tort law, in responding to social needs within a legal framework, acts as a mirror for the concerns of society and its individual members and interest groups.[130] The examples of workplace accidents and road traffic accidents, in particular, demonstrate the overlapping roles of both formal and informal participants in the legal process. The provisions of the Civil Code, whilst initially respected, have been interpreted with extraordinary flexibility to give results often at odds with their literal meaning. This, however, is considered a price worth paying.

As Saleilles comments in his note to the *Teffaine* decision:

> The function [of case law] is not to limit legislation to the application that it could have in view of the limited scope of the economic situation that inspired it, but to give it all the progressive vitality of a principle that both operates and acts; it is vital that legislation, thanks to case law, adapts according to the progress of time.[131]

[130] A further example may be found in relation to liability for fire under art. 1384, Cass. civ: see Civ. 16 November 1920, D. 1920.I.169, note R. Savatier. By the 1920s, insurance companies had expressed concern at the possible application of art. 1384 to claims by neighbours due to fires in nearby buildings, and threatened an increase in insurance premiums as a result. To avoid placing an excessive burden on property owners, the Act of 7 November 1922 added the following paragraph to art. 1384: 'However, a person who possesses, regardless of the basis thereof, all or part of a building or of movable property in which a fire has originated is not liable towards third parties for damages caused by that fire unless it is proved that the fire must be attributed to his fault or to the fault of persons for whom he is responsible.'

[131] D. 1897.1.433, 439.

6

The impact of institutions and professions in Germany

JENS M. SCHERPE

The principal approach to liability in German law has been expressed quite succinctly by Rudolph von Jhering: 'Kein Übel ohne Schuld' ('No wrong without fault')[1] and 'Nicht der Schaden verpflichtet zum Schadensersatz, sondern die Schuld'('It is not the occurrence of the harm which obliges one to make compensation, but fault').[2] In the liberalist thinking of nineteenth-century German academia this premise was never truly challenged. The law, it was felt, had to be pure, devoid of social and political considerations.[3] It was to be a logical construct in which these considerations had no place. Even in the modern German law of today, (non-contractual) liability without fault is almost entirely to be found in special statutes, but not in the *Bürgerliches Gesetzbuch* (*BGB*), the German Civil Code.

The philosophy of enlightenment in the nineteenth century put freedom and duty at the centre; thus the law of contract was to be a tool for the use of freedom, while the law of torts was to deal with the abuse of freedom.[4] Only a breach of a duty was perceived to be legally relevant and a sufficient basis for liability; all other damages had no place in the 'pure'

[1] R. von Jhering, 'Das Schuldmoment im römischen Privatrecht' in R. von Jhering (ed.), *Vermischte Schriften juristischen Inhalts* (Leipzig: Breitkopf and Härtel, 1879), p. 163.

[2] *Ibid.*, p. 199. Translation by Tony Weir in K. Zweigert and H. Kötz, *Introduction to Comparative Law*, 3rd edn (Oxford: Oxford University Press, 1998), p. 630. The quote continues: 'This is as simple as the chemical fact that what burns is not the light but the oxygen in the air.'

[3] F. C. von Savigny, *System des heutigen römischen Rechts*, 8 vols., Vol. I (Berlin: Veit, 1840), p. 54. See also R. Ogorek, *Untersuchungen zur Gefährdungshaftung im 19. Jahrhundert* (Cologne and Vienna: Böhlau, 1975), p. 11; and J. Esser, *Grundlagen und Entwicklung der Gefährdungshaftung* (Munich and Berlin: Beck, 1941), pp. 55, 62ff.

[4] F. C. von Savigny, *Das Obligationenrecht als Theil des heutigen römischen Rechts*, 2 vols., Vol. II (Berlin: Veit, 1853), pp. 330ff. Cf. Esser, *Grundlagen*, pp. 50ff.

German law of torts.[5] Esser therefore distinguished between a wrong (*Unrecht*) for which the culpable wrongdoer was to be held liable, and accident (*Unglück*) where the damage was to lie where it fell, i.e. the injured party had to bear the damage; only a wrong should lead to liability.[6]

This 'pure', apolitical approach was very much a rational, academic construct with little influence from legal practitioners,[7] and the social reality of the growing industrialisation soon made it clear that such an approach was unsustainable. Therefore, gradually in many areas exceptions to or circumventions of fault liability were created, partly by the legislature, partly by the courts. In the following, four such areas will be looked at.

I Von Savigny and the introducation of strict liability for railway operators in Prussia in 1838

One of the first and most striking incursions into the realm of the fault principle was §25 of the *Preußisches Gesetz über die Eisenbahnunternehmungen* (*PGE*; Prussian Railway Act) of 3 November 1838.[8] It was enacted only four days after the first Prussian railway line from Berlin to Potsdam, a mere 3.5 miles (5.6 km) in total, was opened. The first railway line in Germany had been opened only three years earlier on 7 December 1835 (Nürnberg–Fürth).[9] As Reinhard Zimmermann reports, there was quite a bit of scepticism about this new technology: a pastor in Berlin had even implored his congregation to keep away from railway trains, which he referred to as 'infernal dragons', for the sake of their eternal salvation.[10]

[5] Esser, *Grundlagen*, p. 2.

[6] *Ibid.*, p. 1. This distinction is criticised, *inter alia*, by C. von Bar, *Verkehrspflichten: Richterliche Gefahrsteuerungsgebote im deutschen Deliktsrecht* (Cologne: Heymann, 1980), pp. 130ff.

[7] Cf. Zweigert and Kötz, *Introduction to Comparative Law*, pp. 136ff.

[8] *Gesetzessammlung für die königlichen preußischen Staaten* 1838, no. 35, 505–516. On this see also Sebastian Lohsse, 'The Development of Traffic Liability in Germany' in Wolfgang Ernst (ed.), *The Development of Traffic Liability* (Cambridge: Cambridge University Press, 2010), pp. 112–150; and Jens Martin Scherpe, 'Technological Change and the Development of Liability for Fault in Germany' in Martín Miquel-Casals (ed.), *The Development of Liability in Relation to Technological Change* (Cambridge: Cambridge University Press, 2010), pp. 134–184, pp. 140–144.

[9] For a description of the historical development of railways in Germany see G. Eger, *Eisenbahnrecht* (Leipzig: Gloeckner, 1910), pp. 26–60.

[10] R. Zimmermann, *The Law of Obligations: Roman Foundations of the Civilian Tradition* (Oxford: Oxford University Press, 1996), p. 1130 n. 261.

Section 25 of *PGE* is not only remarkable because it – at a very early stage of legal and technological development[11] – stipulated a strict liability rule, but also because it is the gamete of a legal division that is still found in place today in Germany: the *BGB* is kept 'pure' and (with only one exception for liability for certain animals, see Section IV below) only contains rules for fault-based liability in tort; the 'alien' concept of strict liability, where it was deemed necessary, has been introduced by special legislation – of which the *PGE* was the first.[12]

The genesis of the Act is documented fairly well, but the role of Friedrich Carl von Savigny in the process was only quite recently revealed when Theodor Baums examined documents in the Zentrales Staatsarchiv der DDR (the central public records office of the German Democratic Republic) in Merseburg. Baums came to the conclusion that while the Act in principle came into existence as a purely ministerial effort, it was von Savigny's contribution as a member of the Staatsrat (State Council)[13] that changed the Bill from one that contained a presumption of fault into one that stipulated strict liability. Therefore Baums even entitled his piece in which he describes this 'The Introduction of Strict Liability by F. C. von Savigny'.[14]

For those familiar with von Savigny's work this must appear somewhat surprising, given that in his *Das Obligationenrecht als Teil des heutigen römischen Rechts* of 1853 he really only engages with obligations arising either from contract or delict (which required fault). Only on the very last two pages, under the heading of '§85 *Variae causarum figurae*' does he touch upon other possibilities of incurring liability, simply stating that these *figurae* were not suitable to derive general principles from – and

[11] Cf. *ibid.*, pp. 1130ff.; F. H. Lawson, *Negligence in the Civil Law* (Oxford: Oxford University Press, 1950), pp. 45ff.

[12] Cf. N. Jansen, *Die Struktur des Haftungsrechts* (Tübingen: Mohr Siebeck, 2003), pp. 370ff. A number of special Acts today establish strict liability under certain circumstances or for certain risks, e.g. the successor of the *Reichshaftpflichtgesetz* (*RHPflG*, Imperial Law of Liability), the *Haftpflichtgesetz* (Liability Act, BGBl. 1978 I, 145), *Straßenverkehrsgesetz* (Road Traffic Act, *BGBl.* 2003 I, 310, 919), *Luftverkehrsgesetz* (Air Traffic Act, BGBl. 1999 I, 550), *Wasserhaushaltsgesetz* (Water Balance Act, BGBl. 2002 I, 3245), *Atomgesetz* (Nuclear Power Act, *BGBl.* 1985 I, 1565), *Gentechnikgesetz* (Act on Genetic Engineering, BGBl. 1993 I, 2066), *Umwelthaftungsgesetz* (Act on Liability for Environmental Damages, BGBl. 1990 I, 2634) etc. (all citations of the BGBl. refer to the latest re-enactment).

[13] Von Savigny was a member from 1817 to 1848; for details see W. van Hall, 'Savigny als Praktiker: Die Staatsratsgutachten', Ph.D. thesis, Bremerhaven (1981).

[14] T. Baums, 'Die Einführung der Gefährdungshaftung durch F. C. von Savigny' (1987) 104 *Zeitschrift der Savigny-Stiftung für Rechtsgeschichte, Germanistische Abteilung* 277, 277–282.

leaves it at that.[15] His unwillingness to include social and political considerations in the 'pure' Civil law has been considered by some as a wilful blindness to the exigencies of beginning industrialisation. This view, according to Baums, fails to consider his contributions as a member of the Staatsrat etc., which for example led to §25 *PGE*.[16]

A The genesis of §25 PGE

The original draft of the *PGE* by the Ministry (then §19) allowed the recovery of damages because of train transportation from the railway operator only when (a) the damage occurred owing to an oversight (*Versehen*) of an employee of the railway operator, and (b) the damages could not be recovered from that individual.[17] The notes to this draft explained that such a subsidiary liability was necessary because otherwise the victim could hold the railway operator liable only when the operator himself had been at fault when selecting or supervising the employee (which was considered virtually impossible to prove for the victim).[18] This clearly shows how deeply the concept of fault liability was ingrained into the legal draftsmen, as they even considered this provision quite daring and necessitating further explanation.

This draft was then considered by the Staatsrat and a scathing response was written by the *Abteilung für Justizangelegenheiten* (Department for Judicial Affairs). The author (as we now know) was Friedrich Carl von Savigny.[19]

First von Savigny considers a proposal by the Minister of Justice, Heinrich Gottlob Mühler, who apparently had suggested a presumption of fault. While this had met with criticism, namely that it was contrary to tradition and 'general principles of law', von Savigny expresses some sympathy and also shows that comparable provisions were included in the *Allgemeines Landrecht für die Preußischen Staaten* (*ALR* II 8 §444ff.)

[15] Von Savigny, *Das Obligationenrecht*, Vol. II (Berlin: Veit, 1853), pp. 330ff. Cf. also Lohsse, 'Traffic', pp. 81–2; Scherpe, 'Technological Change', pp. 141–142.

[16] Cf. also J. Rückert, *Idealismus, Jurisprudenz und Politik bei Friedrich Carl von Savigny* (Ebelsbach: Münchner Universitätsschriften, 1984), p. 40 with further references.

[17] See G. Lehmann, *Körperverletzungen und Tödtungen auf deutschen Eisenbahnen und die Unzulänglichkeit des Rechtsschutzes* (Erlangen: Enke, 1869), p. 45; and Baums, 'Die Einführung der Gefährdungshaftung', p. 278 (including an excerpt from the explanatory notes).

[18] Baums, 'Die Einführung der Gefährdungshaftung', p. 278.

[19] The response is reproduced in Lehmann, *Körperverletzungen*, pp. 45–48 (without reference to von Savigny); and Baums, 'Die Einführung der Gefährdungshaftung', pp. 278ff.

in a different context (for innkeepers) and thus were not completely alien to the law. He then continues to dissect the draft and make suggestions of his own. He thought that it was unjust that the victim should first sue the employee; it should rather be the other way round: the railway operator should be held liable and then possibly recover from the employee. Von Savigny also stated that it would be almost impossible for the victim to identify the employee who might be at fault, while it was much easier for the employer to do so. Finally, the railway operator should also be liable for damage occurring without anyone being at fault. This, von Savigny explained, was appropriate as, despite the operator's best efforts in the technological circumstances of the day, it was often impossible to prevent harm from occurring. A railway by its very nature was dangerous and it seemed inequitable to make travellers and landowners of adjoining plots bear the burden of this danger. Here he refers to England, where 'several times this has led to great damage' to landowners and travellers.[20]

This response apparently had an enormous impact. In the proceedings of the plenary session of the Staatsrat on 6 June 1838 the delegates considered Mühler's proposal of a presumption of fault on behalf of the railway operator, who would also be primarily liable.[21] This approach, it was argued, was not only to be found in the *ALR* (albeit in a different context), but also in sterner form in France and also in England.[22] This was criticised by some of the delegates present; while primary liability was acceptable to them (because of the impossibility of determining which employee was at fault), a presumption of fault would take things too far and be contrary to the 'general principle of law that all liability needs to be founded upon the finding of fault'. Also, a difference should be made between those who paid for the services of the railway – with respect to whom the railway operator incurred an obligation to prevent harm – and other persons. The critics, however, lacked sufficient support, and a resolution was passed without a formal vote that the railway operator should be liable for *all* damage occasioned during train transport unless he presented proof that the damage was coincidental.

[20] Lehmann, *Körperverletzungen*, p. 46; and Baums, 'Die Einführung der Gefährdungshaftung', p. 278.

[21] Reproduced in Lehmann, *Körperverletzungen*, pp. 46–48 (without reference to von Savigny); and Baums, 'Die Einführung der Gefährdungshaftung', pp. 280ff.

[22] For an account of French and English law in 1869 on this point see Lehmann, *Körperverletzungen*, pp. 48ff. Lehmann's work was widely read and quite influential in the debates leading up to the *Reichshaftpflichtgesetz*. On this see Scherpe, 'Technological Change', pp. 148–149.

In the same session, some departments then proposed what von Savigny's response had contained: that even where the damage was coincidental, there should be liability because of 'the nature of the enterprise'. Against this it was argued that it was unfair to single out railway operators; other enterprises created comparable risk and had not and should not be burdened with such a rule. This was countered with the observation that von Savigny had made: that the operation of a railway inevitably created risks and that complete prevention of the harm was impossible. Because of this, the State was under a duty to safeguard the welfare of the citizens, particularly those residing close to the railways, 'as has been done in England'. The dangerous nature of the enterprise needed to be expressly recognised by the law and provide remedies according to the general sense of justice. In the following vote, the Staatsrat, with a majority of 29 to 4, passed a resolution that a railway operator should be held liable for damages arising from the nature of the enterprise, unless the victim was at fault himself or they came about by an inevitable event. Von Savigny's view had prevailed and the *PGE* was enacted shortly after.

B The content of §25 PGE

Section 25 of the *PGE* read as follows:

> The company is liable for all damages occurring during train transport to transported goods and persons as well as to other persons and goods, and the company can only exonerate itself from this liability by proving that the damage was caused through fault of the claimant or by an inevitable event. The dangerous nature of the undertaking as such is not such an event exonerating from liability.

Similar provisions were quickly enacted by other German states (but not all; see below, p. 121).[23] Section 25 of the *PGE* was applicable to both privately and publicly owned railways[24] and claims could be based on

[23] Lehmann, *Körperverletzungen*, pp. 17ff. The Duchies and Grand Duchies of Saxony and Anhalt brought §25 *PGE* into force with regard to the Thuringian and Anhaltian railways. Holstein adopted a comparable provision in the declaration of 19 May 1840 (§22), as did Mecklenburg by a statute dated 23 May 1855. Austria also implemented similar rules – *Eisenbahnbetriebsordnung*, 16 November 1851 and 5 March 1869 (cf. the account by Lehmann, *Körperverletzungen*, pp. 18ff.) – as did Switzerland in 1875 (cf. H.-P. Benöhr, 'Zur außervertraglichen Haftung im gemeinen Recht' in D. Medicus and H. H. Seiler (eds.), *Festschrift für Max Kaser zum 70. Geburtstag* (Munich: Beck, 1976) pp. 689, 707 n. 87); Baums, 'Die Einführung der Gefährdungshaftung', p. 277.

[24] Cf. *Preußisches Obertribunal, Entscheidungen des königlichen Ober-Tribunals*, Vol. 37 (1858), 42ff. no. 3 (14 December 1857); M. Eckardt, 'Technischer Wandel und

contract as well.[25] As the second sentence makes clear, the fact that the operation of the railway was an allowed activity (and actually required a State concession) did not in any way allow for arguments to exclude liability.

The primary reason for the enactment of §25 was to cover personal injury cases (and personal injury of employees of the companies in particular), but the provision also covered claims to transported goods and 'any other goods', the latter including neighbouring land and premises, as long as the damage occurred 'bei der Beförderung auf der Bahn' (during train transport), which was interpreted rather broadly. However, any form of contributory negligence by the victim immediately ruled out the entire claim, as the wording of §25 *PGE* makes clear. Unsurprisingly, railway operators therefore often –and successfully – tried to argue contributory negligence. According to the data available, only 52 per cent of the passengers injured 'during train transport' were counted as having been injured without being at fault themselves and were eligible for damages under §25 *PGE*.[26] The situation for employees of railways seems to have been even worse, with only 12 per cent[27] receiving compensation in personal injury cases.[28] Further, §25 *PGE* was often interpreted rather narrowly by Prussia's courts. For example, it was held that there was no liability for consequential damages, particularly loss of present or future income because of the injury.[29]

Rechtsevolution: Ein Beitrag zur ökonomischen Theorie der Rechtsentwicklung am Beispiel des deutschen Unfallschadensrechts im 19. Jahrhundert', Ph.D. thesis, Friedrich-Schiller-Universität Jena (1998; later published, Tübingen: Mohr Siebeck, 2001), p. 288.

[25] Eger, *Eisenbahnrecht*, p. 131.

[26] See Eckardt, *Technischer Wandel*, pp. 289, 316, 333.

[27] See M. Eckardt, 'The Evolution of the German Tort Law in the Nineteenth Century: An Economic Analysis of the Evolution of Law' in O. Volckart (ed.), *The Institutional Analysis of History* (Munich: Accedo, 2004), p. 83, 105ff.; Eckardt, *Technischer Wandel*, Table 12 (p. 411).

[28] Mostly because their contracts of employment contained provisions that excluded strict liability by the employers. §25 PGE was not seen as part of the mandatory legal rules as it 'clearly' established an exception. Cf. Jansen, *Die Struktur des Haftungsrechts*, p. 369; Eckardt, 'Evolution', pp. 98, 105ff.; Prinz, 'Der Ausgleichsanspruch bei Funkenflugschäden' (1929) *Zeitung des Vereins deutscher Eisenbahnverwaltungen* 473, 478ff.; Scherpe, 'Technological Change', pp. 146–7.

[29] *Preußisches Obertribunal, Entscheidungen des königlichen Ober-Tribunals*, Vol. 28 (1854), 270 no. 33 (24 April 1854); *Preußisches Obertribunal, Entscheidungen des königlichen Ober-Tribunals*, Vol. 37 (1858), 42 no. 3 (14 December 1857).

C Liability of railway operators outside Prussia

As already mentioned, similar provisions were soon passed in other German states; but even in those states that had no comparable legislation in place, there was apparently considerable social pressure to award damages even in the absence of proof of fault.[30] It seems that this led some courts to resort to curious constructs, as they struggled to award damages and uphold the formal requirement of fault at the same time.

For example, the Oberappellationsgericht München held in 1853 that the railway company was liable for the damages because the 'sparks could only be explained by the employees' negligence or insufficient measures to prevent such sparks'.[31] The court allowed the claim under the *lex Acquiliae*.[32] Quite remarkably (and similarly to what was contained in §25 *PGE*), the defence that the company's activity was lawful and within the concession obtained (*qui iure suo utitur, neminem laedit*) was denied because this could not amount to a right to damage another's property and thus effectively to expropriation without compensation.

The Oberappellationsgericht Braunschweig held in 1856 that the operation of a railway was 'necessarily dangerous' and awarded damages;[33] it was simply assumed that the instructions of the railway operator must have been faulty if harm occurred, without much further explanation.

The Oberappellationsgericht Lübeck held in 1858 that because of the special nature of railways the operator was under such an exceptional duty of care that the smallest mistake by one of the employees would lead to liability.[34] In a complete reversal of established principles, the court stated that it was not for the claimant to prove fault but that the onus was on the operator to prove the absence of fault! The court found support for this in the rules on liability deriving from the *receptum*, and in the legislation of other German states (especially §25 *PGE*) and the court decisions following from them. This reversal of the burden of proof effectively amounted to a presumption of fault and rendered the fault requirement almost meaningless.

[30] For an extensive account see Ogorek, *Untersuchungen zur Gefährdungshaftung im 19. Jahrhundert*, pp. 63ff.; Scherpe, 'Technological Change', pp. 144–6.

[31] OAG-München, Seufferts Archiv, Vol. 10, 220, no. 164 (11 May 1853).

[32] The court referred to Gaius D.19.2.25.7.

[33] OAG-Braunschweig, Seufferts Archiv, Vol. 10, 221, no. 165 (10 January 1856).

[34] OAG-Lübeck, Sammlung der Entscheidung des Ober-Appellationsgerichtes zu Lübeck in Frankfurter Rechtssachen, Vol. 6, 116, no. 259 (27 September 1858). Cf. Zimmermann, *The Law of Obligations*, pp. 397ff., 1124ff.

In an 1859 case the Oberhofgericht Mannheim awarded damages, explicitly disallowing the defence of the railway operator that he was acting under a State concession and that he undisputedly used state-of-the-art technical equipment to prevent harm as far as technically possible. The claimant could not be worse off than someone who was expropriated and could claim compensation accordingly.

The most spectacular reduction of the fault requirement can be found in the famous 1861 decision of the Oberappellationsgericht München.[35] The court in theory upheld the fault requirement, but if the defendant knew that his acts could lead to harm and he acted nonetheless, this was sufficient to find him at fault. As the operation of a locomotive inevitably contained the risk of harm, the mere operation of one was seen as necessarily constituting a culpable act![36] It is difficult to see how this in any way differs from strict liability for harm occasioned by the operation of a railway.

D *A 'revolution'?*

The enactment of §25 *PGE* for the first time in Germany stipulated a form of strict liability, in breach of the traditional approach to the problem, and indeed was, as Zimmermann has stated, 'revolutionary'.[37] Interestingly, the Act was created by the ministerial administration, hardly an institution to start revolutions, and there was almost no input from the legal profession and very little from academia. Even von Savigny, the mastermind behind §25 *PGE*, apparently distinguished clearly between his academic work and that in the ministry. While in his academic writing strict liability received almost no attention, in his administrative role he clearly argued for the State's duty to safeguard the welfare of the citizens.

Section 25 of the *PGE* clearly met an existing social need, as similar provisions were quickly adopted in other German states; where there were no comparable provisions, the courts stretched the boundaries of the fault requirements to the limits – if not beyond. Indeed, as Christian von Bar has written,[38] decisions like the one of the Oberappellationsgericht

[35] OAG-München, Seufferts Archiv, Vol. 14, 354, no. 208 (16 April 1861).

[36] *Ibid.*, p. 358. See also Ob. LG für Bayern, Seufferts Archiv, Vol. 41, 403, no. 271 (1 April 1886).

[37] Zimmermann, *The Law of Obligations*, p. 1131.

[38] Von Bar, *Verkehrspflichten*, p. 106. Cf. also Esser, *Grundlagen und Entwicklung*, pp. 23ff.; and E. von Caemmerer, 'Wandlungen des Deliktsrechts' in E. von Caemmerer, E. Friesenhahn and R. Lange (eds.), *Hundert Jahre deutsches Rechtsleben: Festschrift*

München in 1861 paved the way for the later development of the *Verkehrssicherungspflichten* where the concept of fault was extended similarly to cope with the narrow constraints of the *BGB* (see Section III below). Still, the dividing line remained intact: strict liability was only to be found in legislation and the courts upheld the fault principle – if only formally in some cases.

II Liability for industrial accidents and social insurance legislation: reaction to the growing social pressure

The growing industrialisation in Germany led to a significant increase in the number of accidents, particularly at the workplace. This lead to a lively debate,[39] not least because of some startling and widely publicised industrial and railway accidents.[40] The starting point – with the exception for certain railway accidents as just described – of course remained that any liability required fault on behalf of the employer. More often than not this was either impossible to prove or the harm was caused by a fellow worker, so that the damages were not effectively recoverable by the victim. This led to growing social unrest and in the end to the *Reichshaftpflichtgesetz.*

A The Reichshaftpflichtgesetz *of 1871*

In 1868 the Nationalliberale Partei zu Leipzig (National-Liberal Party of Leipzig) called in the Reichstag des Norddeutschen Bundes for a reform of the law regarding accidents and liability. It was argued that a general feeling of injustice and uncertainty was generated by the fact that in different parts of Germany different legal rules applied to accidents and

zum hundertjährigen Bestehen des Deutschen Juristentages 1860–1960, 2 vols, Vol. II (Karlsruhe: Müller, 1960), p. 49 (pp. 62ff.).

39 See Lehmann, *Körperverletzungen*, esp. pp. 65ff., 84ff., with interesting data comparing Prussia and England; G. Lehmann, *Der Nothstand der Schädensprocesse und der Entwurf der königl. sächsischen Civilproceßordnung* (Leipzig: Fischer, 1865) and the debates and reports at the Deutsche Juristentage (e.g. *Verhandlungen des 4. Deutschen Juristentages* (1863), Vol. II, p. 278; report by Schaffrath in *Verhandlungen des 6. Deutschen Juristentages* (1867), Vol. III, pp. 252ff.; report by Karsten, in *Verhandlungen des 9. Deutschen Juristentages* (1871), Vol. I, pp. 390ff.); Benöhr, 'Zur außervertraglichen Haftung', p. 696.

40 For an account of some railway-related accidents see Lehmann, *Körperverletzungen*, pp. 22ff., 28ff., 76ff., 85 (table) and further data pp. 86ff., including a comparison of Prussian with English data, pp. 65ff., 84ff; Eckardt, *Technischer Wandel*, Table 5, pp. 406ff.

liability.[41] The petition by the party demanded, *inter alia*, new liability rules for certain undertakings, namely railways, mines and factories; a change of the procedural rules; and a duty to compensate not only for personal injury as such but also for the harms arising therefrom. Further it was stated that, as the grievances were well known, it was the 'economical, social, political and moral duty of the Government' to provide functioning remedies. The petition won the support of the responsible commission of the Reichstag.[42] The Government prepared a draft Bill which was presented to the first *deutschen Gesamtreichstag* (all-German Reichstag) in the 14th session on 13 April 1871 after consultations with German State Governments. Of those, only three opposed the general idea: Hamburg (stating that industry should not be burdened with disproportionate costs), Sachsen-Weimar (denying the necessity of such legislation) and Mecklenburg-Schwerin (suggesting that this problem should be dealt with in a general reform of the law of obligations).[43]

The Bill effectively proposed a two-tier system for liability. Section 1 established strict liability for railways quite similar to §25 *PGE*.[44] But instead of requiring damage to occur 'during train transport' ('bei der Beförderung auf der Bahn') like the *PGE*, it was proposed to use the wording 'in the conduct of a train' ('bei dem Betriebe einer Eisenbahn'), thus allowing for a greater scope of application. This clearly was a reaction to the narrow interpretation of §25 *PGE* by the courts and intended to broaden the application of the provision.[45]

41 *Drucksachen des Reichstages*, 1868, no. 56. See also Lehmann, *Körperverletzungen*, pp. 109ff.; and Benöhr, 'Zur außervertraglichen Haftung', pp. 695ff.

42 The commission even stated that the description of the situation of victims of personal injuries actually was worse than described by the petitioners. Cf. Lehmann, *Körperverletzungen*, p. 110; and Eckardt, 'Evolution', pp. 105ff.; and especially the data cited above in n. 26.

43 Ogorek, *Untersuchungen zur Gefährdungshaftung*, p. 101 n. 16.

44 In 1871 there were some 30,000 km of railways in Germany; cf. Table 1 in Eckardt, *Technischer Wandel*, p. 402.

45 The *Preußisches Obertribunal, Entscheidungen des königlichen Ober-Tribunals*, Vol. 28 (1854), 270ff. no. 33 (24 April 1854), for example, had interpreted 'during train transport' to mean that the train had to be in motion (p. 273), thus excluding liability for loading/unloading under §25 *PGE*. Therefore it was felt that the wording had to be changed to include such activities; see MP Dr Schwarze, *Stenographische Berichte über die Verhandlungen des deutschen Reichstags* (Berlin: Sittenfeld, 1871–1939) (hereafter *RT-Sten. Ber.*), 1871, Vol. 1, pp. 444ff. For details see G. Eger, *Das Reichs-Haftpflicht-Gesetz*, 6th edn (Hannover: Helwing, 1906), pp. 3–42; A. Heucke, *Haftpflichtgesetz*, 2nd edn (Berlin: Heymann, 1937), pp. 10–23; F. Seligsohn, *Haftpflichtgesetz*, 2nd edn (Berlin and Leipzig: Springer, 1931), pp. 24–46. On the *Reichshaftpflichtgesetz* generally see Lohsse, 'Traffic', pp. 85–90; and Scherpe, 'Technological Change', pp. 160–168.

Also, unlike §25 *PGE*, the proposal did not extend to damage to goods. Transported goods, however, were already covered by the rules in §§422ff. of the *Allgemeines Deutsches Handelsgesetzbuch* (*General German Commercial Code*) of 1861, which was deemed satisfactory.[46] Damages to other goods, for example those caused by escaping sparks, therefore had to be dealt with under the general rules.[47]

According to §2 of the Bill, operators of mines, quarries, pits and factories were subject to a much more lenient liability regime. There was only to be a liability if it could be established that an authorised agent or representative, or anyone[48] employed in the direction or supervision of the workmen or the undertaking, through his fault had caused the damage in the execution of his contractual duty or in the carrying out of the service arrangements ('in Ausführung seiner Dienstverrichtung').[49] The distinction between railway operations and other industries was justified by citing the already existing, 'historical', law.[50]

Unsurprisingly, the Bill was met with resistance by industry representatives. It was argued that such legal rules would worsen the conflict between employers and employees. The Verein der Privat-Eisenbahnen (Association of Private Railway Operators) particularly opposed the strict liability rule of the draft.[51]

The distinction between railways in §1 and mines, quarries, pits and factories[52] in §2 was also much criticised, as was the fact that all other

[46] See Eger, *Eisenbahnrecht*, pp. 181ff.

[47] On this see Scherpe, 'Technological Change', p. 167.

[48] As is made clear in a decision by the Reichsgericht in 1882 (Entscheidungen des Reichsgerichts in Zivilsachen (RGZ) 8, pp. 30–35, no. 7 (3 November 1882)), this comprises any worker, even 'ordinary factory workers', as long as they have a supervisory or instructing function at that moment. It is not necessary that they were hired to have such a function and it is sufficient that such a function at that point in time was delegated to them.

[49] For details see Eger, *Das Reichs-Haftpflicht-Gesetz*, pp. 204–317, esp. pp. 298ff.; Seligsohn, *Haftpflichtgesetz*, pp. 185ff.

[50] Dr Achenbach, *RT-Sten. Ber.* 1871, Vol. 1, p. 449; Ogorek, *Untersuchungen zur Gefährdungshaftung*, p. 104 n. 26.

[51] *Ibid.* For a debate on whether a duty to pay damages actually can be seen as an infringement of freedom see Jansen, *Die Struktur des Haftungsrechts*, pp. 60ff.

[52] The use of the word 'factory' was also criticised heavily, as it was unclear which undertakings exactly were meant to be included. Cf. Ogorek, *Untersuchungen zur Gefährdungshaftung*, pp. 113ff. For a discussion of the cases ensuing from this see Eger, *Das Reichs-Haftpflicht-Gesetz*, pp. 221–234; Heucke, *Haftpflichtgesetz*, pp. 70ff.; Seligsohn, *Haftpflichtgesetz*, pp. 160–163.

industries were left out.[53] Statistical data, it was argued, did not support this distinction, as railway accidents did not occur more frequently than other industrial accidents.[54] The suggestions on how to deal with this distinction differed. Some supported the view that strict liability should extend to all undertakings,[55] while others suggested that the more lenient rules in §2 apply to railways as well, so that this particular business would not be burdened with excessive costs.[56] Some MPs favoured developing a general solution for the problem of industrial accidents and it was said that the Act was a short-sighted and inadequate reaction to public pressure.[57]

In the end the Bill was passed on 7 June 1871 with a large majority of votes and the *Reichshaftpflichtgesetz* (*RHPflG*; Imperial Law of Liability) came into effect.[58] The large majority can be explained by the position of the major interest groups: those advocating stronger liability rules for industrial accidents and a general reform of the law of obligations saw the Bill as a first stepping stone and only accepted it because otherwise most accident victims would be without any effective remedy at all until such a reform came about;[59] those who thought the Bill actually went too far nevertheless voted for it because it provided some relief from the complaints of the working class and a preventative measure against the rising 'spectre' of socialism[60] – an argument that also triggered the next reform of this area of law, the creation of a public insurance scheme.

[53] See *RT-Sten. Ber.* 1871, especially the MPs von Unruh (pp. 201ff.), Becker (pp. 210ff.), Bamberger (p. 212), Bethusy-Huc (p. 213), Duncker (p. 214), Ulrich (p. 441) and Schulze (pp. 446ff.).

[54] See *ibid.*: von Unruh (p. 202) and Duncker (p. 214). Cf. also O. von Mühlenfels, *Die Haftpflicht der Eisenbahnen und die Unfallversicherung* (Berlin: Reimer, 1884), pp. 56ff. But see Eckardt, *Technischer Wandel*, pp. 311ff. (esp. pp. 335ff.: the highest number of accidents actually seemed to occur in railway operations) and Table 5 (pp. 405ff.).

[55] Namely Becker, Bamberger, Bethusy-Huc, Duncker, Ulrich and Schulze (see above, n. 53).

[56] Von Unruh (n. 53).

[57] See for example Schulze (n. 53), calling the *RHPflG* a *Notstandsgesetz* (emergency Act), owing its existence to recent industrial accidents that could not possibly be the last word in this matter. Cf. also Zimmermann, *The Law of Obligations*, pp. 1133ff.; Jansen, *Die Struktur des Haftungsrechts*, p. 370; Ogorek, *Untersuchungen zur Gefährdungshaftung*, pp. 103ff.

[58] *Reichs-Gesetzblatt*, 1871, pp. 207–209, no. 652. An English translation of the Act can be found in Lawson, *Negligence in the Civil Law*, pp. 195ff.

[59] See *RT-Sten. Ber.* 1871, Vol. 1,: Russel (p. 456), Bamberger (p. 212), Becker (p. 211).

[60] E.g. Bethusy-Huc, *ibid.*, p. 213; von Unruh, pp. 201ff.

B *The* Unfallversicherungsgesetz *(Accident Insurance Act) of 1884*

Space precludes a detailed discussion, but the *RHPflG* failed to live up to expectations; it proved largely ineffective and the situation of workers did not improve significantly.[61]

In 1878 a proposal was advanced in Parliament to reverse the burden of proof. If the employers had to prove that they acted with due care, it was argued, this would be an incentive for employers to implement precautionary measures, and thus reduce the overall number of accidents and lead to an overall better social security for workers.[62] In the following debates[63] the social democrats suggested the extension of §1 *RHPflG* to all dangerous undertakings,[64] whereas the conservatives proposed to abandon private law liability altogether and to implement a mandatory general insurance for all businesses, modelled on the social miners' and mine-employees' insurance (*Knappschaft*).[65] In the end the question was referred to a commission whose final report led to the Bill for the *Unfallversicherungsgesetz* (*UVG*; Accident Insurance Act) in which essentially the conservative proposals prevailed.

Despite continuing objections by liberal and social democrat MPs[66] the third draft of the Bill was adopted on 27 June 1884.[67] The following years saw a gradual extension of the public law model,[68] which is essentially still in place in Germany today.

It was openly stated that the Act of 1884 was meant to appease the social democrat and socialist groups in Germany, who were seen as 'dangerous to the public safety',[69] by improving the social situation of the workers.

[61] For an account of the reasons for this failure see Scherpe, 'Technological Change', pp. 165–168.

[62] Hirsch MP, *RT-Sten. Ber.* 1878, Vol. 2, pp. 838ff.

[63] For a detailed description of the debates cf. Ogorek, *Untersuchungen zur Gefährdungshaftung*, pp. 115ff; Eckardt, *Technischer Wandel*, pp. 362ff. (here particularly the table at p. 370).

[64] The MPs Kapell, Hasenklever *et al.*, *RT-Sten. Ber.* 1878, Vol. 3, no. 128 (Appendices).

[65] Stumm MP, *RT-Sten. Ber.* 1878, Vol. 2, pp. 844ff.; cf. Eckardt, *Technischer Wandel*, pp. 367ff.

[66] Cf. for example *RT-Sten. Ber.* 1882, Vol. 1, p. 200.

[67] *Ibid.* 1884, Vol. 2, p. 1129.

[68] See Ogorek, *Untersuchungen zur Gefährdungshaftung*, pp. 119ff. (beginning on 28 May 1885 with the *Gesetz über die Ausdehnung der Unfall- und Krankenversicherung*, RGBl. 1885, 159 ff., and eventually leading to the *Reichsversicherungsordnung* of 30 May 1911, RGBl. 1911, 509ff).

[69] For the rising number of votes and seats in Parliament of the social democrats see the table in Eckardt, *Technischer Wandel*, p. 344.

This was not only a 'humanitarian and Christian duty', but would also serve 'the interest of the State'.[70]

The Act was a clear statement that private law liability should not be widened and should not embrace strict liability rules. Instead a public law solution was preferred. The member of Government and minister of State Hofmann stated that the new Act would forge a 'social bond' between the employers and workers, unlike private law liability, which, because of its very structure, would create animosity between the parties and worsen the conflict.[71] Strict liability was unacceptable as this would impede the ability of German industrial undertakings to compete in the international market.[72] Other solutions like reversal of burden of proof would not solve the underlying problem.[73] Hence a public law solution was considered the only way forward.

The *UVG* covered all personal injuries at the workplace, regardless of fault and even if the worker himself had been negligent. However, the damages paid were only to ensure that the victim received equitable compensation that covered his future needs.[74] Therefore the claim was limited to compensation for the damage actually suffered, especially loss of income and medical costs, as well as a pension in case of invalidity or alimony for dependants in case of death; property damage was not covered.

C *Appeasement legislation*

It is one of the great paradoxes in German legislative history that the most important Acts for the social protection of workers were in fact created by people that were openly hostile towards the working class, while those opposing them most strongly were representatives of the social democrats.[75] The 1871 and 1884 Acts were passed reluctantly, with Parliament giving in to the mounting social pressure, and were meant to be a safety valve against social unrest and to appease the working classes – something

[70] Cf. *RT-Sten. Ber.* 1881, Vol. 3, Anlagen, no. 41, pp. 222ff.; Ogorek, *Untersuchungen zur Gefährdungshaftung*, pp. 116ff.; H. Kötz, 'Haftung für besondere Gefahr' (1970) 170 *Archiv für die civilistische Praxis* (*AcP*) 6ff.

[71] *RT-Sten. Ber.* 1879, Vol. 1, pp. 141ff.; cf. Eckardt, *Technischer Wandel*, p. 352.

[72] Hirsch MP, *RT-Sten. Ber.* 1878, Vol. 2, p. 841. As Eckardt, *Technischer Wandel*, p. 347, puts it quite accurately, these are the same arguments used today in similar debates.

[73] *RT-Sten. Ber.* 1881, Vol. 3, Anlagen, no. 41, pp. 229ff.; and Eckardt, *Technischer Wandel*, p. 352.

[74] Cf. the explanatory statements to the third and final draft of the Act, *RT-Sten. Ber.* 1884, Vol. 3, Anlagen, no. 4, pp. 66ff.

[75] Ogorek, *Untersuchungen zur Gefährdungshaftung*, p. 120.

that the courts apparently felt unable to do within the existing legal framework.

With the *UVG*, questions of liability were to a very large extent removed from the private law sphere. This started a development in which tort liability was replaced by public insurance schemes that we still find in place in Germany today. Yet again the general civil law was kept 'pure' insofar as the fault principle remained intact and strict liability remained constricted to special Acts.

III The courts attempt to work within the system of fault liability of the *BGB*: *Verhehrssicherungspflichten*

Liability for torts under the *BGB* was almost entirely based on fault.[76] Unsurprisingly the courts after 1900 were increasingly confronted with cases where fault as such could not be established but not awarding damages seemed manifestly unjust. Thus the gaps in the system of the *BGB* soon became apparent.[77] But the legal rules were clear: fault was required and nothing else would do unless a special statute stipulated something different. But these special statutes were the exception and quite a large number fell into one of the 'gaps' in the *BGB* if the rules were stolidly applied. Therefore a certain amount of judicial creativity was needed to bring those claims into the system.

One of those examples of judicial creativity is the development of the so-called *Verkehrssicherungspflicht*,[78] which helped to replace the maxim *casum sentit dominus* with a system based on spheres of responsibility. In these spheres, the person in control of them was under a duty of care to prevent harm from occurring. The *Verkehrssicherungspflichten* were developed on a case-by-case basis and in essence turned what appeared to be 'accidents' into 'wrongs'.

[76] For §833, the only provision stipulating strict liability, see below, Section IV, pp. 135–141.

[77] See von Caemmerer, 'Wandlungen des Deliktsrechts', pp. 52ff., 71ff.; von Bar, *Verkehrspflichten*, pp. 102ff.

[78] In modern legal language usually referred to as *Verkehrspflicht*; see for example von Bar, *Verkehrspflichten*; H. Kötz and G. Wagner, *Deliktsrecht*, 10th edn (Munich: Beck 2006), pp. 53ff.; E. Deutsch and H.-J. Ahrens, *Deliktsrecht: Unerlaubte Handlungen, Schadensersatz, Schmerzensgeld*, 4th edn (Cologne: Heymann, 2002), pp. 123ff.; and von Caemmerer, 'Wandlungen des Deliktsrechts', pp. 71ff. Sometimes authors distinguish between *Verkehrspflicht* and *Verkehrssicherungspflicht*, but the distinction has no discernible practical consequences.

A Definition of Verkehrssicherungspflichten

In decisions by the Reichsgericht we can find abstract definitions of what a *Verkehrssicherungspflicht* is: 'A person is under a duty to ensure that movables and immovables that he owns or controls are not endangering orderly human interaction.'[79] In more modern times, the Bundesgerichtshof regularly applies the approach that anyone who creates a sphere of risk 'in principle is responsible for taking all necessary and reasonable precautions to prevent a possible harm to others'.[80] The *Verkehrssicherung* required by law comprises such measures that would be considered necessary and sufficient by a prudent, knowledgeable and, within reasonable limits, careful person; therefore it is required that a knowledgeable observer would have realised that there is a risk that harm might occur.[81]

In determining the content of a *Verkehrssicherungspflicht*, a certain minimum standard of acceptable behaviour is set. If a person – by act or omission – falls short of that standard he will be held liable. This is not very different from the legal definition of *Fahrlässigkeit* (negligence) in §276 II *BGB*: 'Fahrlässig handelt, wer die im Verkehr erforderliche Sorgfalt außer Acht lässt' ('A person acts negligently if he fails to take ordinary care').[82] Indeed, one can therefore say that violation of a *Verkehrssicherungspflicht is* fault, and the apparent 'accident' becomes a 'wrong'. With this remarkable dogmatic tool the courts were able to establish fault and could therefore award damages *within* the existing system.

While *Verkehrssicherungspflichten* have become an integral part of the German law of tort, they cannot be defined with absolute certainty. Over time certain criteria have developed, for example the gravity of the possible consequences, the likelihood of harm and reasonableness of preventative measures.[83] Even so, the exact scope of a

[79] E.g. Reichsgericht 13 October 1916, RGZ 88, 433; cf. also Esser, *Grundlagen und Entwicklung*, pp. 32ff.; Kötz and Wagner, *Deliktsrecht*, pp. 53 ff.; Deutsch and Ahrens, *Deliktsrecht*, pp. 123ff.

[80] See for example Bundesgerichtshof 15 July 2003, *NJW-RR* 2003, 1459; Bundesgerichtshof 19 December 1989, *NJW* 1990, 1236; Bundesgerichtshof 17 December 1992, *NVwZ- RR* 1993, 337; all with further references.

[81] Bundesgerichtshof 4 December 2001, *NJW-RR* 2002, 525 with further references.

[82] Formerly §276 I 2 *BGB*. By the *Gesetz zur Modernisierung des Schuldrechts* of 26 November 2001, BGBl. I 2001, 3138, the former second sentence of the first paragraph of §276 was moved and became the second paragraph. The wording has not changed.

[83] See Kötz and Wagner, *Deliktsrecht*, pp. 70ff.; Deutsch and Ahrens, *Deliktsrecht*, pp. 124ff.; von Caemmerer, *Verkehrspflichten*, pp. 77ff. with comparative observation, particularly to the common law tort of negligence at pp. 79ff.; von Bar, *Verkehrspflichten*, pp. 112ff.

Verkehrssicherungspflicht is difficult to determine in the abstract, and regularly could only be established on a case-by-case basis when the breach was found because of a harm occurring.[84] German commentaries consequently list potential spheres of risk in alphabetical order and refer to appropriate court decisions.[85] This of course makes it rather difficult for those who might potentially be liable to determine what their duty comprises and what they need to do to be sure of avoiding liability.

The paradigm textbook example is the obligation of a landowner to disperse sand or salt if there is black ice.[86] In 1909 the Reichsgericht had to decide a claim made against a parish.[87] In the case the black ice had appeared very suddenly, only some 15 to 30 minutes before a church service. The sexton, whose duty included keeping the paths to the church in order, had at the time – quite understandably – been busy with preparations for the service. The court held that it was the duty of the owner of the land – here the parish – to make sure that everyone who could reasonably be expected to walk on the paths thereon was protected from the danger of slipping. A very sudden change of weather that leads to black ice was not completely unforeseeable in winter and if the sexton was busy elsewhere the parish should have hired someone else for the task. In 1932 this was confirmed in a case with almost identical facts.[88] The case law that was developed for this specific *Verkehrssicherungspflicht* has later been incorporated into statutes by the German states.[89]

A typical approach to the *Verkehrssicherungspflichten* is exemplified by another decision of the Reichsgericht in 1932. It held that a football club was liable for injuries suffered as the consequence of someone kicking a football over the fence around the pitch owned by the club. The ball smashed a window and the claimant sustained an eye injury due to the flying shards. It was considered irrelevant whether the persons kicking the ball were allowed to play on the pitch or not. A higher fence had been built before the accident, but balls nevertheless had flown over it, albeit

[84] See Esser, *Grundlagen und Entwicklung*, p. 32.

[85] See O. Palandt, *Kommentar zum Bürgerlichen Gesetzbuch*, 67th edn (Munich: Beck, 2008), commentary by H. Sprau, §823 *BGB*, nos. 185ff. (hereafter: Palandt–Sprau); and Kötz and Wagner, *Deliktsrecht*, p. 70.

[86] For a brief summary of the *Verkehrssicherungspflicht* on public roads and footpaths see H. Schmidt, 'Der Umfang der Räum- und Streupflicht auf öffentlichen Straßen und Wegen', *NJW* 1988, 3177–3184.

[87] Reichsgericht 1 March 1909, *JW* 1909, 218.

[88] Reichsgericht 27 February 1932, *JW* 1933, 1454.

[89] See for example §§29, 31, 33, 34 *Hamburgisches Wegegesetz* (*HWG*) of 22 January 1974; *HmbgGVBl.* 41, 83.

in smaller numbers. The defendant club knew this and had apparently accepted that risk. Additionally, they had not taken any precautions to prevent unauthorised persons from playing on their premises. It had been open to them to build even higher fences or to move their pitch elsewhere. The fact that the pitch etc. had been approved by the local authorities[90] and that the police had been present at a number of games and not complained about the balls flying over the fence could not exculpate them; it was the duty of the defendant alone to make sure that no harm emanated from their premises, by erecting a fence that was high enough.[91]

In a comparable case in 1983, the Bundesgerichtshof held the organiser of an ice hockey game liable for injuries sustained by a spectator when hit by a puck.[92] The court stated that there should have been Plexiglas walls in place, despite the fact that German regulations (unlike international ones) at the time did not require such walls – hence they were not very common in Germany – and that such walls were quite expensive. While admittedly even with such a wall in place it would still have been possible for pucks to hit people in the stands, a Plexiglas wall would at least have reduced the danger of this happening. That the spectators knew that there was a danger of pucks flying into the stands and accepted this when they attended a match could not exclude the liability of the organiser;[93] it was their duty to protect the spectators with a Plexiglas wall and they had failed to do this. Interestingly, the court briefly refers to an unreported decision by the Oberlandsgericht München of 1964, when Plexiglas did not yet exist and erecting wire netting was the only possibility.[94] The Oberlandesgericht in that decision apparently had held that it could not be expected that this means of protection be employed as this would impair the view of the spectators too significantly, and thus it dismissed a claim for injury by a puck. This seems odd, as the risk of injury owing to the lack of a barrier must have been more or less the same in 1964 as in 1983;[95] but the feasibility of employing protective means apparently made a difference in the legal evaluation. So despite the fact that protection in principle was possible in 1964 a breach of a *Verkehrssicherungspflicht* was

[90] On this see also von Bar, *Verkehrspflichten*, pp. 106ff.: public licences or 'official approval' are not sufficient to rule out liability.

[91] Reichsgericht 20 April 1932, RGZ 138, 21.

[92] BGH 19 November 1983, *NJW* 1984, 801.

[93] After all, retrieving a puck is generally considered a marvellous souvenir and spectators therefore are very eager for this to happen!

[94] Reference number 4 U 284/63, dated 9 July 1964.

[95] The Bundesgerichtshof states that the 'increased competitiveness in professional ice hockey' might also have increased the likelihood of a puck flying into the stands.

denied by the Oberlandesgericht as wire netting would have defeated the purpose of an ice hockey game, which is supposed to be watched. The Bundesgerichtshof in its 1983 decision expressly refused to comment on whether the decision by the Oberlandesgericht was 'correct', as this was unnecessary in the present case now that Plexiglas was available.

B *The courts extend the concept of* Verkehrssicherungspflichten

Normally *Verkehrssicherungspflichten* comprise situations and examples, as can be seen from the definitions above, where the defendant was in a position in which he could reasonably be expected to take measures that would have prevented the harm. It is important to note that *Verkehrssicherungspflichten* also are independent of the 'normal standard', public licences, concessions etc.; the standard set by the *Verkehrssicherungspflichten* is a purely private law one and a public concession or approval will not be sufficient to be exempt from liability; nor will 'general practice'.[96] But occasionally the standard expected by the courts seems overly strict and onerous, and it appears unlikely that the reasonable man of ordinary prudence could have adhered to it.[97] While it needs to be said that these cases remain rare exceptions, it is nevertheless a tool that appears to have been used to establish liability in situations where not awarding damages seemed unfair or unjust. Christian von Bar even remarks that the standard applied by the courts was particularly strict where the courts would have considered liability without fault as appropriate.[98] He also states that it was the spirit of the above-mentioned 1861 decision of the Oberappelationsgericht München (see p. 122, above) that made the development of the *Verkehrssicherungspflichten* possible.[99]

One such example where the borders of the *Verkehrssicherungspflicht* have been pushed quite far is a decision by the *Amtsgericht Gelsenkirchen*.[100] Meat from pigs infected with red murrain was sold by the defendant, who

96 Von Bar, *Verkehrspflichten*, pp. 106ff.

97 Cf. von Caemmerer, 'Wandlungen des Deliktsrechts', pp. 63ff., citing Reichsgericht 11 April 1935, RGZ 147, 353 as an example (cable falling off power supply line). Here the court, referring to the events as 'accident', held that the greater the potential danger, the greater the *Verkehrssicherungspflicht* (p. 356) and that therefore – despite the fact that no fault could be proved but that the parties agreed that the weather conditions played a role – liability was possible. See also von Bar, *Verkehrspflichten*, p. 129ff.; Zimmermann, *The Law of Obligations*, pp. 1132ff.; Zweigert and Kötz, *Introduction to Comparative Law*, p. 650.

98 Von Bar, *Verkehrspflichten*, p. 130. 99 *Ibid.*, p. 106.

100 *Geschäftszeichen* 2 C 195/38, apparently unreported officially, but reproduced by Esser, *Grundlagen und Entwicklung*, pp. 29ff. as an example for this point.

knew about the infection. It was established that all possible precautions had been taken, particularly that the meat had been sterilised according to proper standards by cooking it for five hours before the sale, which was by the standards of the time deemed to be sufficient to make it safe for consumption. The meat was then sold for a low price and it was made clear where it came from. This apparently was a very common practice. The claimant was infected by meat a friend had bought (therefore there was no claim in contract). The court held that if it was certain the infection derived from the meat, the defendant could not exculpate himself by having taken all the required and reasonable precautions and adhered to all necessary procedures: 'Whoever takes the risk of selling meat from infected animals is held to such a high standard of duty of care that even adhering to standards prescribed by health regulations would not be sufficient to exculpate him.'[101] It can hardly be said that the defendant was 'at fault' here, although this is what the decision amounted to. He was held liable because the court imposed a special duty of care for the sphere of risk created by him. As Esser remarks, the same line of argument could apply to the person eating such meat: whoever takes the risk of eating cheap meat, knowing that it came from infected animals and had been sterilised for consumption, should be liable for the damage himself as this fell within his sphere of risk. That the court decided to hold the seller liable appears to be a policy decision, not least based on the fact that poor people often could only afford such meat.[102]

C *Creating liability by extending duties of care*

Verkehrssicherungspflichten in principle determine a standard of acceptable behaviour, and if the defendant falls short of this standard he is 'at fault' and liable for the harm that occurred. Yet, in a way it can be said that the courts on (admittedly rare) occasion have 'deconstructed' the rigorous fault requirement of the *BGB* by extending the *Verkehrssicherungspflichten* to a remarkable degree,[103] almost in the way of a general clause,[104] and thereby turning certain types of 'accidents', for which there would have been no liability in a fault-based regime, into compensable 'wrongs' in a fault-based system of liability.

[101] Cited by Esser, *Grundlagen und Entwicklung*, p. 29.

[102] *Ibid.* [103] Cf. von Bar, *Verkehrspflichten*, pp. 129ff.

[104] Von Caemmerer, 'Wandlungen des Deliktsrechts', p. 80; Deutsch and Ahrens, *Deliktsrecht*, p. 124.

In addition it can be said that certain *Verkehrssicherungspflichten* that were originally created by the courts eventually found their way into some statutes.[105] For example, the *Straßenverkehrsordnung* (*StVO*; Road Traffic Regulation) contains in §1 a general duty to conduct oneself in a way that does not endanger, harm or impede others more than is acceptable under the circumstances.[106] This general duty was developed by the courts under a so-called *allgemeine Verkehrspflicht*. Another example is the already mentioned obligation of landowners to disperse sand or salt (see above, p. 131).

In any event, the courts generally have considerably widened the scope of application of German fault-based tort law by the creation of *Verkehrs sicherungspflichten*[107] – and actually in a way that quite closely resembles the duty of care in the common law tort of negligence.[108]

IV How strict liability for animals (almost) disappeared from the *BGB*: an example of successful lobbying

A *The genesis of animal liability in the* BGB *of 1900*

In the deliberations leading up to the *BGB*, the liability for animals[109] received a remarkable amount of attention.[110] The first draft commission

[105] Von Caemmerer, 'Wandlungen des Deliktsrechts', p. 70.

[106] *Straßenverkehrsordnung* §1 reads as follows:

(1) Die Teilnahme am Straßenverkehr erfordert ständige Vorsicht und gegenseitige Rücksicht.

(2) Jeder Verkehrsteilnehmer hat sich so zu verhalten, dass kein Anderer geschädigt, gefährdet oder mehr, als nach den Umständen unvermeidbar, behindert oder belästigt wird.

[107] Von Caemmerer, 'Wandlungen des Deliktsrechts', pp. 62ff.; Deutsch and Ahrens, *Deliktsrecht*, pp. 123ff.

[108] As expressly noted for example by von Caemmerer, 'Wandlungen des Deliktsrechts', pp. 71ff.; and Deutsch and Ahrens, *Deliktsrecht*, pp. 123ff.

[109] For a full account of liability for animals in the *BGB* see R. Schmalhorst, *Die Tierhalterhaftung im* BGB *von 1896: Die Entstehung und Änderung des §833* BGB *sowie eine Analyse der Rechtsprechung des Reichsgerichts bis 1908* (Frankfurt: Lang, 2002); H. H. Seiler, 'Tierhalterhaftung, Tiergefahr und Rechtswidrigkeit' in K. A. Bettermann *et al.* (eds.), *Festschrift für Albrecht Zeuner zum siebzigsten Geburtstag* (Tübingen: Mohr Siebeck, 1994), pp. 279–293; and F. Litten, *Die Ersatzpflicht des Tierhalters im Rechte des Bürgerlichen Gesetzbuches, zugleich ein Beitrag zur Lehre von der Kausalität im Rechtssinne* (Berlin: Bahlen, 1906).

[110] On the discussions see Litten, *Die Ersatzpflicht des Tierhalters*, pp.1ff.; H. H. Jakob and W. Schubert, *Die Beratung des Bürgerlichen Gesetzbuches in systematischer Zusammenstellung der unveröffentlichten Quellen, Recht der Schuldverhältnisse III, §§652 bis 852* (Berlin: De Gruyter, 1983), pp. 949ff.; W. Schubert, *Die Vorlagen der*

of the *BGB* had proposed that – in line with the rest of the provisions – there should only be liability for animals where the keeper was at fault.[111] It was felt that a rule stipulating strict liability would be contrary to the system of the *BGB* as a whole and 'beyond tort law'.[112] This is somewhat surprising, given that the *BGB* is permeated with Roman law principles and strict liability for animals indeed was very much in line with the Roman *actio de pauperie*.[113] Under the *actio de pauperie* there was a strict liability for an animal when it caused harm 'against its nature', i.e. that was uncharacteristic for the type of animal in question.[114] But apparently for the commission the 'internal logic' of the *BGB* was more important than its Roman roots.

The proposal by the first commission was much criticised, not least because it was contrary to 'ancient Indo-Germanic legal tradition' and 'simply unjust',[115] and because it was an almost complete renunciation of Roman law.[116] During the deliberations[117] the first draft was changed and the second commission proposed a reversal of the burden of proof for

Redaktoren für die erste Kommission zur Ausarbeitung des Entwurfes eines Bürgerlichen Gesetzbuches, Recht der Schuldverhältnisse, Teil 3, Besonderer Teil II (Berlin: De Gruyter, 1980), pp. 932ff.

111 In the so-called *Erster Entwurf* (first draft) the liability for animals was to be found in §734 ('Wer ein Thier hält, ist verpflichtet, unter Anwendung der Sorgfalt eines ordentlichen Hausvaters diejenigen Vorsichtsmaßregeln zu treffen, welche erforderlich sind, um das Thier an der Zufügung von Beschädigungen zu hindern. Wird diese Pflicht verletzt, so ist der Halter des Thieres zum Ersatze des daraus einem Dritten entstandenen Schaden … verpflichtet').

112 Jakob and Schubert, *Die Beratung des Bürgerlichen Gesetzbuches*, p. 957; N. Habermann *et al.* (eds.), *J. von Staudingers Kommentar zum Bürgerlichen Gesetzbuch mit Einführungsgesetz und Nebengesetzen*, 12th edn, 7 vols., Vol. II: commentary by D. Belling and C. Eberl-Borges on §833 *BGB*, no. 2 (Berlin: De Gruyter, 2002), hereafter: Staudinger–Belling/Eberl-Borges.

113 On this see Zimmermann, *The Law of Obligations*, pp. 1096ff.; Staudinger–Belling/Eberl-Borges, §833 *BGB*, no. 1.

114 Zimmermann, *The Law of Obligations*, pp. 1102ff.; Staudinger–Belling/Eberl-Borges, §833 *BGB*, no. 1. On the even wider liability under the *edictum de feris* see Zimmermann, *The Law of Obligation*, pp. 1104ff.

115 O. von Gierke, *Der Entwurf eines Bürgerlichen Gesetzbuches und das deutsche Recht* (Leipzig: Dunker & Humblot, 1889), p. 270.

116 Cf. Seiler, 'Tierhalterhaftung, Tiergefahr und Rechtswidrigkeit', pp. 282ff.; Litten, *Die Ersatzpflicht des Tierhalters*, p. 11.

117 See for example the very mixed positions of the German states in Reichsjustizamt, *Zusammenstellung der Aeußerungen der Bundesregierungen zu dem Entwurf eines Bürgerlichen Gesetzbuchs* (Osnabrück: Zeller, 1967 [1891]), 2 vols., Vol. I, pp. 87ff.

domestic animals (*Nutztiere/Haustiere*).[118] It was thought that thus the victim would not be overly burdened, yet the usefulness of those animals for society as a whole could be taken into account by allowing the keeper to prove that he acted with due care.[119] But liability for animals not falling into those categories should be strict.[120]

But the Reichtstagskommission (Commission of the Reichstag) held that in the interest of 'public safety' liability for all animals, including farm and domestic animals, should be strict. Even domestic animals, particularly 'big luxury dogs' (*große Luxushunde*), which astonishingly featured quite prominently in the deliberations, but also all animals used for commercial purposes, were potentially dangerous, and the keeper in keeping them had to accept this risk.[121] Interestingly, as another reason why such an approach should be accepted, the Commission expressly stated that 'an equivalent provision in French Law had proved itself'.[122] Therefore the Commission decided to strike out the second sentence, which contained the privilege for domestic animals.[123] Opponents, namely the governments of the German states, argued that this would be contrary to the rules of Prussian law[124] and would also disadvantage those who had to keep animals because of their occupation.[125]

In the third reading in the plenary session of the Reichstag, the strict liability proposal was criticised heavily, as it was considered much too

118 In the so-called *Zweiter Entwurf* (second draft) §56 read:

> Wird durch ein Tier ein Mensch getötet oder der Körper oder die Gesundheit eines Menschen verletzt oder eine Sache beschädigt, so ist derjenige, welcher das Tier hält, verpflichtet, dem Verletzten den entstandenen Schaden zu ersetzen. Die Ersatzpflicht tritt nicht ein, wenn der Schaden durch ein Haustier entstanden ist und derjenige, der das Tier hält, bei dessen Beaufsichtigung die im Verkehr erforderliche Sorgfalt beobachtet hat oder der Schaden auch bei Anwendung dieser Sorgfalt entstanden sein würde.

This is also the wording of §818 Bundesratsvorlage and §817 Reichstagsvorlage. On the latter see H. Jäntsch, *Denkschrift zum Entwurfe eines Bürgerlichen Gesetzbuchs nebst drei Anlagen*, 5th edn (Berlin: Guttentag, 1896), p. 152.

119 Staudinger–Belling/Eberl-Borges, §833, n. 2; Litten, *Die Ersatzpflicht des Tierhalters*, p.12.

120 Litten, *Die Ersatzpflicht des Tierhalters.*

121 *Ibid.*; L. Enneccerus, *Bericht der Reichstagskommission über den Entwurf eines Bürgerlichen Gesetzbuches* (Berlin: De Gruyter, 1896), §817, p. 103.

122 Enneccerus, *Bericht der Reichstagskommission*; Litten, *Die Ersatzpflicht des Tierhalters*, p. 12. Unfortunately the reference to French law was not elaborated upon.

123 Enneccerus, *Bericht der Reichstagskommission.*

124 This refers to *ALR* I, 6 §72 (see p. 139 and n. 136).

125 Enneccerus, *Bericht der Reichstagskommission*, p. 103.

harsh on keepers of domestic animals. Therefore Parliament decided to return to the version of the second commission/second draft (see above, p. 137 and n. 118), but limited further, such that only 'animals necessary for the occupation or the business of the keeper' should be subject to a milder liability standard.[126] The point remained contentious, yet somewhat surprisingly, in the next session dealing with the matter, Parliament reverted to the proposal by the Commission of the Reichstag[127] and the liability for animals was included in §833 *BGB* as strict liability when the *BGB* came into force on 1 January 1900: 'If a person is killed, or the body or the health of a person is injured, or a thing damaged, by an animal, the person who keeps the animal is bound to compensate the injured party for any damage arising therefrom.'[128]

B The reform of 1908

The controversy about this provision, however, continued. For example, Ludwig von Bar wrote in a short piece in 1906 that §833 '... is indeed a rarity that has caused theory and practice embarrassment on many occasions and, despite heated efforts from different sides, has led to a number of decisions that violated one's natural sense of justice.'[129] Ludwig von Bar considered the provision a complete failure, which he deemed regrettable considering that the codification was new and generally very impressive, and suggested changing the provision to one that would allow the keeper of the animal to exculpate himself if he could prove that he had acted with proper care.[130] This rebuttable presumption of fault was employed in other provisions in the *BGB* like §§831, 832 and 836, so was not unknown to the system of the *BGB*. Interestingly, Ludwig von Bar based his proposal *inter alia* on the fact that legal practice in the Anglo-American countries, while 'starting from different legal principles', had developed towards a system of liability solely based on 'real fault' (*wirkliche Schuld*).[131]

126 Litten, *Die Ersatzpflicht des Tierhalter*, p. 13.

127 Staudinger–Belling/Eberl-Borges, §833, no. 2; Litten, *Die Ersatzpflicht des Tierhalter*, p. 13.

128 Translation by I. S. Forrester, S. L. Gorenon and H. M. Illgen (trans.), *The German Civil Code: Translated with an Introduction* (Amsterdam and Oxford: North Holland, 1975).

129 L. von Bar, 'Die Haftung des Tierhalters' (1906) 51 *Die Nation: Wochenschrift für Politik, Volkswirtschaft und Literatur* 485.

130 *Ibid.*, 486.

131 *Ibid.*

Under pressure from lobbyists representing the agrarian sector[132] the provision was amended in 1908[133] and a second sentence was added. The provision since then remained unchanged until today, despite continuous criticism. The second sentence resembles the version originally suggested by the above-mentioned second Commission (and the suggestion made by Ludwig von Bar). It reads as follows:

> The duty to make compensation does not arise if the damage is caused by a domestic animal which aids the business, the earnings or the prosperity of the keeper of the animal, and if the keeper of the animal has either exercised necessary care in supervising the animal or if the damage would have occurred notwithstanding the exercise of such care.[134]

In the *travaux préparatoires* the reasons given for the reform openly state that the change was mainly due to the demands by the agrarian sector, but also by manufacturers and tradesmen. It was deemed that strict liability was particularly harsh on these groups. It had been reported that 28 per cent of those found liable under §833 were agricultural undertakings and 44 per cent general tradesmen. So the vast majority of those were engaged in some form of commercial activity. Also, while insurance against these risks in principle was possible, full coverage was either not possible or not economically feasible. This, it was argued, led to significant hardships for those concerned that the courts were unable to mitigate because of the strict nature of the provision.[135] In a decision of 1912 the Reichsgericht expressly declared that the purpose of the 1908 reform had been to introduce milder standards of liability for those concerned, namely small and medium agricultural and commercial enterprises. It also stated that the reform brought the *BGB* closer to the rules of the old *ALR* (I, 6 §72), which stipulated that anyone keeping an animal simply for his amusement was to be liable for any damages, irrespective of fault.[136]

[132] *Münchener Kommentar*, Wagner commentary §833, no. 3; K. H. Johannesen *et al.* (eds.), *Das Bürgerliche Gesetzbuch mit besonderer Berücksichtigung der Rechtsprechung des Reichsgerichts und des Bundesgerichtshofes, herausgegeben von Mitgliedern des Bundesgerichtshofes*, 12th edn (Berlin: De Gruyter, 1982), commentary by G. Kreft (hereafter *RGRK*–Kreft) on §833, no. 5; Staudinger–Belling/Eberl-Borges §833, no. 3; Seiler, 'Tierhalterhaftung, Tiergefahr und Rechtswidrigkeit', p. 284.

[133] *Reichsgesetz betreffend Änderung des §833 des* BGB, 30 May 1908, RGBl. 1908, 313.

[134] Translation from Forrester, Gorenon and Illgen, *The German Civil Code.*

[135] Reichstags-Verhandlungen 1905/1906, Nr. 255, 3230ff., as reported in Bundesgerichtshof 27 May 1986, *NJW* 1986, 2501, 2502.

[136] Reichsgericht 18 April 1912, RGZ 79, 246, 249ff. This was also remarked upon in Jäntsch, *Denkschrift*, p. 152, where at §817 Reichstagsvorlage was explained and defended.

That the 1908 amendment came about is somewhat surprising, given that the 28th Deutsche Juristentag of 1906 had passed a resolution rejecting such a change to §833, opting for a narrower range of exceptions,[137] and respected German academics and practitioners had proposed different solutions.[138] As can be seen from the text of the added second sentence, the milder liability was not applicable to all animals but to certain domestic animals, either those kept for commercial purposes[139] or those that in a different way are necessary for the livelihood of the person concerned,[140] which suited the interests of the agriculturists who had pressed for this reform. But also the frequently occurring accidents caused by cart horses[141] could now be dealt with by applying the second sentence, so that exculpation was possible here, too. Essentially, as students these days still learn, the strict liability for animals was limited to 'luxury animals':[142] animals that served no productive purpose and were kept for the sheer enjoyment by their owners.

[137] *Verhandlungen des 28. Deutschen Juristentages 1906*, Vol. III, 1907, pp. 130ff., following a motion by the chairman Professor Dr Enneccerus (pp. 71ff.); Staudinger–Belling/Eberl-Borges, §833, no. 4.

[138] Cf. P.-A. Marwitz, 'Gutachten des Herrn Oberlandesgerichtsrats Marwitz zu Kiel über die Frage: Empfiehlt sich eine Änderung der Vorschrift des §833 *BGB* über die Haftung des Tierhalters' in *Verhandlungen des 28. Deutschen Juristentages 1906*, pp. 86–114, proposing exemptions if liability was to be considered *contra bonos mores* or if the injury occurred in the fulfilment of a contractual obligation and the injured person had exposed himself to the risk; L. Traeger, 'Gutachten des Herrn Professors Dr L. Traeger in Marburg über die Frage: Empfiehlt sich eine Änderung der Vorschrift des §833 *BGB* über die Haftung des Tierhalters' in *Verhandlungen des 28. Deutschen Juristentages 1906*, pp. 115–160, proposing a possibility of exculpation if the animal had been employed for the benefit of the injured person, and other limitations, including maximum amounts for property damages.

[139] Which, for example, has been found to include cats that are kept to keep rodents away, Landgericht Kiel 8 May 1984, *NJW* 1984, 2276; and an ox that a butcher led to an abattoir, Reichsgericht 18 April 1912, RGZ 79, 246.

[140] This presumably encompasses guide dogs for blind people (cf. E. Deutsch, 'Die Haftung des Tierhalters' *Juristische Schulung* 1987, 679; Palandt–Sprau, §833 *BGB*, n. 17), and in any event any animal that is bred for consumption, Reichsgericht 18 April 1912, RGZ 79, 246.

[141] See the data provided by Marwitz, 'Gutachten des Herrn Oberlandesgerichtsrats Marwitz', p. 103; and Traeger, 'Gutachten des Herrn Professors Dr L. Traeger', pp. 126 ff.; and for example the Reichsgericht decisions of 20 February 1901, RGZ 50, 217, and of 26 February 1903, RGZ 54, 73.

[142] A term that was used by a Staatssekretär (Under-Secretary of State) of the Reichsjustizministerium (Imperial Ministry of Justice) in the debates; see *RT-Sten. Ber.* 1907/1908, pp. 2338, as referred to by Reichsgericht 18 April 1912, RGZ 79, 246 (250).

C *Further calls for reform*

Numerous academics have proposed a return to strict liability, arguing convincingly that the underlying social and economic facts that originally justified the renunciation of strict liability for animals have changed.[143] The Bundesgerichtshof has expressly supported this criticism and called for reform, but clearly stated that it was not the task of the courts to initiate it.[144] But so far the German legislature has not shown any inclination to reinstate strict liability for animals. Thus §833 remains as it has been since 1908, a remarkable example of successful lobbying that even managed to convince the German legislature to accept a rule that was contrary to the otherwise sacrosanct principles of Roman law.

[143] H. Kötz, 'Gefährdungshaftung' in Bundesminister der Justiz (ed.), *Gutachten und Vorschläge zur Überarbeitung des Schuldrechts*, 2 vols., Vol. II (Cologne: Bundesanzeiger, 1981), p. 1779 (pp. 1802ff.); E. von Caemmerer, *Reform der Gefährdungshaftung* (Berlin: De Gruyter, 1971) pp. 20ff.; *RGRK*–Kreft, §833, no. 6; C. von Bar, *The Common European Law of Torts*, 2 vols., Vol. I (Oxford: Oxford University Press, 1998), pp. 230ff.

[144] Bundesgerichtshof 27 May 1986, *NJW* 1986, 2501.

7

The impact of institutions and professions in the Netherlands

ESTHER ENGELHARD AND IVO GIESEN

I The impetus to reform tort liability

The current Dutch legislation and rules regarding fault liability are basically a product of case law, indirect influences such as academic writings and legal practice left aside.[1] This may seem remarkable as legislation is the primary source of law in the Netherlands: constitutionally legislation is formed by the Government and approved by Parliament.[2] Courts give applications of the law. From that perspective, one might expect legal developments to be governed and led substantively by statutory provisions and *iudex est lex loquens*: the court as the mere *bouche de la loi*.[3] But in reality the development of fault liability has always been left to the judiciary, albeit within the elastic frame of an open statutory ruling. This can best be illustrated by focussing on the legal development

1 W. H. D. Asser, 'Over rechtsvorming door de Hoge Raad' (2005) *Ars Aequi* 223, 224. Cf. the general observation by C. C. Van Dam, *European Tort Law* (Oxford: University Press, 2006), no. 607–2 (p. 121) that 'tort law is mainly case law which implies that the power of developing this part of the law has been with the courts rather than with the legislator'. See more generally for the field of private law J. B. M. Vranken and I. Giesen, *De Hoge Raad binnenstebuiten* (Den Haag: Boom Juridische Uitgevers, 2003), p. 6.

2 Article 107, s. 1 of the Constitution (*Grondwet*) holds that civil law, civil procedural law, criminal law and administrative law are ruled by general law books and (only) specific topics may be dealt with in specific legislation. See on this I. Giesen, 'Codificatie en dynamiek in het schadevergoedingsrecht' in J. M. B. Vranken and I. Giesen (eds.), *Codificatie en dynamiek: Instrumenten ter begeleiding van de omgang met codificaties* (Den Haag: Boom Juridische Uitgevers, 2004), p. 139 (p. 142).

3 We are using this metaphor as it is generally understood, free from historical interpretations. Notably, R. Foqué, 'Evenwicht van machten en rechtsstatelijke vernieuwing' in A. Alen and L. J. Wintgens (eds.), *De Trias Politica ruimer bekeken, Staatsrechtconferentie 1999 Vlaamse Juristenvereniging* (Brussel: Larcier, 2000), p. 1 (pp. 3–4) argues this 'one-liner' tends to be misinterpreted so as to characterise Montesquieu as a too absolute legist ('statute fetishism', p. 14).

of the concepts of fault and unlawfulness; our contribution will focus on the latter. To explain the role of the courts and the legislature in this respect, we must go back to the ruling on fault liability in arts. 1401 and 1402 of the former Civil Code that was put in force in 1838 (hereafter CC (1838)).[4] First we will discuss how the concept of unlawfulness was given its first meaning in jurisprudence and the subsequent wrestle between the legislature and the judiciary (and how this resulted in the landmark judgment of *Lindenbaum* v. *Cohen*). Then we will point to factors that have led to its codification in the current Civil Code of 1992 (Section III). In Section IV we will explain how more recently the meaning of unlawfulness was furthered by case law. As an integral part of the discussion we will draw attention to the persons within the judiciary that were particularly influential. In Section V we will face the challenge of unravelling to some degree how judges view their role. After we have looked into regulatory changes that have led to a shift away from fault liability (Section VI), we will end with a summary of our main conclusions.

But first it will be noted that the former Civil Code, the CC (1838), was mostly a 'codification'[5] of the Napoleonic *Code civil*, which had stayed in force after the French oppression.[6] Not surprisingly therefore the old arts. 1401 and 1402 were almost a copy of the articles 1382 and 1383 of the *Code civil*. In one important aspect however both sets of rules differed. Article 1382 of the *Code civil* stated that 'any act' caused by someone's fault (*faute*) made the latter liable to pay damages.[7] Article 1401 CC (1838) gave the exact same ruling with the exception that – instead of 'any' act – only

[4] Our report is mostly based on secondary sources: dissertations and other (legal historical) writings of authoritative lawyers, including non-judicial writings of persons that had a central role in the topic of discussion themselves.

[5] For our purposes this 'Benthamian' expression means no more than written law with exclusive meaning (to be interpreted by courts). For a refined analysis of the term, see J. H. A. Lokin and W. J. Zwalve, *Hoofdstukken uit de Europese Codificatiegeschiedenis* (Den Haag: Boom Juridische Uitgevers, 2006), I.

[6] After the French occupation (1795–1815) hardly any account was given of earlier existing customary law: see J. Drion, *Verzamelde geschriften van J. Drion* (Deventer: Kluwer, 1968), p. 12. Out of hatred towards the French occupier (A. Pitlo, *Het Verbintenissenrecht naar het Nederlands burgelijk wetboek*, 5th edn (Haarlem: Tjeenk Willink, 1961), p. 23) the Dutch made their own code, albeit a mere copy of the French one.

[7] Article 1382 *Code civil*: 'Tout fait quelconque de l'homme, qui cause à autrui un dommage, oblige celui par la faute duquel il est arrivé, à le réparer.' In relation to this, art. 1383 *Code civil* specified 'any act' as either active acts or mere negligence. G. E. van Maanen, … *om te doen ophouden de menigvuldige twistgedingen: Opmerkingen omtrent de historische*

'unlawful' acts gave rise to liability.[8] Van Maanen has shown how in the words of the legislature, in the explanatory memorandum, this new element of unlawfulness served: 'to end the many disputes that article 1382 of the French Civil Code has brought about; as it goes without saying that not any act that causes damages gives ground for compensation; only the unlawful nature of the act can bring this about'. [9] In reality there had only been a few actual legal proceedings.[10] Clearly this statement was a product of its Enlightenment time: the element of unlawfulness was expected to clarify the law and subsequently to *limit* the number of cases. Ironically, in reality adding this vague element to the ruling of fault liability by itself opened new doors for an endless body of legal disputes and case law. New interpretations of the concept of unlawfulness were used to create new results in a changing society with its modern risks.[11] As a result court decisions were gradually given more weight as an autonomous and separate new source of law in this field.

II The judicial change: the courts' contribution to reforming fault liability

Certainly in the first century after 1838 courts had fewer *guidelines* to enable them to give meaning to the concept of unlawfulness. To some degree they could consult earlier published case law.[12] Prior judgments in other cases were (and are) not binding, but the Supreme Court is generally

achtergrond van de onrechtmatige daad (Nymegen: Ars Aequi Libri, 1995) p. 27 argues that the distinctive factor was the actor's intention (which had to be either careless, intentional or something in between).

8 Article 1401 CC (1838) (our translation): 'Any unlawful act that causes damage to another obliges the person by whose fault this was caused to compensate damages.' Similar to the French art. 1383 *Code civil*, art. 1402 CC (1838) ensured this not only covered active acts but also mere negligence.

9 Our translation; as cited by Van Maanen, *Opmerkingen*, p. 40 ('om te doen ophouden de menigvuldige twistgedingen, welke art. 1382 van het Franse Wetboek heeft opgeleverd; daar het van zelf spreekt, dat elke daad die schade veroorzaakt, geenen grond tot schadevergoeding oplevert, en dat de onregtmatigheid der daad daartoe alleen kan aanleiding geven', taken from J. J. F. Noordziek, *Geschiedenis der beraadslagingen gevoerd in de Tweede Kamer der Staten Generaal, over het ontwerp Burgerlijk Wetboek*, 2 vols., Vol. II (The Hague: Nijhoff, 1878), p. 531).

10 *Ibid.*, pp. 42–43.

11 E.g. the risks inherent to industrialisation: the capitalist market based on competition with, more recently, innovative technical modifications and globalisation.

12 Originally only a number of judicial decisions from the Supreme Court (then Hoog Geregtshof) were collected and later published, but from 1839 onwards many more

followed by lower courts as it is its role to examine whether the lower court has observed a proper application of the law in reaching its decision and to promote unity of the law.[13] If lower courts do not follow the Court's jurisprudence, their decisions will most likely be quashed in the last instance. Second, various public law rules and regulations (e.g. criminal law, administrative law etc.) give legislative indications that behaviour was or ought to be unlawful. Needless to say, particularly in the nineteenth and early twentieth centuries the scope and meaning of regulatory rules of conduct were modest compared to today. Also case law (prior to 1838) and academic writings were not clear on the matter. The Supreme Court held at one point that 'unlawfulness' meant no more than that any legal ground or justification for harmful behaviour was missing,[14] but that still left the courts with great discretion to give meaning to the concept of unlawfulness.

In the legist *second* half of the nineteenth century the Civil Code was perceived to be the only source of law in this area; the judiciary merely dealt with its ambiguities.[15] Florijn cites lawyers (including the president of the Supreme Court) who claimed that further development of the law was not for the judiciary but rather for the legislature (in the full acknowledgment that the latter was subjected to a political slow-down).[16] This legist approach is also said to have influenced the courts' interpretation of the concept of 'unlawfulness' as meaning: against *written* law.[17] In the famous *Singer* v. *Ivens* case the Supreme Court held that only careless behaviour that violated written rules of conduct and violations of plaintiffs' subjective rights could give rise to fault liability.[18] This case was

courts' decisions were published on a larger scale in the 22 editions of *Nederlandsche Regtspraak*. This latter project ended in 1913 and was followed by the (still existing) weekly editions of *Nederlandse jurisprudentie (NJ)* and other written periodicals, and more recently internet portals, of which the main one is www.rechtspraak.nl.

[13] In most cases it is possible to contest the Court of Appeal's decision by appealing in cassation to the Supreme Court of the Netherlands.

[14] This was shown by Van Maanen in his Ph.D. dissertation of 1986, published as G. E. van Maanen, *Onrechtmatige daad: Aspekten van de ontwikeling en structuur van een omstreden leerstuk*' (Kluwer: Deventer 1986); and again in Van Maanen, *Opmerkingen*, pp. 14ff.

[15] E. M. Meijers, 'De Honderdjarige burgerlijke wetgeving' in *Verzamelde privaatrechtelijke opstellen*, 3 vols., Vol. I (Leiden: Universitaire Pers Leiden, 1954), pp. 137, 141 (speech originally published in 1939).

[16] E. O. H. P. Florijn, *Onstaan en ontwikkeling van het nieuwe Burgerlijk Wetboek*, (Maastricht: UPM, 1994), pp. 65 and 67.

[17] W. L. P. A. Molengraaff, note discussion regarding *Lindenbaum* v. *Cohen Weekblad van het Recht* (1919) 10365, 2–3, p. 3. See also G. E. van Maanen, *De Zutphense juffrouw en de ontrouwe bediende van Lindenbaum* (Nymegen: Ars Aequi Libri, 1995) p. 13.

[18] Although in some cases negligence liability *was* accepted based on art. 1402 CC (1838).

on unfair competition,[19] but also in other cases the Court's restrictive approach led to remarkable results. In the so-called *Zutphen neighbour* case, the defendant, who lived above the storage house where there was a water leak, had refused to shut down the main water supply, saying it was midnight and she needed her sleep. As a result the plaintiff was not able to prevent his property from being ruined by the water leak. The defendant had not violated any law by refusing to turn off the water supply, nor had she (directly) violated the plaintiff's property. She had merely been negligent for refusing to help him when she could. But following the approach taken by the Supreme Court mere negligence was not enough to establish unlawfulness.[20]

In a noteworthy discussion on how to revise private law, Gratama and Loder, two of the Justices that had ruled the *Zutphen neighbour* case, objected a few years later to the idea that courts could freely interpret the law; the contemplation or rethinking of the law should be left for the legislature.[21] In non-judicial writings a third Justice on this case, Eyssell, the conservative president of the private law chamber of the Supreme Court from 1886 to 1912, expressed firmly his 'true dislike' towards a wider approach. Interestingly, Eyssell *did* call the result of the case unattractive. But accepting that by mere carelessness persons or companies could act unlawfully would negatively affect the freedom of competition (and subsequently the economy). He also objected to labour law protection and to leaving all fault cases to lower courts: the Judiciary's chair should not be taken by idealists.[22] But there were also other voices. In a famous article in 1887 Molengraaff favoured a less narrow view regarding article 1401 CC (1838) so that the law would offer more protection against unfair competition.[23] After the *Singer* judgment and the *Zutphen neighbour* judgment

[19] Copying American Singer stitching-machines was not unlawful as no statutory duty was violated; HR 6 January 1905, *Weekblad van het Recht* 1905, 8163 (*Singer* v. *Ivens*). See Van Maanen, *De Zutphense*, p. 31.

[20] HR 10 June 1910, *Weekblad van het Recht* 1910, 9038 (*Zutphen neighbour*).

[21] Cited by Florijn, 'Onstaan', 69, with reference to *Handelingen NJV* 1912, pp. 114ff. and p. 146.

[22] A. P. Th. Eyssell, 'Het wetsvoorstel omtrent de onregtmatige daad en de regtszekerheid' (1911) *Themis* 568, 597–598. Van Maanen has shown this in earlier profound studies, *inter alia*. Van Maanen, *De Zutphense*, p. 38.

[23] W. L. P. A. Molengraaff, 'De "oneerlijke concurrentie" voor het forum van den Nederlandschen rechter' (1887) *Rechtsgeleerd magazijn* 373, 386 (earlier was G. Belifante, 'Wat is onrechtmatige daad en wat is schuld, volgens art. 1401 B.W.', *Themis* 1865, p. 341; see Molengraaff, note discussion regarding *Lindenbaum* vs. *Cohen*, p. 2).

many lawyers supported Molengraaff's views.[24] It was felt that the outcome would be more reasonable if *any* negligent act or omission could in principle be qualified as unlawful.[25]

The weight of these voices led to a legislative proposal, proposed by Minister Regout, which aimed at expanding the meaning of the concept of unlawfulness of art. 1401 CC (1838). The requirement of unlawfulness would, on the basis of this proposal, not only cover violations of written rules or subjective rights but would also cover all acts that were contrary to 'public order, good morality or the care taken by a *pater familias*'. This phrase was made more concise in a new and revised proposal by Minister Heemskerk in 1913. Clearly the legislature sought to alter the restrictive approach followed by the Supreme Court, but before the legislative procedure even started, the Court changed its position. In the landmark case *Lindenbaum* v. *Cohen* the Supreme Court accepted the more extensive interpretation of the requirement of unlawfulness in art. 1401 CC (1838).[26] This case dealt with a printer named Cohen who had persuaded an employee of the competition (Lindenbaum) to give him the price quotations for potential customers. As a result Cohen was able to offer lower prices. At that time there was no statute to sanction this behaviour; still the district court thought it unlawful, but the Court of Appeal quashed this judgment. Following the earlier line of case law it held that only those acts that are in violation of a written rule can be unlawful. The Supreme Court took the view that this restrictive approach was supported '*neither* by the words of art. 1401 *nor* by the legislative notes underlying it'. An unlawful act is 'an act or omission that is in violation of a subjective right *or* in violation of a legal duty imposed on the defendant *or is contrary to the norms of proper social behaviour*'.[27]

The fact that in earlier years the then president of the Supreme Court, Eyssell, had worded his aversion to a wide interpretation of the element of unlawfulness rather strongly makes the proposition by Van Maanen likely, that the judgment in *Lindenbaum* v. *Cohen* was made possible by the fact that Eyssell was no longer in post.[28] But what had made the Supreme Court change its mind is not entirely clear. The Court hardly explained this, and extra-judicial writings are exceptional in the Netherlands: the

[24] Molengraaff, note discussion regarding *Lindenbaum* vs. *Cohen*, p. 2 (with many references) claims these supporters were 'young' academics.

[25] Molengraff, 'De "oneerlijke concurrentie"', 24.

[26] HR 31 January 1919, *NJ* 1919, 161 (*Lindenbaum* v. *Cohen*).

[27] *Ibid.* (our italics).

[28] Van Maanen, *De Zutphense*, p. 47.

Court as such decides the case and individual views of the Justices can rarely be found. Clearly the great number of opponents of the narrow view had put pressure on the Court. Surely its decision reveals to some degree how the authoritative Justices on the case viewed their role. In Florijn's study we have also found the statement made prior to this case by one of its Justices, Feith, that in his view courts *had* a role to play in the development of the law.[29]

III The extent and importance of legislative change

Owing to this changed point of view of the Supreme Court, following the broader concept of unlawfulness, the heat was taken out of the prior legislative proposal by Heemskerk. The *Lindenbaum* v. *Cohen* ruling was applauded by those who thought it was impossible for the legislature to regulate the entire legal community (under the *Singer* case law the unlawful character of the act needed to be based on the violation of a written rule or subjective right).[30] But critics argued that the Supreme Court had overstepped its boundaries by coming to a result that the legislature, by adding the requirement of unlawfulness next to fault, had clearly not wanted. To Kappeyne van de Coppello, former advocate and member of the Senate, this had been a result of the poor state of the Civil Code that forced the legislature to revise it. It was he who, in 1919, right after and with reference to *Lindenbaum* v. *Cohen*, first initiated this.[31] Since the turn of the nineteenth century, there had been many voices that the CC (1838) was not suited for the changed, industrialised society and its new social needs, especially in other fields of law such as labour law and rent law.[32] The CC (1838) was known for its many lacunae, and together with the many unclear writings and contradictions of the Code this prompted further calls to have these deficiencies eliminated by a governmental committee, led by Kappeyne. Several years before, in 1880, the then Minister of Justice, Modderman, had formed another governmental committee to draft a new Civil Code (formally the initiative to create new legislation is taken by the Government or by Parliament). But this project, though supported by the most prominent legal periodical, *Weekblad van het Recht*,

[29] Florijn, *Onstaan*, p. 69.

[30] Molengraaff, note discussion regarding *Lindenbaum* vs. *Cohen*, p. 3: 'those, to whom striving for laying down the entire law in the Civil Code is delusional, will welcome this decision that allows harmful acts to be judged by unwritten law as well' (our translation).

[31] Florijn, *Onstaan*, p. 74.

[32] Meijers, 'De Honderdjarige burgerlijke wetgeving', p. 140.

never saw the light of day.[33] Similarly the committee led by Kappeyne, later by Limburg, failed to make the necessary changes. Even further went the plea, at the celebration in 1938 of the 100th anniversary of the Code, by former advocate and prominent Leiden professor Eduard Meijers for a complete recodification of the Code.[34] Meijers argued that as a result of the many lacunae and technical ambiguities in CC (1838), the law was formed by the judiciary. In his view this caused a lack of uniformity as well as legal uncertainty.[35] An argument for this could also be found in the Constitution, as it obliged the State to codify the law.[36] But the other speakers at the celebration felt that a recodification was impossible and preferred to leave it to the judiciary to deal with the lacunae of the existing Code. One of them was Scholten, Meijers' colleague at the University of Amsterdam. He claimed that the quest for a new Civil Code could only be political.[37]

Because of the Second World War, the decision was left to rest. In 1940 Meijers (along with all 2,500 Jewish civil servants in our country, among which there were 41 professors and the Chief Justice of the Supreme Court) was suspended, and two years later he was arrested and transported to Westerbork. In these years Meijers managed to continue some of his academic work, which even included certain drafts for a new Civil Code. After the war, in 1945 he came back to Leiden and started to work again. According to another great lawyer of that time, the Amsterdam law professor Pitlo (who was later found controversial because of his alleged anti-Jewish beliefs), the postwar legal practice and enterprises were not at all in favour of a recodification because of the legal uncertainty this would bring.[38] But in the spirit of 'rebuilding the nation' the old criticism in the legal arena finally found political gain.[39] Also other factors seem to

[33] Drion, *Verzamelde geschriften*, p. 12; Florijn, *Onstaan*, pp. 52 and 54; V. J. A. Sutö, *Nieuw Vermogensrecht en rechtsvergelijking: Reconstructie van een wetgevingsproces (1947–1961)* (Den Haag: Boom Juridische Uitgevers, 2004), p. 1, n. 1.

[34] Meijers, 'De Honderdjarige burgerlijke wetgeving', p. 139.

[35] *Ibid.*, p. 141.

[36] Drion, *Verzamelde geschriften*, p. 11.

[37] P. Scholten, 'De codificatie-gedachte vóór honderd jaar en thans' in P. Scholten and E. M. Meijers (eds.), *Gedenkboek Burgerlijk Wetboek 1838–1938* (Zwolle: W. E. J. Tjeenk Willink, 1939), p. 30. This is also noted by Florijn, *Onstaan*, p. 101.

[38] Pitlo, *Het Verbintenissenrecht*, p. 32.

[39] *Ibid.*, p. 22 mentions the postwar sentiment as a substantive argument for recodification. Florijn, *Onstaan*, p. 97 warns this should not be given much weight as such but rather as a circumstantial cause. His study shows the real reasons came from the technical dissatisfaction with the old Code.

have played a role, such as the dissatisfaction with the Supreme Court's role during the war.[40] A member of the Senate requested in 1947 that the Minister of Justice have the Civil Code 1838 fully revised or even have a new Code drafted by Meijers for the reason that the former was outdated, given the great social changes.[41] Drion, who later played a leading role in the codification process, referred to the role of politicians in those days as the 'pushing power' in drafting the new Code.[42]

In 1947 Meijers was assigned the task to draft a complete codification. He was assisted first by Drion, then Franken. The (then) Minister of Justice, Van Maarseveen, felt that owing to the CC (1838)'s obsolete rules and deficiencies, written law would gradually be overridden by lawyers' law. He shared Meijers' concerns that it was unfit to deal with society's complexities and would result in legal uncertainty. It would suffice to make the old code more coherent and to codify case law.[43] The purpose was a thorough technical revision to make clear what the law was again. It would then be for the judiciary to apply and interpret the law, not to make it. The recodification of the Civil Code is seen as the largest and most ambitious Dutch legislative project of the twentieth century,[44] but Meijers' working method was strikingly simple. He used the old Code, reformulated the rule and examined whether it had to be maintained for practice. If so, he studied it and if necessary he codified existing case law. For specific legal matters he sought the opinion of experts and if they differed internally he asked Parliament. Other national laws were studied and incidentally used as a source of inspiration.[45] Meijers' drafts were critically assessed by a committee of about ten academics and legal practitioners.[46] For each topic two of them were approached: one to report and comment and another

[40] Generally it was felt the Supreme Court had been disappointing as it had not protested in any way or even raised any argument in its decisions against the undermining effects of the occupation on our law system.

[41] W. G. Belinfante, 'De Totstandkoming van het Nieuwe Burgerlijk Wetboek' in *Het Ontwerp B. W. Voordrachten gehouden op het Landelijk Congres 1961 voor Juridische Faculteitsverenigingen* (Deventer: Kluwer, 1961), p. 35. Cf. Sutö, *Nieuw Vermogensrecht*, p. 1 (with reference to the *travaux préparatoires (Part I. Algemeene. Deel)*, p. 1).

[42] Drion, *Verzamelde geschriften*, p. 18. His brother, H. Drion, Professor of Law in Leiden, was from 1969 onwards Justice of the Supreme Court and from 1981 even deputy chairman of the Supreme Court.

[43] Florijn, *Onstaan*, p. 95. Belinfante, 'De Totstandkoming van het Nieuwe Burgerlijk Wetboek', p. 36 explains the fact that Meijers was asked to draft a new Code for three reasons. First, he was 'the greatest lawyer' of those days in our country, and second, he had been a known proponent of a revision, while lastly he had placed himself at the Minister's disposal for this task. All three reasons are also pointed at by Florijn, *Onstaan*, p. 105.

[44] Florijn, *Onstaan*, p. 1. [45] *Ibid.*, p. 113.

[46] Belinfante, 'De Totstandkoming van het Nieuwe Burgerlijk Wetboek', p. 37. See also Florijn, *Onstaan*, p. 117.

to criticise the comments made by the former. The results were discussed with special experts who were invited to participate in the discussion. The first draft for the chapter on the law of obligations (Book 6), including the section on fault liability, was finished in 1950.[47] But there were concerns in Parliament that Meijers would single-handedly make too many choices with regard to the new draft. To ensure his drafts would merge with the wishes of Parliament and therefore gain sufficient political support, Meijers posed questions for Parliament to answer.[48] Partly based on this, he prepared his final drafts and, reputedly without influence of the Ministry Departments, these were finally sent to Parliament.

Meijers' work had been expected to reach completion in two years. However, partly owing to these lengthy procedures it took a good seven years (at least) to finish the introductory title and the first four books of the new Civil Code.[49] After Meijers' death in 1954, a committee was appointed to continue this work, despite calls to end the project. It was formed by three active members of Meijers' governmental committee: Leiden professor J. Drion (who as an academic had preferred to be joined by the two latter, *inter alia* given their practical knowledge) and the Advocate-General of the Supreme Court J. Eggens, together with Justice of the Supreme Court F. J. de Jong. They are referred to as the 'Triumvirate' (*het 'Driemanschap'*). Drion was in charge of the tort law section. Attempts were now made to codify the existing case law and doctrine, which made the final drafts of Book 6 look quite detailed and academic.[50] From the 1970s onwards this process progressed considerably by virtue of the fact that one person, Government Commissioner Wouter Snijders, who was also Justice at the Supreme Court, was primarily in charge of the recodification of Books 6 and 3.[51] Snijders is said to be the *auctor intellectualis* of many legislative notes, including those regarding Book 6, but the provision on fault liability was hardly changed.[52] Tort law, and the rest of Book 6, passed Parliament in 1980 before they became law in 1992.[53]

[47] Florijn, *Onstaan*, p. 107.

[48] Belinfante, 'De Totstandkoming van het Nieuwe Burgerlijk Wetboek', p. 38. On special topics, for instance notary law, Meijers would consult certain professions (p. 38). See also on this Florijn, *Onstaan*, p. 124.

[49] How much of the eventual result (our current Civil Code) was actually based on Meijers' work and personal notes is not entirely clear; see Florijn, *Onstaan*, pp. 106ff.

[50] *Ibid.*, p. 207. [51] *Ibid.*, pp. 363ff.

[52] *Ibid.*, 384; and Sutö, *Nieuw Vermogensrecht*, p. 253. Article 6:162 CC has not been changed dramatically compared to Meijers' draft.

[53] The same is true for Book 5 and parts of Book 7 of the Civil Code 1992. Book 4 (law of succession) has only been completed very recently, owing to the many objections of the notary profession after its first draft.

The new ruling on fault liability, art. 162 of Book 6 CC, is, dogmatically and in its terminology, different from the text of art. 1401 CC (1838), but it is based on a codification of the existing (case) law and academic writings.[54] Different from the old provision, art. 6:162 CC defines the requirement of unlawfulness as to include mere negligence, based on the revolutionary change brought about by *Lindenbaum* v. *Cohen*. Only minor textual changes were made in this respect. In *Lindenbaum* v. *Cohen* the Supreme Court mentioned both behaviour in violation of good morals *and* behaviour contrary to norms of proper social conduct as separate grounds for unlawfulness. In line with the earlier proposal of Heemskerk,[55] which never gained force, the legislature has chosen *not* to take over the first part of the criterion as formulated by the Court (violations of good morals: in Dutch *goede zeden*), as in case law this had hardly received any substantive meaning.[56] As a result, in the words of art. 6:162 CC an act or omission is unlawful if, without justification, it violates the victim's subjective right, or if it breaches a statutory norm, *or* if it is 'contrary to norms of proper social conduct' (i.e. negligent).

What matters more than these exact words is that this third criterion (negligence) leaves it to the judiciary to decide its meaning. In terms of lawmaking it differs substantially from the two other criteria for unlawfulness: violation of a subjective right or breach of a statutory norm.[57] Surely these latter two criteria need *interpretation* by the courts, but they each have a more concrete and a more definite meaning; they are embedded in statutory norms and treaties that guarantee the protection of personal rights or impose certain duties. Subsequently there is a distinction between the lawmaking tasks of courts regarding these two unlawfulness criteria and the third criterion. The latter requires more than mere interpretation; courts need to create rules that enable them to decide when behaviour is negligent (while for the violation of a subjective right this is to a good degree decided by looking at whether other written norms offer protection of such rights). This seems to run parallel with Meijers' perception of lawmaking, incorporated in the Code. To Meijers, courts must in principle only 'interpret' – that is, in his view, explain – the words and rules found

[54] For example, it requires that the tortfeasor can be held 'accountable' for his unlawful acts or omissions. This concept of accountability has replaced the old requirement of fault that courts had been determining by objective factors (the test was not 'Was the defendant personally to blame?', but 'What can we expect of the average prudent man in his shoes?').

[55] See above, p. 147.

[56] *Parl. Gesch.*, Book 6, pp. 614 and 617.

[57] E. Engelhard, 'Toerekening van een onrechtmatige daad' (2000) *NTBR* 514, 514ff.

in written law (what does 'subjective right' mean, does the injunction to give priority to traffic members on a major road include pedestrians?). But for matters that are too difficult to capture by written rules, courts must be given room to create new rules themselves through the use of legal terms or phrases in the Code that have no definite meaning, such as the phrase 'contrary to norms of proper social conduct'.[58] By introducing many open norms such as these, the legislature, as principal lawmaker, enables courts to decide cases freely based on their appreciation of the facts and circumstances.[59] Based on this idea of 'free lawmaking' the Civil Code has many examples of such open norms next to the third criterion for unlawfulness, compared to the CC (1838). Article 6:2 CC, for example, has replaced art. 1374 CC (1838) by ruling that debtors and creditors are bound not only to contractual agreements and/or the law, but also to the law and to 'good faith standards' (*eisen van redelijkheid en billijkheid*: standards imposed by reasonableness and fairness). A similar rule for contractual obligations was laid down in art. 6:248 CC. While through the use of these open norms the courts are free to make further rules, the legislature has the final say.[60] But as was said before, in reality, tort law is generally viewed as *de facto* judiciaries' law; that means: the courts as a factual lawmaker.

How far the judiciary's role in lawmaking goes compared to the legislature is still debated.[61] The constitution leaves courts room critically to assess written law; it solely prohibits courts to question formal legislation and treaties.[62] The strict distinction that Meijers made between the interpretations of written rules on the one hand and 'free lawmaking' came from a less steady perception of courts as lawmakers than today.[63] But

[58] J. M. Smits, 'E. M. Meijers (1880–1954)' in C. J. H. Jansen, J. M. Smits and L. C. Winkel (eds.), *Zestien juristen en hun filosofische inspiratie* (Nijmegen: *Ars Aequi*, 2004), pp. 61–74 (p. 64), with further references to J. H. A. Lokin, 'De plaats van Meijers in de legistische traditie' in *Tekst en uitleg* (Groningen: Chimaira, 1994), pp. 143–170, and L. Reurich, 'Pragmatische rechtswetenschap' (2003) *RM Themis* 126–131.

[59] *Parl. Gesch.*, Book 6, p. 66.

[60] In art. 3:12 CC Meijers has even – albeit in general terms – laid down *how* courts in their role of 'free lawmaking' should come to their judgment of what is fair or reasonable: 'by taking account of common principles, of Dutch legal views and beliefs and of the public and private interests at stake'.

[61] Asser, 'Over rechtsvorming', 224; and I. Giesen and H. Schelhaas, 'Samenwerking bij rechtsvorming: De instelling van een Periodiek Overleg van Rechtsvormers (POR)' (2006) *Ars Aequi* 159, 159.

[62] Article 120 of the Constitution (*Grondwet*).

[63] S. K. Martens, 'De grenzen van de rechtsvormende taak van de rechter' (2000) *NJB* 747 notes how in the early fifties no mention of any role of lawmaking was made: only of keeping unity and certainty of law, when legislation was proposed to extend the grounds for

even in those days critics argued that both were inseparable, as the 'mere' application of written rules too required a critical assessment and, if needed, *contra legem* decision by the judiciary.[64] In case law a few, admittedly more exceptional, examples of this can be found: instances where the Supreme Court took the liberty of setting the legal result of a clear-cut rule aside for more fair results. Famous are the cases regarding the prescription of asbestos claims (where the Court first allowed the plaintiff's claim despite the fact that the prescription period had expired) and cases concerning accidents with motor vehicles (where the Court has created serious limitations for principal defences).[65] Also the Court seems to have accepted proportionate liability: in 2006 an asbestos claim of a smoker was awarded although he had *not* shown that his lung cancer could not have been caused but for the exposure to asbestos (the 'but for' causality test, as read in article 6:162 CC).[66] Although the results in all these cases were welcomed, the legal doctrine is critical of the idea of courts, or better yet the Supreme Court, deciding cases contrary to what written rules dictate. The judiciary should be neutral and not change the law based on singular cases brought forward by singular parties. It is not equipped to do so and not subject to parliamentary control. Also, the (technical) reasoning by the Court gives hardly any insight into the political choices behind its decisions.[67]

IV Further changes by the judiciary

Before we will explain how the process of 'free lawmaking' has developed further based on the negligence criterion for unlawfulness, it must be noted that the explanatory notes by the legislature did give some indications to help courts to decide the unlawfulness question under art. 6:162 CC. More particularly an important note was made in respect of the first criterion for unlawfulness: violations of a subjective right. The legislature noted that the fact that the defendant has caused property damage or an injury to the plaintiff does not by itself make his or her behaviour

cassation (while much later, in the late eighties, the lawmaking role *was* mentioned by the Minister).

64 Smits, 'E. M. Meijers', p. 65.

65 See for example HR 28 April 2000, *NJ* 2000, 430 (*Van Hese/Koninklijke Schelde*); and on the traffic liability cases see Ernst, *Traffic*, pp. 137–139, and below, p. 158.

66 HR 31 March 2006, *JAR* 2006, 100, LJN AU6092 (*Karamus/Nefalit*).

67 See G. J. Wiarda, *Drie typen van rechtsvinding*, 4th edn, ed. T. Koopmans (Deventer: W. E. J. Tjeenk Willink, 2005), pp. 78ff.

unlawful.[68] This was in line with existing case law. For the rest the legislature left it to case law and academic writings to set the boundaries for this unlawfulness criterion.[69] Courts were thus faced with many cases raising the question when there was negligence in terms of unlawfulness.

Based on the open formulation of the third criterion for unlawfulness ('contrary to norms of proper social conduct') various sub-rules for various fault cases can be deduced from case law. For this purpose the cases on fault liability have been categorised into various types, dependent on the context in which the damage was caused: for example cases that deal with dangerous operations, cases that deal with professional wrongs, cases that deal with sport activities and the like. These sub-rules must help courts to decide when negligent behaviour in a certain context may or may not be qualified as unlawful. A landmark case in this respect was and is the so-called *Cellar hatch* (*Kelderluik*) case in 1965. In this case a delivery boy of the Coca Cola company had left a cellar hatch open that was close to the toilet in an Amsterdam bar. He had merely placed a few chairs around it, while he was carrying the crates up and down from the cellar and in and out of the bar. Was leaving the hatch open unlawful to the customer (the plaintiff) who, while headed for the toilet, had fallen down and was seriously injured? The Supreme Court laid down criteria by which this question should be answered according to whether the behaviour in question has caused a direct risk to life, body or property.[70] In remarkably general wordings the Court gave four criteria that need to be taken into account when deciding if negligent behaviour that increases the risk of property or injury damage is unlawful.[71] These '*Cellar hatch* criteria' are even today the leading criteria for courts to decide whether dangerous behaviour may lead to fault liability.[72]

The Supreme Court has further distinguished between acts that are unlawful and acts that are a mere 'unfortunate matter of events' for which the actor cannot be held liable in law. For example, accidentally hitting a tennis partner in the eye with a tennis ball,[73] swinging a branch during a walk with friends in the woods[74] and making the wrong move while

[68] *Parl. Gesch.*, Book 6, p. 614. [69] *Ibid.*

[70] HR 5 November 1965, *NJ* 1966, 136 note GJS (*Cellar hatch*).

[71] These criteria are: the probability of this negligent behavior for the victim, the chances that damage would result from this, the seriousness of the result if damage occurred and the costs of taking precautionary measures to avoid damage.

[72] See for example HR 28 May 2004, *NJ* 2005, 105 note CJHB (*Jetblast*).

[73] HR 19 October 1990, *NJ* 1992, 621 and 622 note CJHB (*Tennis*).

[74] HR 9 December 1994, *NJ* 1996, 403 note CJHB (*Swinging branch*).

moving a heavy cupboard[75] have been qualified as 'unfortunate matters of events', which means there can be no risk of liability for these acts in similar situations. On the other hand, not warning trainees before roll-erblading to wear helmets,[76] and, after feeding sheep in the vicinity of crops, leaving onion remainders behind that subsequently start rotting and spreading a plant disease[77] were in the circumstances of the case each qualified as 'unlawful behaviour'. In making these choices, using the *Cellar hatch* criteria, the Supreme Court *in fact* gave directions to society: these cases put a price tag on certain activities. At the same time however these case decisions (with the exception of the *Cellar hatch* case) can hardly be seen as general rules, given that situations are rarely *exactly* alike: a slight difference of the circumstances could lead to a different outcome.

In some other lines of cases the Supreme Court's interpretation of the concept of unlawfulness has gone further; the Court has laid down general rules that have introduced special conditions for fault liability. We will briefly point at the three most common examples of cases: those concerning liability for pre-contractual negotiations, traffic liability and State liability. As far as pre-contractual liability is concerned the legislature left it openly to case law to make law,[78] although it was never doubted that parties have the right to decide not to continue their negotiations with others. But the Supreme Court has, case by case, created a far-going and rather detailed system of rules regarding different stages of pre-contractual negotiations.[79] Earlier attempts to create a special rule for this in the Civil Code had failed.[80] Technically this was brought under the umbrella of fault liability or, as an alternative option, under the general good faith clause, but that was considered of secondary importance. The latter in our view seems indicative of a growing inclination to perceive case law as having to do with what really matters and thus supreme over legislation, which is of a more technical and thus lesser importance. Not because of a lack of a proper legal basis but rather (seemingly) influenced by critical

[75] HR 12 May 2000, *NJ* 2001, 300 note JH (*Sisters moving a cupboard*).

[76] HR 25 November 2005, *JA* 2006, 1 (*Skeelers*).

[77] HR 25 November 2005, *NJ* 2007, 141 note CJHB (*Rotting onions*).

[78] *Parl. Gesch. Inv.*, p. 1448.

[79] J. M. Barendrecht, 'Pure Economic Loss in the Netherlands' in E. H. Hondius (ed.), *Netherlands Reports to the Fifteenth International Congress of Comparative Law* (Antwerpen/Groningen: Intersentia Rechtswetenschappen, 1998), pp. 115–135, §3.1; M. R. Ruygvoorn, *Afbreken van onderhandelingen* (Deventer: Kluwer, 2005).

[80] Meijers had convinced his working committee to draft a rule, but in the continuing process after his death this was decided otherwise; Florijn, *Onstaan*, p. 123 (with references).

voices in literature, the Court is nowadays more reluctant to allow pre-contractual liability.[81]

Governmental liability cases form another field of fault liability cases in which the Supreme Court has created special rules that go beyond a mere interpretation of art. 6:162 CC. The Court has shown a miraculous interpretation of the concept of unlawfulness in cases in which the State had operated on good grounds (e.g. by bringing criminal proceedings against a person who cannot be found guilty of the alleged crime or by enforcing a regulation that farmers have to kill stock). Originally in such situations civilians that suffered damages and asked compensation based on art. 6:162 CC would see their claim refused by dint of the fact that the State's operation is not unlawful. But in some of these situations[82] the Supreme Court has sought ways to circumvent this by arguing, for instance, that based on the principle of *égalité devant les charges publiques* the State should have offered compensation, and the fact that this was not done made its operations unlawful after all.[83] Also, administrative decisions that have been quashed in an administrative procedure are without further ado – by that mere outcome of the administrative procedure – regarded as unlawful acts.

The most far-going line of cases that introduced jurisprudential sub-rules in respect of art. 6:162 CC, and that challenge its basic understanding, deals with traffic liability. To explain this we must first briefly touch upon the fact that throughout the 1990s the Supreme Court has (also) laid down a system of *strict* liability that seriously exceeds the protection already offered by the legislature in the statutory ruling (the strict liability laid down in article 185 WVW). Based on this entirely jurisprudential system the owner or keeper of a motor vehicle will always be liable for at least 50 per cent or even 100 per cent of the damages to non-motorised traffic members (cyclists, pedestrians) who were run over, unless the latter acted intentionally or with gross negligence (see, more extensively on this, below, p. 158). In the context of *fault* liability, however, in the reverse situation – in which a motor vehicle is damaged by a non-motorised traffic member (now being the defendant) – the Court has held analogously that

[81] *Inter alia* HR 18 June 1982, *NJ* 1983, 723 (*Plas* v. *Valburg*); HR 14 June 1996, *NJ* 1997, 481 (*De Ruiterij* v. *MBO*); and HR 12 August 2005, CO4/163HR (*CBB* v. *JPO*).

[82] Not always: in the case where a convict who was rightfully sent on leave had committed assaults, the court did not accept the principle of *égalité devant les charges publiques* to back up (indirectly) the fault liability claim vis-à-vis the institution; HR 28 May 2004, *NJ* 2006, 430 (*Convict on leave*).

[83] HR 30 March 2001, *NJ* 2003, 615 (*Staat* v. *Lavrijsen*).

the latter can only be held liable based on art. 6:162 CC if he has caused the damage by intent through gross negligence.[84] As a result, contrary to what art. 6:162 CC promises, mere fault will not entitle the motorist victim to compensation unless he can show the damage was due to intent or gross negligence on the part of the non-motorised defendant. Further, he will only be entitled to *full* compensation if *he* (the plaintiff!) can prove that he has *not* been at fault himself, for example by driving too fast.[85] It is doubtful, to say the least, whether the court has not overstepped its authority by limiting the motorised victim's right to compensation based on the general art. 6:162 CC to this extent.

Also outside the scope of art. 6:162 CC there have been occasions on which the Supreme Court was criticised in academic writings for having displayed a too far-reaching understanding of its role as lawmaker.[86] A famous example of this concerns the strict liability of keepers of motor vehicles towards non-motorised traffic members: here, the Supreme Court has reduced the possibility of raising the Act of God and the contributory negligence defences laid down in written law (art. 185 of the Traffic Act and art, 6:101 CC of the Civil Code respectively). The Court used several cases to create a whole new system, holding basically that unless the non-motorised victim was grossly negligent there can be no Act of God or contributory negligence for more than 50 per cent (the so-called '50 per cent rule'). For children below the age of 14 years old, the contributory negligence defence has been set aside by the Court completely: no contributory negligence, unless the child acted intentionally or with gross negligence (the '100 per cent rule'). This extraordinary regime of protection inspired the legislature to draft an even more protective ruling, but this was subject to interest groups and after a few revisions the legislative process was frozen again.[87]

The cases mentioned above are all examples of occasions on which the Supreme Court has created rules that gave a completely new and/or challenging meaning to written liability rules. In general it is its task to judge whether the law has been applied correctly by the lower courts in the

[84] HR 6 February 1987, *NJ* 1988, 57 (*Saskia Mulder*); HR 4 May 2001, *NJ* 2002, 214 (*Chan* v. *Maalsté*).

[85] HR 4 May 2001, *NJ* 2002, 214 (*Chan* v. *Maalsté*).

[86] See, in general, Giesen and Schelhaas, 'Samenwerking bij rechtsvorming'.

[87] E. Engelhard and G. E. van Maanen, 'Een nieuw voorstel verkeersaansprakelijkheid in de maak: De belangrijke – ook minder voorzienbare – consequenties van Korthals' ingreep in het wetsvoorstel Verkeersongevallen' (1999) *VR* 353.

individual case and to promote the development and unity of the law.[88] To give an accurate picture though we have to admit these examples are of challenging cases; in fact most judgments of the Supreme Court are less innovative and concerned with the specific motivation of concrete judgments. Second, the arguments used by the Supreme Court tend to be rather technical and lack much colour as far as the underlying factual and/or political interests of the legal issues at stake are concerned.[89] In this respect Vranken and Giesen have pleaded that the Supreme Court puts more weight on its task of furthering the development of the law and promoting unity of law.[90] But how do the Court or its justices see their task themselves?

V How judges consider their role vis-à-vis the legislature

In general it seems that both the Supreme Court and the legislature do not cross swords.[91] The Court (formally) takes the view that it is its task to do justice and explain the law in individual cases, in a way that promotes legal consistency and coherence. In various instances it has refused to accept legal results that are not consistent with written law or with the systematic or dogmatic choices behind this, because it has felt that it is the role of the legislature to make those changes – even in respect of changes that it thought might be socially desirable.[92] As said, the three lines of cases that we referred to above thus do not represent our everyday jurisprudence. Rather they are concerned with special areas of law in which the Supreme Court has created new, general rules on top of the existing written framework of open rules. In the examples that we used, this often ran counter to the legal results that would normally have followed from

[88] J. B. M. Vranken and I. Giesen, *De Hoge Raad binnenstebuiten* (Den Haag: Boom Juridische Uitgevers, 2003), p. 5.

[89] This was also one of the points of criticism mentioned by Vranken and Giesen, *ibid.*, p. 1 in their experiment of having some grand decisions of the Supreme Court rewritten by themselves and a number of other academics.

[90] *Ibid.*, p. 6.

[91] Giesen and Schelhaas, 'Samenwerking bij rechtsvorming', p. 166.

[92] In 2002 the court was presented with a dreadful case (HR 22 February 2002, *NJ* 2002, 240 note JBMV) of a mother confronted with the crushed skull of her child, who had been run over by the defendant. Although the court allowed the nervous shock claim, it refused to award damages for 'mere' bereavement (affectionate damages) with reference to the statutory regime by which these damages are excluded. It admitted that this regime might be socially unacceptable ('onvoldoende tegemoet komt aan de maatschappelijk gevoelde behoefte') but it felt it was not for the judiciary to decide how to revise it. See also Giesen and Schelhaas, 'Samenwerking bij rechtsvorming', p. 163.

the written rule (or the system of written rules or rationale behind it). For that reason it has been argued that in doing so it was sitting in the legislature's seat.

Interestingly, even the critics have hardly given any account of the persons that were influential in the development and change of fault liability in the above cases. This seems particularly interesting when the courts are faced with controversial political matters: that is, matters that would require an exercise of power giving direction to society that clearly exceed the interests of two individuals involved in court proceedings.[93] To give an example, in the eighties the Supreme Court was asked whether the – politically controversial – decision of the State regarding the stationing of cruise missiles was contrary to rules of international law (and, based on that violation of written law, unlawful). The Supreme Court ruled that it was *not*, but the Advocate-General Mok had argued that NATO's policy to use the missiles to protect peace was a political choice that was not to be judged by the courts in the first place.[94] Other such cases of a political character have come before the courts, such as claims after strikes and the so-called 'wrongful life' claims, but even those have hardly raised any debate as to the *person* of the judge. The critical notes and discussions concern the outcomes (the judgment of the Court), rather than the persons behind the judgments.

This is not surprising. First, it would not be just if only the judges who decide the case were held (individually) accountable for the outcome; the lawyers arguing the case may in some situations be the real force behind the changes of the law.[95] Surely it is the judge who decides the outcome. But even then the Dutch court system[96] works in such a way that decisions are formally given by the court as such, not by personal judgments. In the lower district courts in civil liability law cases the vision of the judge, albeit not necessarily corresponding with his or her personal vision, is clear, as

93 Cf. J. Bell, *Policy Arguments in Judicial Decisions* (Oxford: Clarendon Press, 1983), pp. 6ff.

94 HR 10 November 1989, *NJ* 1991, 248 (*Cruise missiles*).

95 Vranken suspects the influence of lawyers who argue their clients' cases on the development of the law is underestimated; J. B. M. Vranken, *Mr C. Asser's Handleiding tot de beoefening van het Nederlands Burgerlijk Recht Algemeen Deel: Een vervolg* (Deventer: Kluwer, 2005), no. 20.

96 The Netherlands is divided into 19 legal districts (areas in which several local communities are united), each with its own court. The districts are divided into 5 areas of appellate jurisdiction, each with its own Court of Appeal. These courts re-examine the facts of the case and will give a new, independent judgment in second instance.

this will be in principle the one judge deciding the case.[97] However, more complex district court cases will be ruled by three judges. Although their names will be mentioned under the judgment there are no deliberations or opinions from the judges separately or in their professional person as such; these only come from the court as such. Also cases that come before the Courts of Appeal will be ruled by three judges. In (the Civil Chamber of) the Supreme Court claims are adjudicated by five or three justices (*raadsheren*), depending on the degree of difficulty and the legal and social importance of the case, but there we do see the (often extensive and more often than not followed) advice of the Advocate-General, preceding each judgment.

There have been examples of judges giving quite extrovert views on legal issues within their authority as a judge but this is (and always has been) quite exceptional. We mentioned the name of Eyssell (see above, p. 146) as one of the driving forces behind the restrictive approach initially taken by the Supreme Court, in the *Singer* case in 1905 and in the *Zutphen neighbour* case in 1910. As said, Eyssell was a conservative lawyer and the president of the Dutch Supreme Court. In 1911, while still head of the Supreme Court, Eyssell published an article in a high-quality legal periodical in which he made strong arguments against the legislative proposal to opt for a wider concept of unlawfulness, a private law disaster as he called it.[98] In this article he advocated the restrictive approach by which mere negligence was not sufficient to found tort liability *in person*. The arguments for this were supported by his conservative political beliefs: if unfair competition was not in violation of any written law and was nevertheless sanctioned with civil liability, this would affect all competition and harm economic growth.[99] As we explained above this makes Van Maanen's view likely that it could only have been after Eyssell had left the Supreme Court, in 1919, that the court gave its ruling in *Lindenbaum* v. *Cohen*, in which the Court opted for a more extensive concept of unlawfulness.

As we have also shown above, this latter decision (in the case of *Lindenbaum* v. *Cohen)* seems to have been influenced by academic writings. However, it is difficult to know whether and how personal contextual circumstances or the system as such may have influenced the case law development of fault liability as described above. As far as fault liability is

[97] More particularly this will be so if the case is decided by the so-called sub-district sector. This deals with cases concerning rent, employment and hire purchase, as well as claims for civil liability below €5,000 (€28,000 as of July 2011).

[98] Van Maanen, *De Zutphense*, p. 38.

[99] *Ibid.*, 39. See also above, p. 146.

concerned we can only speculate as to whether there is any influence at all. With regard to the personal contextual circumstances this is extremely difficult to grasp, as factors such as the judge's social and religious background, political preference and individual way of life are hardly known or found relevant.[100] As far as training is concerned, judges are trained and promoted separately from attorneys and, once in the job, there is a system where, if a judge sits in the civil section, as is the case at most courts, he can only do so for a number of years. Judges then generally will be asked to move to a different section of the court.

Rather than speculate on this we would like to point at three more general factors that seem to be of influence. First, there might be an influence – namely strengthening the meaning and role of the judiciary – coming from the fact that from 1913 onwards case law was systematically published and annotated. Second, developments with regard to the limited grounds for cassation may influence the role and position of the judiciary.[101] For example, originally this did *not* include situations where the legal grounds that the court used in the motivation of its decision could not have the legal result as envisaged by the court.[102] But currently it recognises motivations that are incomprehensible as a ground for cassation as well. A third factor of influence regarding the role and position of the judiciary may be the changing style of judicial decisions. Over the last century the Supreme Court has made a shift from the concise – French-style – model to the more elaborate – German-style – model of court decisions.[103] This is not just in the *number* of words: a change of style can also be noticed with regard to the content of the decisions.

VI Regulatory changes

A *The importance of 'regulatory change'*

It must be noted that during the period studied legislation and regulations seem to have gained importance, although this is not special to liability

[100] C. J. J. M. Stolker, 'De politieke rol van de rechter in het burgerlijk recht' in M. G. Rood (ed.), *Rechters en politiek: Nationale en internationale beschouwingen* (Zwolle: Tjeenk Willink, 1993), pp. 53–83.

[101] Grounds for cassation are either procedural mistakes by the court (*error in procedendo*) or violations of substantive rules (*error in iudicando*).

[102] L. E. H. Rutten, 'De cassatiegronden van art. 99 RO en de motiveringsplicht' in *Rechtspleging* (Deventer: Kluwer, 1974), pp. 237, 239.

[103] Van Dam, *European Tort Law*, no. 607.

law. Over the last two centuries several parts of civil liability law have been removed from the scope of fault liability. The fault liability rules in those areas were then replaced by stricter forms of liability or even ruled by forms of public regulation and/or (mandatory) insurance systems. Below we will discuss some of those areas briefly. In most areas, however, we see combinations of systems, as Dutch basic compensation comes from social security rules (and liability law therefore only offers special protection as a 'second layer of protection'). Fault liability is thus operative next to a form of no-fault liability and certain types of social and/or private insurance as well as private or public law funds and regulations.

A good example of this is the recovery of damages caused by workplace injuries. This part of law is to a great extent governed by statutory rules on public and/or private insurance and liability law. The Netherlands – as most other European legal systems, including the UK – has a long history of legislative endeavours to regulate the employee's right to compensation for workplace accidents.[104] Also, in each country several of these public and private law systems are in operation, therefore each has different 'layers' of protection.[105] More concrete, in 1901 the Dutch Government proclaimed the Industrial Accidents Act (*Ongevallenwet*), amended in 1921. This served to replace the special regime of employers' fault-based liability by a public law duty imposed on employers to take out mandatory insurance for damages to their employees arising from workplace accidents. Prior to this, employees struggled with several problems. From the beginning of the nineteenth century they had been in a position of having to sue their employer for accidents due to the latter's negligence but in practice such claims only gradually started to take hold in the last quarter of the nineteenth century, from 1871 onwards. In the Dutch transport, catering, medical and chemical industries, for instance, special funds covered damages, which – after a modest start in the seventeenth and eighteenth centuries – slowly grew to become professional insurances only covering those who paid contributions.

In 1967 this system was replaced by one of social insurance that covered the basic risk of medical expenses and income loss regardless of the way they were caused, and liability law covering the rest of the damages.

[104] E. Engelhard, 'Shifts of Work-Related Injury Compensation. Background Analysis: The Concurrence of Compensation Schemes' in S. Klosse and T. Hartlief (eds.), *Shifts in Compensating Work-Related Injuries and Diseases* (Vienna/New York: Springer, 2007), p. 9.

[105] *Ibid.*

Interestingly, employers now face the – much wider – financial risk of disability *regardless of its cause*, as they are required to continue the employee's salary payments during the first two years of work-related disability (as well as most of the social security premiums). Based on special reimbursement rules the employer has the right to claim the salary back from the liable person (art. 107a of Book 6 of the Civil Code); similar rules in social security law provide for reimbursement rights of social insurance carriers. It must be noted though that many employers take out additional private insurance for their employees, which is limited to the risk of workplace accidents, although on a voluntary basis. As employers' risk of civil liability for accidents caused by violations of safety rules or of good employment is, however, very strict, with a very limited contributory negligence defence (art. 658 of Book 7 of the Civil Code), the system is not as different from the former insurance model as one might expect. There are still voices promoting the reintroduction of a special no-fault insurance for the *risque professionel*, similar to that in Belgian or German law. Why, it is asked, should the employer have to pay for personal risks run by his employees in their private lives such as going on a skiing trip? But these voices, raised in parliamentary debates and literature, are not likely to be heeded in the near future.

A similar trend is noticeable for traffic liability (dealt with above, p. 158) and product liability. As for product liability law, this has evolved, owing to the EU Directive on Product Liability, into a strict liability regime. Concepts such as defect and causal link were no longer interpreted by national standards but, at least partly, by European standards.[106]

B Techniques used in place of fault liability

As was seen above, in the early twentieth century a no-fault compensation scheme was introduced to remove fault liability for workmen's compensation. Fault liability was now replaced with a statutory duty for employers to take out insurance for the personal damages of their workmen. The employer could in principle not be held liable for any damages

[106] J. H. Nieuwenhuis, 'De verwoestende kracht van de rechtswetenschap' (1988) 6 *Justitiële Verkenningen* 23, 25; I. Giesen and M. Loos, 'Liability for Defective Products and Services: The Netherlands' in E. Hondius and C. Joustra (eds.), *Netherlands Reports to the Sixteenth International Congress of Comparative Law* (Antwerpen/Oxford/New York: Intersentia, 2002), pp. 75–113 (also published at www.ejcl.org/64/art64-6.html).

of the victim-employee, certain exceptions (intentional wrongdoing, property damage etc.) left aside. The obligation to pay compensation was now *not* primarily an individual employer's responsibility but was shared collectively, by *all* employers, based on this statutory insurance.[107] Employers were now faced with the statutory obligation to pay for the entire insurance, in the form of insurance contributions (premiums). Certain employers could also offer their employees direct relief instead of taking out private insurance. Where the insurance had been taken out, the insurance contributions were calculated based on the accident risk of their branch: the higher the risk, the higher contributions would be (which can be taken to give employers good incentives to minimise this risk). In practice, however, most companies that had their own medical service would handle claims themselves and pay directly to the victim, without reporting the accident to the public institution in charge of controlling and securing insurance protection, the *Rijksverzekeringsbank* (Public Insurance Bureau).[108]

C *Reasons for the removal from fault liability*

This 'shift' from civil liability was the result of a growing social awareness of the problems employees faced within the system as it stood, and employers' fear of a flood of claims.[109] It was inspired by similar shifts in other European countries (Germany, France). More and more, the risk of accidents caused by employment was perceived as a risk inherent of the production process. Therefore, its costs were part of the production costs that were to be borne by the one who also gained the profits: the employer.[110] This line of thinking seems similar to German law (though different from the English – political – view of industrial accidents as being a shared responsibility of both the employer and employee). Not surprisingly, therefore, the Dutch statutory insurance resembled greatly the German statute.

[107] E. Engelhard, *Regres* (Deventer: Kluwer, 2003), pp. 163ff; and 'Shifts of Work-Related Injury Compensation', pp. 28–32.

[108] The State inspectorate authority that granted pensions or benefits based on the Industrial Accidents Act was then entitled to collect these back from the liable party. For those purposes it was given an action for reimbursement. See *ibid.*, p. 164.

[109] E. Engelhard, 'Shifts of Work-Related Injury Compensation', nos. 6 and 33 (with references).

[110] *Ibid.*, no. 43.

The fact that this shift has not lasted was for a small part related to difficulties in case law regarding the question of what made an accident fall under the special protection of the insurance model. More fundamentally, in 1945 the so-called Van Rhijn Committee was formed by the Minister of Justice, to examine the options for forming a scheme of social insurance. This committee felt that public insurance would have to be carried by the public at large; to put it bluntly, the more collective the paying community the more certain the insurance would be. For this reason it was doubted whether the *risque professionnel* would still serve as the foundation for public insurance, and the committee also pointed at the benefits of not having to decide when and if the cause of the accident was in fact work. Nevertheless it decided *not* to extend the *risque professionnel* protection of the Industrial Accidents Act 1901 and 1921 to all injuries regardless of their cause. It feared this would cost too much and also hesitated to deprive employees of their special treatment. Towards the end of the fifties however, the more favourable position of victims whose injuries were caused at work received more criticism. The idea took hold that the State should guarantee a minimum living standard for all its citizens in all situations, as general as possible, based on the so-called *risque social*. This led to the (former) WAO of 1967 and other social security legislation. In addition to social security benefits the victim can obtain damages by civil liability law. In more recent years serious cuts in these benefits have been accompanied by a strong emphasis on the citizen's own personal responsibility. Arguably, in doing so the Government indirectly stimulates its citizens to claim damages.[111]

It seems difficult to identify the politicians behind the changes, or the particular bureaucrats that have been influential in the way that the regulatory system operated. For the development of liability without fault Paul Scholten (1875–1946) has played a significant role. In 1899 Scholten pointed in his dissertation to the fact that statutory provisions gave rise to liability in many instances based on other grounds than fault. The need for liability without fault was caused by the fact that many accidents could not be linked to any personal fault but were due to legal persons and their business processes. Therefore he also predicted that 'in the future' the legislature would have to expand those instances of no-fault liability

[111] *Ibid.*, no. 87.

with many more.[112] Further, in his opinion it would be up to the courts to establish rules for liability if – based on ethical beliefs and socio-economic relations – there were reasons to impose liability, even in the absence of fault. At this point the legislative proposal for the Industrial Accidents Act had already been made. Scholten thus also referred to this legislative proposal to argue that certain forms of responsibility based on other grounds than personal fault were already recognised. For him that was an extra argument to accept liability on other grounds than personal fault.

VII Conclusions

Let us briefly summarise the main points and then draw some overall conclusions from this. We started our survey by explaining why the requirement of unlawfulness of the defendant's behaviour was added to the 1838 CC, next to the requirement that this behaviour was due to his fault. To the late-nineteenth-century courts this implied that the defendant's behaviour needed to have violated a *written* law or a subjective right of the plaintiff; liability could not simply be based on mere negligence (fault). The Supreme Court felt that it was beyond its authority to change the law in this respect. At the same time this conservative approach strengthened the political views of its then president, who strongly adhered to the idea of free competition (not to be hindered by the risk of negligence liability). But after he retired, the growing number of calls to expand fault liability to cases of mere negligence, followed by sluggish legislative proposals, led a new chamber of Justices to revise the law. In the landmark case *Lindenbaum* v. *Cohen* the Court stretched the requirement of unlawfulness to include mere negligence.

With reference to this decision, politicians claimed that the 1838 CC was outdated, and voted for the recodification of the Civil Code. The ruling on fault liability, drafted by Professor Meijers, was based on existing case law: it not only included the traditional criteria for unlawfulness but also the third criterion as formulated in *Lindenbaum* v. *Cohen*: mere negligence. The first two were left to further interpretations by the courts, but the third criterion allowed courts more freedom in lawmaking, as it would be impossible to capture all negligent behaviour by written rules (although we have shown that in the legal reality, where judges, in part

[112] P. Scholten, 'Schadevergoeding buiten overeenkomst en onrechtmatige daad' Ph.D. thesis, Amsterdam (1899), p. 151.

led by academics, critically assess the law, this dichotomy between mere interpretations and 'free lawmaking' is not at all clear-cut). This process of 'free lawmaking' with regard to the question of when merely negligent behaviour is unlawful has led to a great number of cases that have been categorised and that each contain special part-rules by which this question in similar cases must be answered. Together with the fact that the other requirements of fault liability (fault and causality) are also typical judge-made law, this shows how the primacy of fault liability really is with the courts.

8

The impact of institutions and professions in Spain

ISABEL GONZÁLEZ PACANOWSKA AND
MARTIN GARCÍA-RIPOLL MONTIJANO

I Introduction

Spanish tort law is divided into four different jurisdictions, submitted to different material and procedural rules: civil, criminal, administrative and labour courts.[1] Therefore, on looking at the influence of legal institutions and professions on the development of fault liability since 1850, a brief outline of the creation of the different jurisdictions seems necessary.

The Spanish Supreme Court was set up by a Royal Decree of 24 March 1834.[2] At that time, its members were recruited among *abogados* (more or less, barristers and attorneys) and professors of law.[3]

The first general provisions on the organisation of the Spanish courts were those of the *Ley Provisional sobre Organización del Poder Judicial* (Organisation of the Judicial Power Provisional Act: 'provisional', although it was in force for more than a century) of 18 September 1870. It established for the first time the necessity of passing an exam (*oposición*) to become a judge. However, the qualifications to become a member of the Supreme Court were soon modified, and it was allowed from 1882 for professors of law with over 20 years' experience to be accepted as members

[1] For an overview see P. Salvador Coderch *et al.*, 'El Derecho español de daños hoy: Características diferenciales' in *Libro homenaje al Profesor M. Albaladejo García* (Murcia: Colegio Oficial de Registradores de la Propiedad y Mercantiles de España; Servicio de Publicaciones de la Universidad de Murcia, 2004), p. 4497.

[2] J. F. Lasso Gaite, *Crónica de la codificación española*, Vol. I: *Organización judicial* (Madrid: Ministerio de Justicia, 1998), p. 18; A. Agúndez, 'Antecedentes, principios básicos y proyección histórica de la Ley Orgánica del Poder Judicial de 1870' (1970) 305 *Información jurídica* 11.

[3] Lasso Gaite, *Crónica de la codificación española*, Vol. I, p. 34; M. Martínez Sospedra, 'El nacimiento del juez reclutado por oposición: El artículo 94 de la Constitución de 1869 y la LOPJ de 1870' (1995) 607 *Revista General de Derecho* 3314.

of the Court (art. 50 *Ley Adicional a la Orgánica del Poder Judicial* of 14 October 1882).

The Act established three kinds of courts: civil, criminal and administrative. The status of the last, however, was subject to changes, until it was definitively established by an Act of 5 April 1904.[4] Labour issues (that is, employment contract and, later on, social security problems) were, to start with, within the competence of the civil courts. Labour courts were finally set up by a Decree of 13 May 1938 (so during the Civil War) and the Act of 17 October 1940.[5]

It is important to bear in mind that each one of the aforementioned jurisdictions will follow and apply its own specific rules and precedent case law, not taking much notice of what is happening next door. Our attention will be focussed on changes in fault liability within civil law, as the civil division of the Supreme Court – notwithstanding the gradual creation of other specific jurisdictions – has traditionally ascertained its own competence on tort law matters over the period considered. Such contribution has been decisive for the present understanding of tort liability (Section I). Nevertheless, a concise summary of the way each of the other jurisdictions has evolved seems to be the best way to explain when and why different compensation schemes have been brought forth by the legislature, and, to a certain degree, how different grounds for recovery may be co-ordinated in the courts' practice (Section II).

[4] Artículo Adicional Primero. On the previous situation and the changes after this Act, see J. R. Fernández Torres, *Historia legal de la Jurisdicción contencioso-administrativa (1845–1998)* (Madrid: Iustel, 2007). The members of the new Administrative Chamber of the Supreme Court were the Administration's officers. The situation changed finally with the Administrative Jurisdiction Act (*Ley de la Jurisdicción Contencioso-Administrativa*) of 1956; the administrative courts were then composed of judges who had to pass an additional exam.

[5] Agúndez, 'Antecedentes, principios básicos y proyección histórica', 32; Lasso Gaite, *Crónica de la codificación española*, Vol. I, p. 214. In 1908 *Tribunales industriales* ('Industrial courts') were set up, with trade unionists and employers; their decisions could be appealed before the Civil courts. For a more detailed survey of the period, see M. Alonso Olea, C. Miñambres and R. Alonso García, *Derecho procesal del trabaj*, 13th edn (Madrid: Thomson–Civitas, 2005), pp. 43ff; and J. J. Generelo Lanaspa, 'La primera Jurisdicción Laboral: Los Tribunales industriales y su documentación (1908–1938)' in *La administración de justicia en la historia de España: Actas de las III Jornadas de Castilla-La Mancha sobre investigación en archivos, Guadalajara, 11–14 noviembre 1997* (Junta de Comunidades de Castilla-La Mancha, 1999), p. 1075.

II Civil law

A Legislative framework and judicial contribution to legal change

The Spanish Civil Code (1889, hereafter CC) provided the legal framework for tort law in arts. 1902–1910. The crucial rule is art. 1902, comprising the general clause of fault-based liability. These dispositions have undergone very few changes in the period under examination.[6] As shown below, legislators have preferred to enact specific statutes as an adequate response to social needs or economic development, introducing different kinds of compensation schemes.

Earlier decisions of the Supreme Court (Tribunal Supremo, hereafter TS) had justified the fault requirement in the name of historical tradition. It was described as an 'unquestionable legal principle admitted as such by Roman Law and by our national legislation (*Partida* 7.15.3) that (a person) who by his fault or negligence brings forth a damage is obliged to repair or compensate it'.[7] However, whilst standing on the fault requirement, courts have responded to social changes and economical development through what has been described as the 'objectifying' process. As to the standard of care, courts applied the contractual model of bonus pater familias, laid down in art. 1104 CC in 1894;[8] by 1922 it was declared that 'legitimate actions' could nevertheless be negligent,[9] and in 1930 the 'concepts of fault and negligence' were deemed to 'encompass such a wholesale or extensive range, that it is not possible to reduce or summarise their broad meaning into a closed set of rules'.[10] Complying with administrative security regulations turned out to be unsatisfactory; at first, it seems,

[6] Only arts. 1903 and 1904, devoted to rules on liability for actions of others, have been reformed, in 1991 (*Ley* 1/1991, of 7 January): first, as a result of the changes in liability of public bodies (see below, pp. 188–189); second, the old rule on liability of *maestros* for wrongdoings of *alumnos or aprendices* was transferred to the teaching institution or school itself (*centro docente*) for acts of minors whilst under their control, limiting eventual recovery actions against the teacher (only in case of intent or gross negligence). The new rule had long been demanded by teachers' unions and associations, and the Government had agreed with the unions to change the law, as required by 'social reality' and the 'daily flow of teaching activities' (*Preámbulo Ley* 1/1991).

[7] STS 12 May 1891, *Colección Legislativa: Jurisprudencia Civil* (hereinafter CLJC) (1891), no. 144.

[8] STS 14 December 1894, CLJC (1894), no. 134. An objective standard of care was thus introduced, that must also attend to the circumstances of 'persons, time and place' (art. 1104. 1 CC).

[9] STS 5 June 1922, CLJC (1922), no. 66.

[10] STS 20 December 1930, CLJC (1930), no. 131.

because evidence showed the poor performance of the defendant, despite official or public supervision: *formulary* fulfilment was not enough. By the second half of the twentieth century, however, lack of deterrent measures could be ascertained despite adherence to legal requirements, as 'damage itself is the best proof that sufficient care has not been exerted to avoid it'.[11] Furthermore, from 1942, the TS gave the assessment of *culpa* the character of *quaestio iuris*, rather than a question of fact, and thereby allowed itself wider space for quashing the trial court's verdict.[12]

Spanish legal writing has analysed in detail this process, highlighting the main arguments that – according to courts – supported what was at first described as 'modern theories' (STS 31 October 1931)[13] or a *desideratum* of 'modern law' (STS 14 May 1968[14]): the so-called *pro damnato* principle, creation of risk along with *cuius commoda eius incommoda*, or allusions to social solidarity or social justice. Up to the 1950s such legal reasoning was scarce, but once it had started it did not turn back. To some extent, one could mark the fields in which a rigorous standard starts to break through: damages caused by electronic or technical dangerous devices, road traffic and train accidents, and harmful substances;[15] or – rather timidly at first – prejudicial emissions.[16] Furthermore, notwithstanding the rather late emergence of medical liability[17] and product liability in Spain,[18] the Supreme Court has not minded applying ideas

11 See I. González Pacanowska, 'The Development of Traffic Liability in Spain' in W. Ernst (ed.), *The Development of Traffic Liability* (Cambridge: Cambridge University Press, 2010), p. 156.

12 S. Cavanillas Múgica, *La transformación de la responsabilidad civil en la jurisprudencia* (Pamplona: Aranzadi, 1987), p. 46.

13 *Repertorio Jurisprudencia Aranzadi* (hereafter *RJA*) 2218.

14 RJA 2699.

15 As in STS 30 June 1959 (RJA 2944), explosion and blaze of a film deposit.

16 SSTS 23 December 1952 (RJA 2673); 24 March 1953 (RJA 913). Looking back into the nineteenth century, however, responsibility for emissions, irrespective of negligence, had been granted applying the provisions of the Act of 6 July 1859 on mine exploitation, damage caused to the neighbouring land being the result not of *vis maior*, but '*voluntary acts*' performed by the defendant '*in his own utility and benefit*'. Compensation was due, on the authority of *Partidas*, because (a person) can do as he pleases on his own property, but only in a manner that does not cause damage to another ('pero develo fazer de manera que non faga daño, nin tuerto a otro' P.3, 32, 13): STS 9 April 1866 (CLJC (1866) no. 142).

17 See M. P. García Rubio and B. Trigo García, 'The Development of Medical Liability in Spain' in E. Hondius (ed.), *The Development of Medical Liability* (Cambridge: Cambridge University Press, 2010), p. 161.

18 See M. Martín-Casals and J. Solé Feliú, 'The Evolution of Product Liability in Spain' in S. Whittaker (ed.), *The Development of Product Liability* (Cambridge: Cambridge University Press, 2010), p. 234.

of 'responsibility for risk' to parents for damage caused by minors, or to employers, even if their activity did not seem to imply any danger at all.

Indeed, one of the problems that have raised wide interest has been parents' liability for damages caused by their children. Like many other issues, this one reached the Civil Chamber of the TS in the second half of the twentieth century. Courts have been rather harsh with parents in what has been described as a 'tribal' attitude;[19] we cannot report a single decision of this Chamber considering parents to have been faultless. The first important decision is of 29 December 1962,[20] in which the father (at the time the single guardian, as mothers were then only subsidiary guardians) pleaded he could not have avoided the damage caused by his son since he was at work at the moment of the accident. The court retorted that, if such defences were to be accepted, the outcome would be complete lack of paternal responsibility for damage brought about by children, but the main ground was still fault.[21] Things changed drastically after the decision of 17 June 1980[22]. The court, notwithstanding references to fault *in vigilando* and *in educando*, proclaimed for parents 'the insertion of an objective nuance in their liability that in practice is due to risk criteria'. This assertion was and is still constantly recalled, in spite of critics who refuse to consider having children a risky and harmful enterprise.[23]

From a general point of view, here it is important to stress that the whole 'objectifying' process has taken place with neither legislative change nor recourse to analogical application of strict-liability provisions, despite their presence in the Civil Code. The judicial 'revolution'[24] was achieved through what has been described as the 'expansion of fault'.[25] The provisions on strict liability within the Code itself, notwithstanding a sometimes broad interpretation of their scope, or other statutes enacted after

[19] M. García-Ripoll, 'La concepción tribal de la responsabilidad civil en la Ley Penal del Menor' in *Estudios jurídicos en homenaje al Profesor Luis Díez-Picazo*, 4 vols., Vol. II (Madrid: Civitas, 2003), p. 1929.

[20] CLJC (1962), no. 974.

[21] For instance, STS 15 February 1975 (RJA 566); and STS 14 April 1977 (RJA 1654).

[22] RJA 2409.

[23] The Supreme Court does not usually tell us the age of the minor, but in STS 8 March 2002 (RJA 1912) the parents alleged in vain that their son was 17 years, 7 months and 22 days old when the injury happened. Playing ball in a public park, he accidentally hit a 16-year-old girl sitting on a bench, who thereby lost vision almost completely; his parents were ordered to pay €60,000.

[24] See F. Pantaleón in C. Paz-Ares, L. Díez-Picazo, R. Bercovitz and P. Salvador (eds.), *Comentario del Código Civil*, 2 vols., Vol. II (Madrid: Ministerio de Justicia, 1991), p. 1995.

[25] See Cavanillas Múgica, *La transformación*, pp. 46ff.

the second half of the twentieth century, were not extended by analogy to events other than those expressly included. At the most, new statute has been mixed as yet another ingredient in providing an objective standard for fault.[26] On the whole it could be said that judges have changed the law without having to change the rule. In doing so, they are deemed to have taken into account the new *realidad social,* adapting the existing legal rules in order to achieve 'justice'.[27] Negligence, indeed, has proved to be a very elastic concept, apt to justify almost any decision. Deep down, it is a problem of preventative measures to avoid the harm, and our judges have raised the level of foresight, but the concept remains the same. The outcome, nonetheless, is not very satisfying from a technical point of view. Scholars, despite admitting that the task falls not only on courts, criticise the *imprecisión* of judicial reasoning in the name of juridical security.[28] As Luis Díez Picazo writes, the *jurisprudencia* on tort law appears to be considerably blurred, making it impossible to define the leading thread in order to predict future decisions. Courts seem intuitively to follow justice criteria, difficult to explain as technical legal arguments.[29]

B *Influential individuals within the judiciary*

Not infrequently, the TS has proclaimed its own 'objectifying' thesis to be in harmony with 'modern' or advanced 'scientific doctrines', but hardly ever mentions any author in particular.[30] Civil law treatises of the second half of the nineteenth century dedicated but a few lines to *cuasidelitos*, briefly explaining the provisions of the Criminal Code on civil liability derived from crime.[31] The most important one, right before the Spanish

[26] González Pacanowska, 'The Development of Traffic Liability in Spain', pp. 180ff.

[27] Cavanillas Múgica, *La transformación*, p. 127.

[28] *Ibid.*, pp. 127ff.

[29] L. Díez Picazo, *Derecho de daños* (Madrid: Civitas, 1999), p. 37.

[30] See Cavanillas Múgica, *La transformación*, p. 30.

[31] See J. Sánchez Molina Blanco, *El Derecho Civil Español en forma de Código* (Madrid: Imprenta J. L. Vizcaíno–Imprenta Manuel Minuesa, 1871), p. 504 ; S. Herrero, *El Código civil Español* (Valladolid: Imprenta y librería Nacional y Extranjera de los Hijos de Rodríguez, 1872), pp. 588ff.; C. Fernández Elías, *Novísimo tratado histórico filosófico del Derecho Civil español* (Madrid: Librería de Leocadio López, 1873), p. 662; E. Bravo, *Compilación del Derecho Civil vigente en España*, 4 vols., Vol. IV (Madrid: Establecimiento tipográfico de P. Nuñez, 1885), pp. 155ff.; J. A. Elías, *Derecho civil general y foral de España*, 3 vols., Vol. II.3, 2nd edn (Madrid–Barcelona: Victorino Suarez, 1884), pp. 323ff. Critical, however, was S. Del Viso, *Lecciones elementales de Derecho Civil*, 3 vols., Vol. III: *De las obligaciones*, 5th edn (Valencia: Imprenta y librería de Ramón Ortega, 1884), p. 512. J. Escriche seems to be the only exception: *Elementos del*

Civil Code was enacted, had seven volumes, but only one page on tort, because 'liability in tort is a question of criminal law rather than one of civil law'.[32] The new provisions of the Civil Code did not seem to excite at first much interest.[33] Apparently, as Federico de Castro has explained, civil lawyers felt as if in a foreign land; Roman law training seems to have lessened their agility and they failed to assimilate the basic principles latent in the new provisions that, however, derive from Natural Law and had been included in the Criminal Code.[34]

In fact, it was not until 1935 that extensive treatment was given in the *Anotaciones* written by Pérez González y Alguer, to the Spanish translation of the German treatise by Ludwig Enneccerus, Theodor Kipp and Martin Wolff.[35] The first monograph, by A. Borrell Maciá, was to follow seven years later.[36] The first three decades of the twentieth century did, however, witness a quite ample doctrinal movement explaining the ideas of 'objective liability', under the strong influence of French, Italian and

Derecho Patrio, 2nd edn (Madrid: Librería de la Sra. Viuda de Calleja e Hijos, 1840), pp. 198 ff.; for more detail see *Diccionario razonado de legislación y jurisprudencia*, 2 vols., Vol. II.3 (Madrid: Imprenta de E. Cuesta, 1874, 1875).

[32] B. Gutierrez Fernández, *Códigos o estudios fundamentales sobre el Derecho Civil español*, 5 vols., Vol. V (Madrid: Librería de Sánchez, 1869), p. 633.

[33] Despite its five volumes, F. Sánchez Román, *Estudios de Derecho Civil*, 5 vols., Vol. IV, 2nd edn (Madrid: Est. Tipográfico sucesores de Rivadeneyra, 1899), p. 1011. Most writers recall García Goyena's words on the 1851 draft – the present rules are based on equity – underlining the difficulty of listing the events of *culpa o negligencia*, which are apt to trigger liability; the task requires taking into account every surrounding circumstance. See for instance L. Bonel y Sánchez, *Código Civil Español*, 4 vols., Vol. IV (Barcelona: A. López Robert, 1891), p. 894. According to J. Robles Pozo, *El Código Civil y su Jurisprudencia*, 2 vols., Vol. II (Madrid: Imprenta de la Revista de Legislación, 1896), p. 896, the CC has enacted what has been known as *cuasidelitos* into clear and precise rules that do not require further explanation, as their justification is well known and, even if any doubt arises, the Supreme Court will provide clarity on the matter.

[34] F. de Castro, 'La indemnización por causa de muerte (Estudio en torno a la jurisprudencia del Tribunal Supremo)' (1956) 9 *Anuario de Derecho Civil* 475.

[35] B. Pérez González and J. Alguer, *Anotaciones* to L. Enneccerus, T. Kipp and M. Wolff, *Tratado de Derecho Civil*, 9 vols., Vol. II.1–2 (Barcelona: Bosch, 1935).

[36] A. Borrell Macía, *Responsabilidades derivadas de culpa extracontractual civil* (Barcelona: Bosch, 1942). An earlier book on traffic accidents, written by and for practitioners – E. Colom and F. Marimom, *Compendio jurídico del accidente de automóvil*, 2 vols. (Barcelona: Librería Bosch, 1933) – supplies a neat outline of French, Swiss, German and British law, as well as information on what the authors considered to be 'a few yankee exaggerations' (p. 63). However, they see no fissure in the reign of negligence in Spanish accident law, despite their awareness that the extensive regulations on road traffic would favour some compensation within criminal proceedings, as any infringement of such regulations would be tantamount to a criminal offence.

German authority.[37] Strict liability, at least for risky or potentially harmful activities, was considered to be progressive and desirable in order to keep up with 'advanced theories', and indispensable for a fair treatment of innocent accident victims of cars or trains used by others in their own interest. The so-called 'professional risk' and strict liability rule laid out for work accidents from 1900 was a beacon to lead the way. Drawbacks and disadvantages, or diffident attitudes, were argued away and appeals made to confidence: 'there are but two things in life that cause alarm, love and new ideas; maybe because the consequences of either escape our foreseeability'.[38] Textbooks of the same period were also giving some notice to this issue, but perhaps only Calixto Valverde seems to have firmly proposed leaving behind interpretations in collision with *países cultos*, urging a socialisation of responsibility and loss spread through compulsory insurance.[39]

Of course, quite a number of academics reached the Supreme Court in this period. One of them was Felipe Clemente de Diego (1866–1945), Professor of Roman Law at the University of Santiago de Compostela (1897), who moved to the University of Madrid in 1906 as a professor of private law. In 1939 (right after the Civil War) he became president of the Supreme Court until his death.[40] His three-volume treatise on civil law[41] reveals a wide knowledge of Continental law (including Germany and Austria). Unfortunately, as was then still usual, not much attention was given to fault liability rules: just 6 pages out of 1706.

As far as the evolution of tort law is concerned, perhaps the most prominent individual was José Castán Tobeñas (1889–1969),[42] who in 1918 had become professor of private law at the University of Murcia. From 1922 onwards he published a treatise (10 volumes) on civil law, perhaps the

[37] Indeed, nearly all tort law papers of the time dwelt on the topic, most of them proposing strict liability for traffic accidents (González Pacanowska, 'The Development of Traffic Liability in Spain', p. 177).

[38] A. Ossorio Gallardo, 'El hecho, generador de obligaciones (Contribución al estudio de la responsabilidad sin culpa)' (1934) 164 *Revista General de Legislación y Jurisprudencia* 282.

[39] C. Valverde Valverde, *Tratado de Derecho Civil Español*, 5 vols., Vol. III, 4th edn (Valladolid: Talleres tipográficos Cuesta, 1937), pp. 783ff., 809, 810.

[40] See D. Espín Cánovas, *Don Felipe Clemente De Diego en la ciencia y la aplicación del Derecho* (Madrid: Centro de Estudios Registrales, 2000).

[41] F. Clemente de Diego, *Instituciones de Derecho civil español* (Madrid: Imprenta de Juan Pueyo, 1929, 1930, 1932).

[42] A. Serrano González, *Un día en la vida de José Castán Tobeñas* (Valencia: Tirant lo Blanch, 2001); G. García Cantero, *El maestro Castán* (Madrid: Centro de Estudios Registrales, 1998).

most popular one for decades; it was widely used by professionals, law students or those preparing for exams to become judges, public notaries and so on. It was known simply as *el Castán*. In 1933 he had delivered a lecture under the title 'Towards a New Civil Law', proposing a cautious approach to 'liability without fault', to be accepted in the name of equity in 'exceptional cases, in which the inequality of those involved would produce notorious injustice, were damage caused without fault not to be compensated'.[43]

José Castán was appointed to the Supreme Court in 1933 and in 1945 became its president until 1967. One of Castán's main aims was to update our legal culture by means of implementing new juridical theories received from other European countries considered as a model (especially France, Italy and Germany). It has even been said that 'it was not unusual for the decisions of the Supreme Court ... to follow *verbatim* Castán's handbook'.[44]

One of the most important decisions in the field of damage compensation was issued on the 12 February 1944,[45] with Castán as *ponente* (that is, the judge who writes the project of decision to be discussed among the members of the Court). A company had got a licence to extract sand from a beach, doing so in such large quantities that a close building of another company suffered extensive damage after a storm. The latter company sued the former for damages in tort, and the defendant asserted that it had been authorised to extract the sand. The Supreme Court decided that the defendant had exercised its right correctly from a external point of view, but not according to the *social limits* that any right has; it was a case of *abuso de derecho* (abuse in the exercise of the use of a legal right). This theory had been imported from France, was soon accepted by all courts in Spain, and was even to be included in the Civil Code in 1974 (art. 7.2). It is worth noting that abuse of rights allowed quasi-objective liability for private nuisance.[46] And still nowadays, art. 7.2 CC appears in courts' decisions as one of the legal bases in emission suits, alongside art. 1908 CC, interpreted, in turn, as a source of strict liability.

43 J. Castán Tobeñas, *Hacia un nuevo Derecho Civil* (Madrid: Reus, 1933), p. 121.

44 C. Petit, 'Por una arqueología de la Civilística española' (1996) 49 *Anuario de Derecho Civil* 1447.

45 CLJC (1944), no. 43, 344ff.

46 See A. Masferrer, 'Relations between Neighbours in Spanish Law' in J. Gordley (ed.), *The Development of Liability between Neighbours* (Cambridge: Cambridge University Press, 2010), p. 173.

In a second outstanding decision – 10 July 1943 – Castán was not the *ponente* but was one of the members of the Civil Chamber who signed it. This decision is usually quoted as being the first one that introduced the reversal of the burden of proof of fault (in this case, a traffic accident).[47]

Another influential judge, this one especially in the field of torts, was Jaime Santos Briz, not an academic, but appointed to the Supreme Court as a promotion in his professional activity as judge. In 1963, at nearly the beginning of his career, he wrote a book on tort: *Derecho de daños* (*Damages Law*).[48] Later on he wrote *La responsabilidad civil: Derecho sustantivo y procesal* (*Tort Law: Civil and Procedural Aspects*), which has reached seven editions (the last in 1993[49]), a considerable amount in Spanish legal literature.

Santos Briz's works were deeply influenced by German scholarship.[50] One of the ideas he followed was the requisite of unlawfulness (*ilicitud* or *antijuridicidad* in Spanish; *Rechtswidrigkeit* in German) to sue successfully in tort. The first decisions reflecting such views – 10 October 1968[51] and 25 October 1968[52] – had Bonet Ramón as *ponente*, well acquainted with the subject, having written the foreword for Santos Briz's first book. Later on, Santos Briz, himself as *ponente*, was to explain in detail the debated requisite in STS 17 March 1981,[53] followed by some other decisions.

Finally we will highlight two contemporary cases. One is Vicente Luis Montés Penadés, former professor of private law at the University of Valencia, and Antonio Salas Carceller, career judge. Both were appointed to the Civil Chamber of the Supreme Court at the beginning of the twenty-first century. In the last two decades part of Spanish scholarship has accepted as a new requisite of liability in torts what is called *imputación objetiva* (in German *objektive Zurechnung*, 'objective imputation', similar to the proximate cause of the common law jurisdictions). This theory developed among German criminal law scholars in the early seventies. The Criminal Chamber of the Supreme Court had incorporated the idea since 1981. Some Spanish tort law scholars have transferred this theory to

[47] RJA 856. For further details, see González Pacanowska, 'The Development of Traffic Liability in Spain', pp. 175–176.

[48] J. Santos Briz, *Derecho de daños* (Madrid: Edersa, 1963). The preface was written by Francisco Bonet Ramón (†2002), professor of law and member of the Supreme Court, also with a deep knowledge of tort law.

[49] J. Santos Briz, *La responsabilidad civil: Derecho sustantivo y procesal*, 2 vols., 7th edn (Madrid: Montecorvo, 1993).

[50] In fact, he translated one edition of the *Schuldrecht* of the German jurist Karl Larenz; J. Santos Briz, *Derecho de obligaciones*, 2 vols. (Madrid: Edersa, 1958, 1959).

[51] RJA 4271. [52] *Ibid.* 4976. [53] *Ibid.* 1009.

the field of torts. Montés Penadés had previously written a paper on this topic.[54] Salas Carceller, on the other hand, was a judge at the *Audiencia Provincial* (Court of Appeal) of Murcia, deciding on private and criminal cases. When either of them has been *ponente* in a tort law case, the objective imputation issue usually appears.[55] To some extent, it seems, working in different jurisdictions can influence judges' criteria.[56]

C *Legislative change*

Not until the second half of the twentieth century did the legislature develop specific rules. The forces or influences behind a new statute can be usually just supposed.

A first period relates to legislation of the dictatorship period (1939–1975). Deviations from the general fault principles of the Civil Code nearly always pursued strict liability for dangerous activities or risks deriving from the development of industry, alongside compulsory insurance and compensation caps. These new statutes have rarely been preceded by extensive doctrinal debate or specific law reform bodies; neither are they particularly shaped by the views of the judiciary; though not infrequently – at least in the field of traffic accidents – legislative intervention attempted to relieve judicial uncertainty. Immediate inducement and substantive inspiration have been varied, which a brief account may enlighten.

Leaving aside the regulation of work accidents,[57] the first complementary rules were those of the Air Navigation Act of 1960, dealing with liability in tort (Chapter 13, arts. 120–125) and compulsory insurance (Chapter 14) in case of damage suffered by passengers, or ruined air-transported goods, as well as damage caused to things and persons on land in case of an air-crash, or pieces detached or thrown from the plane. Liability has its objective base in the accident or damage, and will take place in any case, even in the occurrence of an act of God, and even when the carrier or his employees acted with due diligence (art. 120). The Act sets up limits to

[54] V. L. Montés Penadés, 'Causalidad, imputación objetiva y culpa en la "concurrencia de culpas"' in *Estudios jurídicos en homenaje al profesor Luis Díez-Picazo*, 4 vols., Vol. II (Madrid: Thomson–Civitas, 2003), p. 2591.

[55] For instance, lately STS 17 April 2007 (RJA 2322); STS 9 November 2005 (RJA 7721).

[56] There is also a third judge recently appointed to the Supreme Court, who was professor of law, and has written a book about torts: E. Roca i Trías, *Derecho de daños: Textos y materiales*, 7th edn (Valencia: Tirant lo Blanch, 2007).

[57] See Section III.C, pp. 189–195.

the damages to be paid by the air company, excepting gross negligence or intent.[58] If we read the provisions carefully, we see that outside the insurance cover the tortfeasor is better off than under the general provisions of the Civil Code, for he is not liable for simple negligence. In any case, the statute was triggered by international conventions, and seems to have closely followed Italian legislation.[59]

The second important change was the Road Traffic Act of 24 December 1962. Up to that moment, courts had had to apply the general provisions of the Civil Code, based on the idea of negligence. Victims, however, usually recovered within criminal proceedings, as traffic accidents could easily be tantamount to a criminal offence of sorts. In addition, injuries suffered by public transport passengers had been provided for, since 1928, by means of compulsory first-party insurance, albeit within rather low limits.[60] Academics had been advocating strict liability and compulsory insurance, finding clear inspiration not only in foreign literature and international proposals but in the legislation on work accidents too, supplying thereby resources from which the legislator would profit. Judges, on the other hand, had relieved the victim of the burden of proof since 1943 and seemed to be less inclined to admit the defence of lack of fault over the following years. The tort law rules of the Act proposal were debated at length, but mostly for technical reasons; as traffic damage spread through all social classes, the yearning for legislative intervention was acutely felt and its arrival was warmly welcomed.[61] The Act not only departed from the traditional rules, but at the same time

[58] The amounts have been updated by the Real Decreto 37/2001, de 19 de enero, por el que se actualiza la cuantía de las indemnizaciones por daños previstas en la Ley 48/1960, de 21 de julio, de Navegación Aérea. About the origin of these limits in the Admiralty Law and its sense nowadays, see E. Mapelli López, 'Historia de la limitación de responsabilidad en el transporte aéreo' in *Estudios jurídicos en homenaje al profesor Luis Díez-Picazo*, Vol. II, p. 2407.

[59] The *Ley de Bases del Código de Navegación Aérea* (Foundations of the Code of Air Navigation Act; a Foundations Act is an authorisation by Parliament to the Government to enact a statute according to the Foundations) was passed in 1947, but was only developed by the 1960 Act. The *Ley de Bases* followed the pattern of the Convention on Damage Caused by Foreign Aircraft to Third Parties on the Surface, Rome 1933 (amended in 1952) and the Italian Codice de la Navegazione from 1942. See E. Casado Iglesias, *La responsabilidad por daños a terceros en la navegación aérea* (Salamanca: Universidad de Salamanca, 1965), p. 75; Y. B. Bustos Moreno, *La responsabilidad civil en la navegación aérea: Los daños a terceros* (Madrid: Dykinson, 2003), pp. 69–70.

[60] See I. González Pacanowska, 'The Development of Traffic Liability in Spain', pp. 162ff.

[61] The discussion is summarised by F. Reglero Campos, *Accidentes de circulación: Responsabilidad Civil y seguro* (Cizur Menor: Thomson–Aranzadi, 2004).

provoked enormous interest in all those involved – practitioners, insurers and judges – to the extent that specific monographs and papers on traffic liability arrived from all sources and easily outnumbered other tort law issues over the next few years. The basic pattern laid down for traffic – compulsory insurance and defences limited to sole fault of the victim and *vis maior* external to the car itself – will be picked up in other fields.[62]

The next significant step was the Nuclear Energy Act of 1964, which was triggered by the project of the Spanish Government to construct nuclear power stations; in fact, building work on the first one – 'José Cabrera' (also known as 'Zurita') – started in 1965.[63] Article 45 states that 'The company responsible for a nuclear power station or any other facility that works with radioactive materials or that has machines that can produce ionising radiation will be liable for any nuclear damages. This liability will be strict [*objetiva*] and limited to the amount of money expressed in this Act.' Should the damage exceed this limit, 'the State will provide the legal means to cover the difference' (art. 51).

In 1970 a new *Ley de Caza* (Hunting Act) was passed. There had been two previous Hunting Acts, one of 10 January 1879, and the other of 16 May 1902. Neither of them had special provisions on tort law. By contrast, the Act of 1970 regulated for the first time the hunter's liability, following the pattern of the Road Traffic Act;[64] it is worth noting this aspect, for scholarship had not claimed before a shift of the previous situation – that is, the general rules of the Civil Code. The exemptions of liability were the same as those set up in the Road Traffic Act, and the limits identical as well.[65]

[62] Subsequent alterations have usually been aimed at settling disputed points in doctrinal work and contradictory court decisions. Others have been directly triggered by European Directives. See González Pacanowska, 'The Development of Traffic Liability in Spain', pp. 181ff.

[63] Nowadays there are six nuclear power stations in Spain, with eight reactors (source: Dirección General de Política Energética y Minas, www.mityc.es/Nuclear/Seccion/Centrales/Espana/). On the origins of the Spanish dictatorship's interest in nuclear reactors, see F. X. Barca Salom, 'La política nuclear espanyola: El caso del reactor nuclear Argos' (2000) 4 *Quaderns d'historia de l'enginyeria* 12. Papers on tort liability in this area are scarce.

[64] M. Fernández Martín-Granizo, 'La deuda legal indemnizatoria en la vigente Ley de Caza' (1973) 26 *Anuario de Derecho Civil* 757.

[65] Following the Spanish Constitution the power on this matter was partly transferred to the autonomous regions (art. 148.1.11ª), which has produced a splitting of regulation, as each autonomous region has its own norms on the topic. Anyway, it seems that the

Since 1978, democracy has brought forth yet another set of innovations, of which three will be examined here, as illustrations of different factors that have spurred legislative choices.

The 1978 Spanish Constitution, within the fundamental rights, recognised the right to honour, privacy and image (art. 18.1), whilst simultaneously protecting freedom of speech and freedom of the press (art. 20.1). Despite the Constitution being directly binding on courts in these matters, the *Ley Orgánica de Protección Civil del Derecho al Honor, a la Intimidad Personal y Familiar y a la Propia Imagen* (5 May 1982) was to be the first Act in Spanish history on this topic. The draft was presented to Parliament as early as 19 December 1979,[66] as press freedom, after a dictatorship, was bound to create friction with the rights of the individual. Very little academic work had been done in the past, so – with some exaggeration – it has been described as 'a very poor Act', with the accusation that 'there was not enough study in its preparation'.[67] One of the most debated novelties pertains not so much to the meticulous description of 'unlawful intrusions', but to the ensuing damage and remedies. Pursuant to art. 9.3, in case of infringement damage is 'presumed', and is to be assessed taking into account the particular circumstances and type of harm, and the benefit to the tortfeasor. Thus, it seems to have introduced, in this field at least, punitive damages, or perhaps a remedy for unjust enrichment (in fact, the Act has been modified in 2010, now explicitly including the unjust enrichment as a remedy along with the damage in tort).

Another statutory regulation worth noting concerns product liability in the *Ley General para la Defensa de los Consumidores y Usuarios* (Consumer Protection Act) of 1984. In 1981 rapeseed (*colza*) oil unfit for human consumption had been sold as cooking oil, poisoning hundreds of people who died or were seriously injured: more than 30,000 were affected. This caused a social shock, one of its aftermaths being the said Act, introducing specific rules for defective products: a strict liability regime for some cases, negligence with a shift of the burden of proof in others. Supreme Court decisions resorting to such rules did not appear until 1993. The so-called '*Colza*-judgments', on the other hand, ensued from criminal courts (in 1992 and 1997), having little impact on subsequent

provisions about tort law remain within the competence of the State. See, for instance, the Region of Murcia's *Ley de Caza y Pesca Fluvial* of 10 December 2003.

66 *Boletin Oficial de las Cortes Generales, Congreso de los Diputados*, I Legislatura, Series A, no. 104–1, pp. 637ff.

67 P. Salvador Coderch *et al.*, *¿Qué es difamar? Libelo contra la Ley del Libelo* (Madrid: Civitas, 1987), p. 19.

case law. After Spain became a member of the European Union, the scope of the 1984 Act was to be very much limited by the 1994 Product Liability Act's implementation of the European Directive, despite 1984 Act's granting consumers a higher level of protection.[68] The strict liability rule of the 1984 Act could still have played an important role for private 'health care services', but Spanish courts, with a few exceptions, have been reluctant to abandon the negligence rule.[69]

Finally, there has been one important change, perhaps the clearest example of the influence of pressure groups – in this case, the insurance lobby – on the legislator, despite not implying anything more than a minor alteration of the basic tort rules, as the main worry was damage assessment: the binding cap system for personal injuries resulting from road traffic accidents, introduced in 1995.[70] Its application is usually confined to traffic issues, though sometimes judges will use it as a frame of reference when deciding in other areas. Some of the very reasons put forth to support it have found an echo among opinions proposing a similar measure for medical liability, basically for the same reason: Spanish courts usually grant global lump sums, without bothering to detail exactly how the different damages are quantified, with wide differences in similar circumstances. Furthermore, they tend to use the umbrella of 'moral damage' to allow the recovery of uncertain or unproven material damage.

III Legislative changes in other branches of the law

A *Tort law in the Criminal Code*

The first tort law provisions in modern times appeared in the Criminal Code of 1848.[71] This requires brief explanation. The French Code of Criminal Procedure (*Code d'Instruction Criminelle*), of 1808, stated in its art. 1, §2, that 'The action in tort deriving from damage caused by a crime or misdemeanour can be sued by all who have suffered this damage.'

[68] For a detailed analysis, see M. Martín Casals and J. Solé Feliu, 'The Evolution of Product Liability', pp. 246, 249, 251ff. The 1994 Act implemented the European Directive 85/374/EEC.

[69] See García Rubio and Trigo García, 'The Development of Medical Liability in Spain', pp. 170, 176. The 1984 Act has been replaced by the *Texto Refundido de la Ley General para la Defensa de los Consumidores y Usuarios y otras leyes complementarias* of 16 November 2007.

[70] See I. González Pacanowska, 'The Development of Traffic Liability in Spain', p. 188.

[71] The first Spanish Criminal Code is from 1822, but it was in force for just a few years, being soon repealed. Besides, it had no rules about tort law.

Shortly after, the French Criminal Code of 1810 established in its art. 51 that 'When restitution should take place, the offender can be likewise condemned to pay the damage to the injured party.' These norms, which could take aback lawyers of other jurisdictions, acted upon the French legislation of the *Ancien Régime*.[72]

The process of codification in Spain followed the French pattern in this issue, but with some specialities, the main one being that the Spanish legislator decided to include specific tort law provisions in the Criminal Code. Scholars usually consider that the reason for this was that criminal codification was the first one to be enacted (the Civil Code is from 1889).[73] But this conclusion is doubtful.

The Civil Code draft of 1836 already stated (art. 1855) that 'Crimes, i.e. actions forbidden by the law that cause harm to a person, impose on the offender the obligation to make good such harm … These obligations are treated more specifically in the Criminal Code.' On the other hand, the draft (art. 1856) also contained a provision on damage not flowing from crime. At this moment the drafter had in mind that both Codes, Criminal and Civil, were to be passed by Parliament more or less at the same time.[74]

The General Commission of Codification was set up in 1843.[75] Soon after, the works of the criminal section commenced. The Criminal Code drafter accepted not only the idea of admitting tort law actions within the criminal procedure, but also the creation of specific provisions. The model was the Brazilian Criminal Code of 1830.[76]

[72] *Ordonnance Criminelle* of 1670 and other previous statutes. See A. Esmein, *Histoire de la procédure criminelle en France* (Frankfurt am Main: Sauer & Auvermann, 1969, repr. of the Paris edition of 1882), p. 111; J. P. Alline, 'Les victimes: Des oubliées de l'histoire du droit?' in Association Française pour l'Histoire de la Justice, *La cour d'assises: Bilan d'un héritage démocratique* (Paris: La Documentation Française, 2001), p. 247.

[73] For instance, M. Yzquierdo Tolsada, *Sistema de responsabilidad civil, contractual y extracontractual* (Madrid: Dykinson, 2001), p. 58.

[74] The Criminal Code is of 1848 and the most important Project of Civil Code is of 1851, which was unsuccessful for reasons that have nothing to do with the problem we are dealing with here.

[75] Lasso Gaite, *Crónica de la Codificación española: Codificación civil*, Vol. I, p. 152.

[76] The Spanish authors used a French translation made by V. Foucher (trans.), *Code Criminel de l'empire du Brésil* (Paris: L'Imprimerie Royal, 1834). The Brazilian Code was a reference not only in this matter, but also in many others concerning criminal questions, strictly speaking. The chief author of the Brazilian Criminal Code was Bernardo Pereira de Vasconcelos (1795–1850). Of course, he followed the patterns of the European codifications of the moment. See E. Magalhães Noronha, *Direito penal*, 4 vols., Vol. I, 19th edn (São Paulo: Saraiva, 1981), p. 66; and B. Bravo Lira, 'Bicentenario del Código Penal de Austria: Su proyección desde el Danubio a Filipinas' (2004) 26 *Revista de estudios histórico-jurídicos* 115.

The Spanish Criminal Code of 1848, therefore, adopted some of the principles inspiring the Brazilian norms. Article 15 stated that 'Any person who is criminally liable is also liable in tort' (if, of course, the offender has caused any damage). Legal writers, at the same time members of the Law Commission that prepared the Criminal Code, described the new section on 'civil' compensation to be most advantageous in securing adequate recovery.[77]

For this reason, it seems, a variety of rules were enacted with the purpose of stating who, in a subsidiary but vicarious manner, could be the target of a tort action within criminal proceedings. Persons not criminally responsible – such as minors or lunatics – would nevertheless have to pay damages (art. 16). This obligation might fall primarily on the wrongdoer himself or subsidiarily on a parent or legal guardian. Damage caused to another's property to avoid a greater evil (what is nowadays called defence of necessity) had to be compensated in the same proportion that it had brought benefit to the owner. Actually the drafter of the Criminal Code bore in mind two cases of Roman law: (a) a house is pulled down to avoid the spread of a conflagration (the owners of the neighbouring houses are benefited; D. 9.2.49.1; D. 43.24.7.4; D. 47.9.3.7); (b) the general average in Admiralty law (the owners of the saved cargo are benefited; D. 14.2).[78] Furthermore, damages could be recovered from the holders of hotels, inns and taverns for crimes committed on their premises, and employers were held vicariously liable for the acts of their employees (arts. 17 and 18).

Finally, art. 121 stated that co-authors of a crime were to be jointly and severally liable in tort (against the *ius commune*'s classic rule, in which there was only several liability, i.e. each one was liable for the share established by the court; D. 9.2.30.4). Nonetheless, the accomplices, if there were any, had their own several share in the liability, as well as the accessories to the crime. Liability was several and joint among the members of each group. Hence, each group was subsidiarily liable for the other group's share.

The 1848 Criminal Code was amended in 1850, and replaced by other Criminal Codes (1870, 1928, 1932, 1944, 1963, 1973). All of them (except that of 1928) maintained the structure of the former, and the tort law

[77] See J. De Castro y Orozco and M. Ortiz de Zúñiga, *Código Penal Explicado*, 3 vols., Vol. I (Granada: Manuel Sanz, 1848), p. 233.

[78] See M. García-Ripoll, *Ilicitud, culpa, y estado de necesidad (Un estudio de responsabilidad extracontractual en los Códigos Penal y Civil)* (Madrid: Dykinson, 2006), pp. 16ff.

regulation was basically the same.[79] The situation changed only with the Code of 1995, today still in force. The tort law rules were modified just in certain details, which are not worth explaining here. Some of them took account of new problems, like the subsidiary liability of the owner of a car for the damages caused by anyone who drives it with his or her permission (art. 120.5.º).

The existing rules of the Criminal Code would lead art. 1092 of the 1889 Civil Code to state that 'Civil obligations arising either from crime or misdemeanour fall under the provisions of the Criminal Code.' This is also the reason why art. 1902 CC, the keystone of fault liability, refers exclusively to damage caused by negligence, not mentioning intentionality (*dolo*); the drafters probably considered that all damage caused on purpose was either a crime or a misdemeanour.

Having two different groups of provisions about the same matter brings about several drawbacks. Owing to diverging rules, the result of the suit may be different depending on which division of the Supreme Court (the civil or the criminal one) decides the matter. For instance, the limitation period in which the plaintiff can sue the tortfeasor is one year according to the Civil Code (art. 1968), but for the criminal division of the Supreme Court this period is 15 years. Such a circumstance can produce situations like this: the action for crime has begun more than a year after the crime was committed; the victim can still recover the damage; suddenly, the defendant dies, so that the criminal trial has to finish. Conclusion: the plaintiff has lost his or her right to recover the damage.

This double regulation has been severely criticised by Civil law scholars, but in vain. The 1990 draft of the current Criminal Code decided not to include any specific provisions on liability derived from crime, although the criminal courts were still to be considered competent to decide on the matter within criminal proceedings. However, important factions of the criminal judges expressed their fear that they would lose said competence, which was not exactly true, because it is granted by the Criminal Procedure Code (*Ley de Enjuiciamiento Criminal*), and nobody pretended to change that situation. Anyway, the criminal judges won the battle, and the Project of Criminal Code of 1992 included again tort law provisions, which finally are part of the present Code of 1995.[80]

[79] It is worth noting that the Code of 1973 considered for the first time recovery for pain and suffering (art. 104).

[80] At great length about this problem, see M. Yzquierdo Tolsada, 'La responsabilidad civil en los últimos proyectos de Código penal (en especial, el de 1994): Más de lo mismo' (1995) 6 *Iniuria* 37.

One specific question concerning the Criminal Code illustrates how it plays a substantial role in the basis of the Spanish tort law system: the liability of minors and mentally ill. The tradition of the Continental law was that these persons were not liable either in crime or in tort (D. 9.2.5.2 Ulpian ad Ed.; in the same sense the Spanish tradition reflected in *Partida* 7.1.9). Nevertheless, as already said, on the one hand the successive Criminal Codes have considered these persons liable in tort. On the other hand the Civil Code does not say a word about this matter, save to establish the liability of parents and guardians if they were at fault (art. 1903). The question is whether minors or the mentally ill are liable when the provisions of the Civil Code are on stage.[81]

Scholars are sharply divided. Some of them deem simply that the argument of analogy is to be applied in this case. Therefore, minors and the mentally ill are always subsidiarily liable, if there are no parents or guardians, or they have behaved without any fault, or are insolvent.[82] For other authors there can be no liability of very young children or insane wrongdoers because they are not capable of fault and the provisions of the Criminal Code are deemed to be exceptional as to this matter.[83] In addition, case-law guidance is scarce, as primarily only liability of parents or guardians is discussed, wrongdoers themselves having usually no goods to be seized. As an exception, the recent STS 8 April

[81] Furthermore, to complicate the situation, a new statute of 2000 (*Ley Orgánica* 5/2000 of 12 January) on Criminal Liability of Minors (older than 14 and younger than 18) also has specific provisions on tort liability, declaring the minors to be directly liable (art. 61.3). Parents are held jointly and severally responsible, with significant nuances, in that lack of intent or gross negligence on their behalf allows courts to reduce recovery.

[82] J. L. Lacruz Berdejo, *Elementos de Derecho civil*, 3 vols., Vol. II.1, 2nd edn (Barcelona: Librería Bosch, 1985), pp. 499–500 thinks that it is not only a question of analogy, but, rather, a sure criterion to interpret the Civil Code, for the rules of the Criminal Code about tort law are exactly civil law norms. With nuances, the same opinion is held by (among others), F. de Castro, *Derecho civil de España*, 2 vols., Vol. II.1ª (Madrid: Instituto de Estudios Políticos, 1952), pp. 188ff., 317 ff.; Santos Briz, *Derecho de daños*, pp. 93ff.; S. Díaz Alabart, 'La responsabilidad por los actos ilícitos dañosos de los sometidos a patria potestad o tutela' (1987) 40 *Anuario de Derecho civil* 852, 876 and 877; R. de Ángel Yagüez, *Tratado de responsabilidad civil* (Madrid: Universidad de Deusto-Civitas, 1993), p. 308; and Yzquierdo Tolsada, *Sistema de responsabilidad civil*, p. 230.

[83] Especially M. Albaladejo, *Instituciones de Derecho civil*, 2 vols., Vol. I (Barcelona: Bosch, 1960), pp. 997–998; A. Borrell Maciá, *Responsabilidades derivadas de culpa extracontractual civil* (Barcelona: Bosch, 1942), p. 23; C. López Beltrán de Heredia, *La responsabilidad de los padres por los hechos de sus hijos* (Madrid: Tecnos, 1988), p. 191; M. García-Ripoll in M. Cobo del Rosal (ed.), *Comentarios al Código penal*, Vol. IV (Madrid: Edersa, 2000), p. 483; E. Gómez Calle in L. F. Reglero Campos (ed.), *Tratado de responsabilidad civil*, 3rd edn (Cizur Menor: Aranzadi–Thomson, 2006), p. 479.

2006[84] considers that minors (whose age is not reflected in the facts) are not liable, but only their parents.

B *Liability of the public administration*

Another field in which confrontation between legislative and judicial power is vivid concerns the liability of the public administration. The 1889 CC stated in art. 1903 that the public administration was liable according to the general rules of vicarious liability (i.e. the public administration was liable for the illegal acts of civil servants, with a shift of the burden of proof). On the other hand, art. 1 *Ley de Responsabilidad Civil de los Funcionarios Públicos* (Civil Liability of Civil Servants Act) of 5 April 1904 stated that any public officer 'who in the performance of his post breaks any provision, by act or omission, *whose observance has been claimed in writing*, will be liable before the claimant for the damages caused by that legal infringement'.

The courts interpreted these provisions in the sense that the public administration was only liable when it acted through a special agent (which was rare), and, on the other hand, the Act of 1904 only foresaw liability of the civil servant, but not that of the public administration itself.[85] To some extent, this outcome belonged to the past, when sovereignty and liability were incompatible (*the king can do no wrong*).[86]

In 1954 the *Ley de Expropiación Forzosa* (Expropriation Act) was passed, and turned the situation upside-down, so to speak. Article 121 (under the heading 'The compensation for other damages') established the liability of the administration for any damage that individuals could suffer 'due to normal [i.e. lawful] or wrongful performance of the public services'. This provision was a consequence of the widespread opinion among scholars (some of whom had had a crucial role in the Act's first draft) that liability of public bodies should *always* be strict; the idea was that the public administration intervenes so much in our everyday life that justice required compensation for damage flowing from its activities,

[84] RJA 1076. For a detailed overview of this topic, see M. Martin-Casals, J. Ribot and J. Solé Feliú, 'Children as Tortfeasors under Spanish Law' in M. Martín-Casals (ed.), *Children in Tort Law Part I: Children as Tortfeasors* (Vienna and New York: Springer, 2006), p. 369.

[85] For instance, Decisions 18 May 1904 (Civil Chamber, CLJC (1904), no. 70, 389 ff.); 8 July 1911 (Civil Chamber, CLJC (1911), no. 20, 146ff.) and 18 February 1914 (Civil Chamber, CLJC (1914), no. 86, 459ff.).

[86] E. García de Enterría, 'Potestad expropiatoria y garantía patrimonial' (1955) 8 *Anuario de Derecho Civil* 1106.

even when it had acted according to the law.[87] Shortly afterwards, in the wake of the quoted Act, art. 40 *Ley Régimen Jurídico de la Administración del Estado* (State Administration Act) of 1957 stated that the State is liable for the 'normal or wrongful performance of public services' when it damages any individual.[88]

Despite these provisions, the administrative chamber of the TS is very reluctant to condemn public bodies in tort when there is no wrongful act: especially in the case of medical treatments, since making them liable for the simple fact of not curing somebody does not seem a reasonable outcome of the lawsuit.[89] However, the administrative courts do not deny compensation by direct rejection of the statutory provisions, but appealing to different grounds, such as lack of causality or *force majeure*.[90]

C *Compensation for work injuries*

Legislation on work accidents started to take shape in the last third of the nineteenth century. Since the creation of the TS in 1834, one single decision (STS 14 December 1894[91]) has been reported as granting

[87] So, one of the Act's inspirers, *ibid.*, 1116.

[88] As a consequence of the previous norms, art. 106.2 Spanish Constitution of 1978 states that 'Individuals, according to the statutory rules, will have the right to be compensated for any damage they suffer in their goods and rights, save the case of *force majeure*, when the damage is due to performance of public services.' It is worth noting that no differentiation is made between legal or illegal performance. Consistently, art. 139.1 *Ley Régimen Jurídico de las Administraciones Públicas* of 1992 (Public Administrations Act, which repeals the previous Act of 1957) states that 'Individuals will have the right to be compensated by the Public Administrations for any damage they suffer in their goods and rights, save the case of *force majeure*, when the damage is due to normal or wrongful performance of public services.'

[89] As to the problem of blood transfusions infected with HIV, and the statutory change it caused in 1999, see M. Martín Casals and J. Solé Feliu, 'The Evolution of Product Liability in Spain', p. 256.

[90] For example: in the decision TS 27 November 2000 (Administrative Chamber, RJA 9409) a patient underwent an angiography or arteriography owing to blood circulation problems. Unfortunately, she suffered a hemiplegia during the catheter insertion into the artery. The woman sued the public hospital for damages due to 'normal' performance of the public service. The Supreme Court rejected the claim because 'the arteriography was performed correctly ... which eliminates any kind of negligence'; and 'on the other hand, it must be pointed out that the state of the patient's arteries influenced crucially ... the outcome'; so, 'there was not a direct cause–effect relationship in the performance of the public service'. But it is easily understandable that 'but for' the angiography the result would not have taken place.

[91] CLJC (1894), no. 134. On this topic see M. Martín Casals and J. Ribot, 'Technological Change and the Development of Liability for Fault in Spain' in M. Martin-Casals (ed.),

compensation for death in the course of work, on the basis of the general fault liability clause of art. 1902 CC and the standard of care provided by arts. 1101 and 1104 CC, referred to contractual liability.

The first steps were taken by politicians with a conservative-liberal background, who encouraged the creation in 1883 of a public body, the Comisión de Reformas Sociales, later turned into the *Instituto de Reformas Sociales* (1903), in order to gather information for future law reform proposals from all kinds of sources (workers' associations, companies, cultural organisations etc.), considering that social reforms must be prepared taking into account the opinion and needs of social organisations.[92]

The first Act on work accidents, of 30 January 1900, was described as a 'legal revolution'. It was promoted by Eduardo Dato, the Government member who presented the law project to Parliament. At the time, industry represented only 16 per cent of the working population, as 68 per cent was still based in agriculture. The turn of the century, however, encountered a nation that had just lost the last sparks of its American Empire, but was facing the future under what were proclaimed to be the basic pillars of liberal-conservative ideology: 'protectionism, State intervention and priority of social problems', as declared by the conservative party leader Cánovas del Castillo in 1892, through the influence of Bismarck and the 'social doctrine' of the Catholic Church (*Rerum novarum*).[93]

Dato had become a member of *Cortes* in 1884, being at the same time a lawyer, engaged in important economic and political issues (trains and banks).[94] He envisaged the need for laws to safeguard workers, as was pointed out in the 'motives' of the law project ('eyes cannot be kept shut before the evidence of suffering and mutilation caused by machines and dangerous substances'), following at the same time the French example ('the French have managed to depart from the codified negligence rule'), so 'liability for work accidents should be considered inherent to industrial exploitation and compensation is to be regarded as a production expense, to be paid by the employer'.

The Development of Liability in Relation to Technological Change (Cambridge: Cambridge University Press, 2010), p. 243.

92 J. Montalvo Correa, *Fundamentos de Derecho del trabajo* (Madrid: Civitas, 1975), p. 143.

93 See J. Velarde Fuertes, 'Reflexión sobre dos circunstancias inseguras: La Seguridad Social española en 1900 y en el 2000. El entorno económico de Dato y Pimentel' in B. G. González *et al.*, *Cien años de seguridad social* (Madrid: Fraternidad Muprespa, 2000), p. 397. On the other hand, the law was clearly aimed at giving response to the social alarm brought about by frequent accidents – namely explosions of steam boilers – at the time. See Martín-Casals and Ribot, 'Technological Change', pp. 241ff.

94 See Velarde Fuertes, 'Reflexión sobre dos circunstancias inseguras', pp. 402ff.

The 1900 Act introduced strict liability, as only *force majeure* external to work was excluded, thus introducing the idea of 'professional risk'. The rule was imperative, contrary contractual clauses were void; insurance, however, was optional and was to be provided by private companies. Furthermore, 'work accident' was described broadly and the definition is still used in current legislation: any kind of *lesion* (injury) arising out of, *or* in the course of, employment. Legal writers of the time and court decisions included work diseases (STS 17 June 1903[95]) and, after 1930 accidents *in itinere* (accidents that take place when travelling from home to work) or caused within work time, even if their immediate cause was not related to work itself.

Benefits (including medical attention), however, were granted within rather low limits. The new legislation has been described as a 'transactional' deal, as employers, whilst having to pay automatically limited damages, were to be preserved from any other claim (the so-called *immunity principle*). Notwithstanding this, if the accident had been caused by the employer's negligence or lack of security measures, the fixed compensation was increased 50 per cent in favour of the victim. Thus the so-called 'surcharge' was introduced.[96]

A minor reform took place in 1922, under the conservative Government of Maura. Spain was going through increasing social instability and conflicts. Since 1918 no fewer than five Governments had been appointed and dissolved after a few months. Dato had been appointed to the Government in 1920, introducing the Ministry of Work, but was to fall under the spiral of violence in February 1921. The 1922 law reform was aimed at settling some debated issues, albeit accepted by scholars and courts: workmen's 'professional imprudence' was not to exclude compensation, a public body (Fondo de garantía – which, however, was not put into practice) financed by employers' contributions was to cover employers' insolvency, and it was clarified that the law did not ban a claim for liability arising from civil negligence or derived from crime.

The Second Republic Constitution (1931) opened the door to wider social protection, extending the work accident regulation to agricultural work (*Ley de Bases* 12 June 1931). Not only national needs, but international

95 CLJC (1903), no. 180.

96 See A. Desdentado Bonete, 'La responsabilidad empresarial y los accidentes de trabajo: Estado de la cuestión sobre el desorden en el funcionamiento de los mecanismos de reparación' in *Congreso de Magistrados del Orden Social: El futuro de la Jurisdicción social* (Madrid: Consejo General del Poder Judicial, 2007), p. 401 (pp. 411ff.).

Conventions (OIT) were taken into account.[97] Insurance was made compulsory by the Law of 4 July 1932. The insurance contract could be agreed with a public body (Caja Nacional del Instituto de Prevision), employer's associations (*Mutuas patronales*) or private companies; the Fondo de Garantía would guarantee subsidiary recourse. Thus, a 'responsibility system' gave way to a 'social insurance system', without forsaking the idea of employer's liability, by means of the surcharge – in case of employer's fault – not covered by insurance.[98]

Franco's dictatorship kept basically the Republican rules regarding work accidents, gradually extending the type of work covered by compulsory insurance (*Ley Fundamental* 17 May 1958) by subsequent Acts in the 1950s, and simultaneously generalising periodic payments, instead of lump sums. The Civil Division of the TS, at the same time, decidedly favoured the so-called 'compatibility doctrine', which enabled the victim to recover damages from the employer by means of a Civil action based on fault and the general tort rules of the Civil Code.[99]

The third step in this evolution took place with what was designed to be a unified system of social security and State insurance (financed by compulsory employers' contributions) through the *Ley de Bases de la Seguridad Social* of 28 December 1963, and *Texto Articulado de la Seguridad Social, Decree* of 21 April 1966. The system was rather complex.

[97] See M. Alonso Olea, 'La Seguridad Social: Presente, pasado y futuro' in González *et al.*, *Cien años de seguridad social*, p. 177.

[98] A. Desdentado Bonete and M. Nogueira Guastavino, 'Las transformaciones del accidente de trabajo entre la Ley y la Jurisprudencia (1900–2000): Revisión crítica y propuesta de reforma' (2000) 24 *Revista del Ministerio de Trabajo y Asuntos Sociales* 31, 37.

[99] A debated issue in this period regarded claims against third persons (for example, accidents *in itinere*, or suffered on the occasion of work; or caused by a fellow worker) and their relationship with benefits to be obtained from the employer or insurer. In 1936 (*Orden* 25 March 1936) it had been clarified that the employer/insurer must pay (medical assistance and other fixed benefits) immediately, but could recover from the wrongdoer with preference over the victim. This provision was included in legislation enacted after the Civil War (*TR Ley de accidents de trabajo, Decreto* 22 June 1956), conferring insurance companies' intervention in disputes, alongside the injured person. Case law and legal writers, however, seem to have disliked the insurer's priority, and contradictory decisions ensued. The reluctance to admit insurer's recoup was favoured from the early 1960s by the Criminal Division of the TS, arguing that labour benefits on the one hand, and tort liability on the other, are based upon different grounds. This allowed the so-called 'compatibility doctrine' to grow and penetrate into the Civil Division (STS 3 October 1961; RJA 1961, 3276), even when the worker sought redress from the employer, under the common tort law rules. See F. Gómez Pomar, 'Indemnización civil e indemnización laboral: Un intento de reconstrucción' (1996) 80 *Revista de Derecho Privado* 935.

The purpose of the 1963 *Ley de Bases* was to leave aside the notion of 'risk', to be replaced by that of event that entitles workers to obtain social benefits. However, the *Texto Articulado* preserved a variety of regulations; contributions for professional contingencies were, and still are, to some extent, connected to the idea of risk insurance.[100] The second important innovation was that social insurance was to be administered directly by a public body or by State-approved managing and collaborating non-profit organisations (*mutuas patronales*, currently *mutuas de accidentes de trabajo y enfermedades profesionales de la seguridad social*), as it still is today. The *Preámbulo* of the 1963 law described the 'fundamental significance' of this measure in order to manage compensation in the most efficient manner and in a way necessary to reduce costs and litigation rates. Subsequent reforms have simplified the 'chaos' of managing bodies and extended – following the requirements of the Spanish Constitution (1978), art. 41 – non-contributory assistance to all citizens, as well as increasing the State's contribution (which in 1977 was only 3.64 %). Work accidents and diseases, however, have always been submitted to a specific regime ('professional contingencies'), more favourable than that applicable to the so-called common risks. In addition, courts and some legal reforms have favoured the so-called 'overflowing of the (notion of) professional accident' and made the defence of external *vis maior* 'extremely infrequent'.[101]

The 1963–1966 innovations could still be described as insurance of employers' responsibility. The issue, however, is controversial. Some authors describe compulsory contributions as 'legal tax obligations'; employers' liability has been assumed by society and loss is spread through social security. Others, on the contrary, consider that the basic idea of responsibility covered by compulsory insurance is visible, despite benefits being automatically granted,[102] without needing a pronouncement on the employer's liability. Work accidents and diseases have been extended, including events that can hardly be described as pertaining to employers' sphere of influence – such as traffic accidents on the public highway

[100] Desdentado Bonete and Nogueira Guastavino, 'Las transformaciones del accidente de trabajo', 39.

[101] See M. Alonso Olea and J. L. Tortuero Plaza, *Instituciones de Seguridad Social*, 18th edn (Madrid: Civitas, 2002), pp. 59, 69.

[102] On this topic, see A. Desdentado Bonete, 'La responsabilidad empresarial y los accidentes de trabajo', pp. 421ff. When the employer has not complied with the legal affiliation, insurance or contribution duties, compensation is automatically anticipated by the *entidades gestoras*, who can recoup from the former.

or 'common' diseases worsened by work (heart attacks, especially); in addition, compensation has been favoured by the (debated and variable) restrictive attitude of courts, when deciding on the reckless imprudence of the victim or if the accident is to be attributed to a third person as not arising from or in the course of work.

The social security system, on the other hand, provided a firm ground for redress through the common rules on tort-civil liability or civil liability derived from crime. Article 97.3 of the 1966 Act stated that benefits provided by social security (or by the collaborating organisations) did not hinder the common (civil or criminal) action for damages to be brought against those responsible, *including the employer.* Article 127.3 of the current social security law has a similar provision. In this way, the so-called immunity of the employer definitely melted away.[103]

The labour provisions, whilst clearly admitting compatibility between public compensation and tort liability have nonetheless received different interpretations in the labour jurisdiction, on the one hand, and the civil (and criminal) on the other. First, it is important to stress that the question on the competent jurisdiction for such claims has been, and still is today, disputed; despite the fact that the predominant view favoured the labour jurisdiction – as according to the rules on the matter, issues flowing from work-contracts are to be judged by labour courts – the civil courts would not dismiss the claim, ascertaining their jurisdiction over claims framed in tort.[104]

Furthermore, labour courts have been perhaps less likely to confer damages above the legal fixed limits of the labour legislation as they seem inclined to require a clear proof of the employer's negligence; even if they do ascertain fault, social benefits (ordinary benefits and voluntary improvements) are currently deducted in full from tort damages, in order to avoid double compensation.[105]

[103] According to the present state of affairs, the injured worker is entitled to receive: public fixed benefits, the surcharge (if the employer failed to comply with safety regulations, as a sort of punitive fixed damages, ranging from 30 per cent to 50 per cent), voluntary improvements (increasing public benefits) plus recovery according to common civil liability rules, to be paid by the employer or a third person. See M. Luque Parra, C. Gómez Ligüerre and J. A. Ruiz García, 'Workplace Injuries and Tort Liability' (2000) 2 *Indret* 10–11 (www.indret.com).

[104] See M. Yzquierdo Tolsada in F. Reglero Campos (ed.), *Tratado de Responsabilidad civil*, 3 vols., Vol. III, 4th edn (Madrid: Thomson–Aranzadi, 2008), p. 804.

[105] See F. Cavas Martínez and F. J. Fernández Orrico, *La cobertura de las contingencias profesionales en el sistema español de seguridad social* (Madrid: Thomson–Aranzadi, 2006), p. 164. The surcharge for infringement of security and health regulations is not deducted.

Civil courts, on the contrary, notwithstanding contrary decisions, have applied in this field the 'risk criteria', thus increasing the employer's duty of care; deduction is rejected, considering – among other arguments – that public benefits are deemed to derive from a 'different source'. This also seems to be the attitude of the Criminal Division.[106] In addition, art. 123.2 LGSS declares the 'surcharge' to be 'independent and compatible with those of any legal order that may derive from the infringement', which, combined with its punitive scope, seems to favour accumulation.[107] Assessing damages without deducting social benefits has been explained by some authors as the manner in which courts have made up for what was considered to be very low public compensation through social security, not including pain and suffering ('moral' damages). However, deduction of damages already covered by labour compensation – notwithstanding the summing up of civil liability for any different kind of damage – appears to be the predominant opinion in legal writing.[108]

IV Conclusion

Courts' decisions are not, at the outset, a formal source of law within the Spanish legal system. The judicial contribution to the evolution of tort law has been, however, decisive – even 'revolutionary'. The Civil jurisdiction, indeed, has never departed from the general fault liability clause of art. 1902 CC, already included in the 1851 draft, but has achieved in some areas a sort of *quasi*-strict liability, where a sense of fairness seemed to require it. In doing so, judges may have been influenced to some extent by academic work, which in turn developed foreign ideas, but it is not easy to trace clearly decisive influential individuals. Basically case law seems to have given response to social necessities, industrial development and public opinion, trying to adapt what could be thought old-fashioned rules to imperatives of justice. No doubt they received support in their quest

[106] Under the influence of the prestigious criminal law professor and judge, A. Quintano Ripollés, 'Seguros y responsabilidad civiles delictuales' (1961) 45 *Revista de Derecho Privado* 3; as pointed out by F. Gomez Pomar, 'Tort Liability and Other Means of Redress: "Collateral Source Rule" and Related Topics' (2000) 1 *Indret* 5 (www.indret.com).

[107] M. Luque Parra, *La responsabilidad civil del empresario en materia de seguridad y salud laboral* (Madrid: Consejo Económico y Social, 2002), pp. 192ff.

[108] S. Cavanillas Múgica, 'Commentary on STS 30 October 1990' (1990) 645 *Cuadernos Civitas de Jurisprudencia Civil* 1158; Díez Picazo, *Derecho de daños*, 173–181; G. Díez-Picazo Giménez, 'Los daños derivados de accidentes de trabajo: Una gran paradoja' (2007) 19 *Revista de Derecho Patrimonial* 33; M. Yzquierdo Tosada in Reglero Campos (ed.), *Tratado de Responsabilidad civil*, Vol. III, pp. 826, 835.

from the ever increasing (optional or mandatory) insurance at hand, to cover the defendant's expenses.

This evolution, despite offering early forerunners in a limited number of fields, grew vigorously only in the second half of the twentieth century. The reasons for this appear to be manifold. Some matters – such as traffic accidents – were nearly always assigned to criminal courts, which, since 1848, could rely on the Criminal Code tort provisions in order to secure damage compensation. Labour accidents compensation had already been, since 1900 – very few years after the enactment of the Civil Code – submitted to a strict liability rule; further legislation not only gradually extended its scope, but judicial interpretation managed to bring most workers' contingencies under the protective umbrella of social benefits through a broad understanding of the legal provisions. The late appearance of other issues, such as product and medical liability, seems to owe much to the relatively recent technical and economical development, and, not the least, to a change in people's attitude towards pain and death.

Over the period considered, several events have changed the shape of our political system: short Republican periods (1873–1874, 1931–1936) mingled with kingdom restoration (1874–1931) and, moreover, two dictatorships (1923–1930, 1939–1975) and a constitutional kingdom since 1978. In our opinion, however, the political situation has not played a decisive role in civil-tort law evolution. Some of the most important legislative innovations, in the way of specific statutes outside the Civil Code, were brought about by economic development and the necessity to meet social demands, as indeed happened with the first regulations on traffic accidents after the second half of the twentieth century. On the whole, the legislator has not moved from a compensation system based on liability, despite eroding the fault principle with strict rules, and using mandatory private insurance as a tool in order to facilitate damage recovery and reduce litigation costs of victims. The legal reforms have received impetus from different sources. Work legislation since 1900 has influenced later regulations, traffic liability in particular; to some extent, both follow today the same pattern, in pursuit of automatic, albeit limited, compensation – public or private, but compulsorily insured. Other innovations were promoted without any kind of prior debate, either academic or judicial (air, nuclear and hunting liability), whilst others had received considerable academic and judicial support, or were the legislature's reaction to a social disaster (consumer protection). There was no systematic approach.

The Spanish development of liability rules could be described – from the beginning – as one of 'multiple juridical regulations'.[109] Different jurisdictions, submitted to a variety of influences and purposes, have created a rather complicated panorama. However, despite many nuances, the opinion of many tort law scholars as to the better understanding of extra contractual liability may be summarised in the following words: primacy of fault, as the basic criterion in order to trigger liability, is still an excellent standpoint, including, especially, liability of the public administration.[110]

[109] See M. Lorente and C. Garriga, 'Certeza jurídica vs. Justicia social: La Ley de accidentes de trabajo y el liberalismo jurídico español' in González *et al.*, *Cien años de seguridad social*, p. 79.

[110] See F. Pantaleón, 'Como repensar la responsabilidad civil extracontractual (también la de las administraciones públicas)' in J. A. Moreno (ed.), *Perfiles de la responsabilidad civil en el nuevo milenio* (Madrid: Dykinson, 2000) pp. 439, 465.

9

The impact of institutions and professions in Sweden

MÅRTEN SCHULTZ

I Introduction

In this chapter some outlines of the development of fault liability in Swedish law from 1850 until now will be presented. The task is difficult, for several reasons. One reason is that the character of Swedish tort law has changed significantly during the period in question. At the beginning of the time period tort law can best be described as a primitive legal discipline, with a legislative support only in some provisions in criminal legislation and with a relatively weak theoretical underpinning. Today, however, the discipline of tort law has been given a clear and rather modern statutory support – in both general legislation (the Tort Liability Act from 1972) as well as in different, specific statutes. Furthermore, the theoretical understanding of tort law has deepened significantly during the period, as a result both of the many Supreme Court decisions that have cast light on the general concepts of tort law, but also because of the treatment of the discipline in legal academia. One can note that tort law has been a favourite subject of the most prominent writers in civil law during the last fifty years.[1]

In this introduction I will start by providing some systematic outlines on Swedish civil law against a comparative perspective. This outline will probably be too brief to achieve its goal, which is to provide a basic understanding necessary for the presentation of the more specific subject of the development of fault liability. After the short introduction, three different lines of development will be mapped: the development of the concept of fault by the courts, with emphasis on the Supreme Court; the development

[1] These writers include law professors Ivar Strahl, Hjalmar Karlgren, Jan Hellner, Bertil Bengtsson, Jan Kleineman and Anders Agell. Both Bengtsson and Karlgren have also served as Supreme Court Justices and several of these authors have also participated in legislative work.

of fault liability in legislation; and the development of different forms of strict liability regimes and other similar institutions that has affected the scope of fault liability.

A *General remarks on the Swedish civil law system*

It is often assumed that European legal systems can be characterised with reference to the division between Civil, Continental law systems and the common law systems. That this broad generalisation of the two 'major legal traditions' fits less well onto the classic mixed systems is well known. However, the Scandinavian systems cannot really be said to belong to the group of mixed systems either. A mixed system is often characterised as bringing together elements of a common law, court-oriented approach to law and codification ideas of the Continental system, and often the latter tradition is also seen in a historical light with reference to the Continental tradition's (at least in its German incarnation) roots in Roman law.[2]

Swedish civil law has not been the subject of a comprehensive codification and it is generally assumed that there are few traces of Roman law in Swedish civil law, even if it has been argued by legal historians that the notion of *culpa* is an exception in this regard.[3] That this simplistic dichotomy is flawed is now generally acknowledged, but it is still often used. It is for instance used by some of the most vocal critics of the Europeanisation movement, albeit with a shift of focus from 'systems' to 'epistemological clusters' or *mentalités*.[4] Among Swedish writers, it is sometimes held that Swedish civil law belongs more to a Civil law tradition than the common

[2] According to Alan Watson, the fundamental feature of a Civil law system is that 'parts or the whole of Justinian's *Corpus juris civilis* have been in the past or are at present treated as the law of the land or, at the very least, are of direct and highly persuasive force; or else it derives from any such system'; A. Watson, *The Making of Civil Law* (Cambridge, MA: Harvard University Press, 1981), p. 4.

[3] S. Jägerskiöld, *Om culpaansvaret under 1600 och 1700-talen* (Lund: Carl Bloms, 1977).

[4] See for instance P. Legrand, 'Against a European Civil Code' (1997) 60 *Modern Law Review* 44. For a Scandinavian reader, Legrand's view seems peculiar. On the one hand Legrand seems to view the existence of a Civil Code as more or less a formative constituent of a civil law system and the apparently collective minds of the civilian systems: '[T]he civilian proceeds to reason from the social and legislative perspective embodied *in the code*', Legrand writes (46). It is the Code that lies at the centre of the civil law *mentalité* – and it is the introduction of such a code on a European level that according to Legrand would destroy the common law tradition. On the other hand Legrand also categorically refers the Scandinavian systems to the Civil tradition, even though he explicitly notes that the Scandinavian systems are not codified (45). One cannot help but wonder

law and this seems to be the dominant view, even if the problem with the black-and-white dichotomy is often emphasised by Swedish writers.[5]

In 1734 a comprehensive law reform took place that led to a division between different 'books' (the Swedish expression *balk* is an archaic word for book), and to some extent these books are still in force, the most important example being the book on commerce (*handelsbalken*). However, most of the old 'books' have been abolished, and also the book on commerce, which still includes many rules that have not been abolished, is to a significant degree obsolete. The old division between different books has some affinities with a modern perception of the civil code, but the different books have not been considered as a comprehensive, 'full' codification. In the most used Swedish collection of statutes, the 'Book of Laws' (*Lagboken*), the structure of the law reform from 1734 is still partly used and one can notice that non-lawyers sometimes think that the collection is comprehensive and complete. Lawyers, however, view the collection as just a collection, a publication of some but not all statutes that the publisher found worthy of inclusion.

B Implications for tort law

These general outlines of Swedish civil law are of special importance when it comes to the law of torts. Tort law is a legal discipline that has gone from being perceived as a part criminal law to a 'pure' civil law subject. There are still remnants of the idea that tort law is connected to criminal law, noticeable for instance in the fact that the rule on defences in the

how we Scandinavian lawyers have come to possess this ephemeral civil law *mentalité* in the absence of a Civil Code, when it is the introduction of such a Code that allegedly would contaminate the common lawyers with Civil law ideas to the very extent of the end of the common law culture. And as a Swedish lawyer one feels even more estranged from Legrand's generalisation of the Civil lawyer after reading this longer characterisation of the legal process in Civil law traditions:

> The civil law is, thus, best understood as a law of the system, where the emerging contingencies of life readily find themselves being subsumed under one or the other of the available categorical umbrellas with all the confidence that comes from the attribution of significance to the act of categorization and to the criteria allowing for a separation of the categories. (50)

This characteristic certainly does not hold for Scandinavian tort law.

[5] This is the conclusion of Jacob Sundberg's thoughtful reflections on this subject; see J. Sundberg, 'Civil Law, Common Law, and the Scandinavians' (1969) *Scandinavian Studies in Law* 179, 181. In the classic introductory book to Swedish civil law, used by most if not all law schools for decades, it is said that Nordic civil law can be seen as a special group, but more influenced by Continental law than by Anglo-American law.

Criminal Code is thought to apply also in tort law, without it even being mentioned in any tort law legislation.[6] Also, tort law has gone from the situation where there were very few statutory rules that directly (that is, without being considered as applied by analogy) dealt with tort liability. This changed in the nineteenth century. The most important legislative input in the development of the current understanding of fault liability is undoubtedly the introduction of the Tort Liability Act.

In 1972 the Tort Liability Act (*Skadeståndslag* 1972:207) came into force. This Act was the first overarching legislation on tort liability in Swedish law. Previously the main source of tort principles in legislation was the sixth chapter of the Penal Act (*Straffslagen*), a predecessor of today's Criminal Code. The Tort Liability Act was never intended to be a full codification of tort law; many basic criteria for liability were left out of the statute. For instance, the general requirement of causation is not mentioned at all in the Act. Still, it is clear from the preparatory works that causation was still to be considered a requirement of liability.[7] Many other basic liability requirements, as well as other tort principles, were also left uncodified.

This general overview of Swedish tort law has implications for the understanding of fault liability in Swedish law. It is traditionally held that *the* main rule in Swedish tort law is the '*culpa* rule', which is the expression for a general rule that liability presumes negligence. This rule has a long history in Swedish law, albeit perhaps a shorter one than in other jurisdictions, and was the main liability rule long before Sweden had any general legislation on liability.[8] There is (now) statutory support for this assumption, but it is generally thought that the scope of the *culpa* rule goes beyond the area covered by legislation. For instance, it is generally held that the *culpa* rule applies also in contractual relationships. To put it in other terms: the *culpa* rule is more important than the legislation from which it partly follows. In this chapter I will give quite a few examples of exceptions from the *culpa* rule, but these should be understood against the background of its high status in Swedish law.[9] On the other hand it is these exceptions to the general *culpa* rule that are often considered most characteristic for Swedish (or Nordic) tort law. The so-called 'Nordic

[6] See J. Hellner and M. Radetzki, *Skadeståndsrätt*, 7th edn. (Stockholm: Norstedts, 2006), pp. 119ff.

[7] Proposition 1972:5, pp. 21ff.

[8] Cf. J. Hellner, 'Compensation for Personal Injuries in Sweden: A Reconsidered View' (2001) 41 *Scandinavian Studies in Law* 249, 251ff.

[9] See for a similar approach Hellner, 'Compensation for Personal Injuries', 250ff.

model' of tort law is for the most part a story of exceptions from traditional tort law doctrines. Still, it seems to be a general consensus that the *culpa* rule is completely fundamental for Swedish tort law. The attitude may thus be considered somewhat schizophrenic.

II Fault liability in the courts

A *Introduction*

It has always been up to the courts to provide content to the *culpa* rule, the commonly used term for the basic fault liability norm in Sweden. To some extent the *culpa* rule receives its content from legislation and other sources of the law, but an understanding of the meaning of the norm can only be achieved through studies of court practice.

In this context I will focus not so much on the content of the *culpa* norm as on the development of fault liability in Swedish law. Only a few examples of the interpretation of the *culpa* norm will therefore be provided.

1 Supreme Court Justices and tort law

Many prominent Supreme Court Justices have had a special interest in tort law. Chief Justice Nils Alexanderson, who served at the Supreme Court from 1922 to 1944, was a professor of civil law and a politician for the Liberal Party, and his lectures on tort law at the Nordic Lawyers' Meetings in 1926 are considered to have had profound influence on the development of tort law.[10] Chief Justice Hjalmar Karlgren, who served at the Supreme Court from 1946 to 1964, was author of the first modern textbook on Swedish tort law,[11] and earlier had been a professor in civil law, which characterised his work also as a judge.

The examples of Alexanderson and Karlgren already show that it is not unusual that academics become members of the Supreme Court in Sweden. Some of the most important writers on tort topics in the twentieth century served for a time at the Supreme Court. A noticeable name here is Bertil Bengtsson, still active as a writer but retired from the Supreme Court. Bengtsson also worked as an expert within the task force set up by the Justice Department in charge of the concrete work of putting together

[10] See regarding this N. Beckman, *Från Calonius till Karlgren, in Teori och praxis, Festskrift till Hjalmar Karlgren* (Stockholm: Norstedt, 1964), pp. 14ff.

[11] H. Karlgren, *Skadeståndsläran* (Lund: C. W. K. Gleerup, 1943).

the Tort Liability Act of 1972; he has been professor at several universities; and is still engaged as an expert in legislative work.

More common in the Supreme Court than the academics are the civil servants: the Justice Department functions partly as a nursery for future Chief Justices. Many – perhaps most – of the Chief Justices that have displayed a special interest in tort law in the last half-century have occupied positions outside the court system before serving in the Supreme Court. Two important names can be mentioned as an illustration. Ulf K. Nordensson was involved as a secretary in the committee appointed to investigate the possibility of the Tort Liability Act; he headed a special task force on the Act in the Justice Department; and he was in charge of the commission on traffic injuries. Nordensson was thereafter a member of the Supreme Court where he was the reporter of what can reasonably be counted as the most important negligence case in modern times, NJA 1981, p. 683. Erland Conradi was chairman of the 'second' Tort Law Committee; chairman of the Product Responsibility Committee, which was set up in 1972; and thereafter Chief Justice and chairman of the Criminal Victim Compensation Board (*Brottskadenämnden*) as well as a prolific writer on tort law.

As these names illustrate there has been a close connection between the legal branches in the development of modern Swedish tort law.[12] One can sometimes find the same name on the list of participants in a preparatory work that became legislation, thereafter among the judges that interpreted the same rule in a decision in the Supreme Court, and thereafter as a commentator on the decision in legal literature.[13]

[12] Furthermore there has been a connection also between the legal branches mentioned and the insurance industry. A prominent example of this is Erland Strömbäck, who was involved in the work on the Tort Liability Act as well as on the reform of the traffic injury system before he became a director for one of the large insurance companies. Strömbäck has also thereafter given valuable contributions to Swedish tort law and tort theory, for instance as a co-writer of the semi-official commentary to the Tort Liability Act: B. Bengtsson and E. Strömbäck, *Skadeståndslagen*, 2nd edn (Stockholm: Norstedt, 2006).

[13] This has sometimes resulted in criticism. See J. Hellner, (1994) *Svensk Juristtidning* 540ff., where Hellner argues that the case note commentaries on tort law cases written by a Supreme Court Justice can lead to a mixing of the roles: what value should the courts attribute to the comments in a law review on a case written by a member of the Supreme Court who was involved in the case? See also J. Kleineman, 'Försäkringsbolagens utredningskostnader som skadeståndsrättsligt metodproblem (1994–1995) 5 *Juridisk Tidskrift* 1009, 1014.

2 The style of Supreme Court decisions

It is generally acknowledged that the style of Supreme Court decisions has changed dramatically during the period in question. In the late years of the nineteenth century and the early years of the twentieth century, decisions from the Supreme Court were generally very laconic and uninformative. This changed gradually during the twentieth century and the open and accessible approach of today's Supreme Court can perhaps be said to have emerged in the sixties or seventies. This means that it is especially decisions from the last forty years that can provide interesting examples of negligence reasoning in the courts.

On a more general level it is often assumed that the development of a fault liability doctrine started relatively late in Sweden. In Denmark and Norway, the influence from the perception of the negligence principle in Continental Europe started to appear in the middle of the nineteenth century. In Swedish law, it is thought that this development appeared at a later time. There are few published precedents from the Supreme Court on issues of fault liability from the nineteenth century. The tort cases that were published are generally concerned with more atypical questions, such as railway liability and the liability between neighbours.[14]

B Two cases

From the courts I will focus only on a couple of decisions that are generally considered as typical of the attitude after the introduction of the Tort Liability Act. From the time period after 1972 the most interesting case is NJA 1981, p. 683, which is the decision where a more theoretical approach to the concept of negligence, inspired by the Hand formula, was taken. A more recent case, NJA 1993, p. 149 will be used to illustrate the connection between norms of conduct, in this case norms of the sport of golf, and the general negligence standard. One could take up older cases here as well, but since these are generally quite laconic and require more or less creative interpretations to fit into any theoretical frameworks it seems more suitable in this context to focus on the institutional factors. However, these two modern decisions can illustrate a couple of interesting factors in modern tort law. The case from 1981 illustrates, I like to think, the first conscious effort by the Supreme Court to establish general criteria for the assessment of fault. The decision is clearly influenced by scholarly suggestions and is the best example of a principled approach

[14] Hellner and Radetzki, *Skadeståndsrätt*, p. 32.

to the concept of *culpa* in Swedish law. The second decision, on the other hand, may illustrate another characteristic of Swedish tort law, namely an instrumental attitude towards the *culpa* concept, when social policy concerns point to a particular decision.

1 The paving stone

A groundbreaking decision is without doubt NJA 1981, p. 683.[15] This decision can probably be described as the most significant example of some sort of Learned Hand-like reasoning by the Swedish Supreme Court.

The circumstances of the case were that a company was doing road work, which caused a paving stone to stick up a couple of centimetres. The company took a break from the work on the road for a long weekend due to holidays, but, before they left, the construction workers put out signs to warn pedestrians that the work on the road was not finished. The warning signs consisted both of cones put around the work area and a warning sign. A pedestrian tripped on the edge of the paving stone that stood up and injured her leg. She sought compensation from the company under the argument that it had been negligent in not making sure that the warnings – the sign and the cones – were not removed from the road. (When the case was tried by the Supreme Court it had been agreed by the parties that the company in fact had taken the precautions just mentioned and that some unknown person or persons had removed the signs.)

In its decision the Supreme Court provided some general clues on its views on the general *culpa* standard in Swedish law. The Court thus stated that the question of how extensive preventative measures someone that has produced a risk of accident should be required to take depends, on one hand, on the nature and extent of the risk of damage, and, on the other hand, on the costs and other inconveniences associated with the preventative measures in question. The risk of damage should, according to the Supreme Court, be assessed with regard to both the risk of an accident in general and the extent of the potential damage.

With these general criteria as a yardstick the Court thereafter examined the situation in the case. It was noted that the risk of damage was relatively low and that the victim's injury in the case was about as bad as it could get; there was thus no significant risk of more serious injuries than the one that had actually occurred. Additional precautions, on the other hand, would have been very costly. All things considered the Court found that the company had done what could reasonably be expected of

[15] The reporter of the decision was Chief Justice Ulf K. Nordensson.

it. The construction company was therefore not considered to have acted negligently.

This decision is widely considered as a landmark in the analysis of the concept of negligence in Swedish tort law.[16] One reason is that the decision lies quite close to a suggestion on how *culpa* assessments can or should be made. It seems fairly clear that the decision is inspired by the account of Jan Hellner in his textbook monograph on tort law, *Skadeståndsrätt*.[17] Hellner's textbook has been the leading presentation of the subject for the last three decades and it is no exaggeration to say that this book has had profound influence on the perception of the discipline of tort law.[18] It is often cited by the Supreme Court; it is used as a textbook by most if not all law faculties; and it is also widely used as a reference by practising lawyers.

In his book, Hellner presents a model for what he calls 'the free *culpa* assessment'. According to Hellner, an assessment of negligence can either take its starting point in legal sources – in legislation, preparatory works or precedents – or it can be carried out more freely. In some situations norms in, for instance, legislation can have great importance for the assessment of negligence. An example of this is traffic legislation that will often provide rather detailed rules of conduct that, if broken, will often mean that the person who broke the rule will be considered to have acted negligently if the offence resulted in damage.[19] Often, however, there will not be any clear guidance for the assessment of negligence in legal sources, and in these situations, Hellner points out, one needs to make a free evaluation. Hellner's suggestion is that the free assessment should be understood in accordance with the ubiquitous Learned Hand formula, in Richard Posner's take on it.[20] However, Hellner adds one important

[16] See A. Agell, 'Kantstenar, plåtbitar, hästboxar och dylikt: Om riskbedömningar enligt culparegeln' in *Festskrift till Ulf K. Nordensson* (Stockholm: Carlssen Law Network, 1999), p. 1.

[17] Hellner and Radetzki, *Skadeståndsrätt*.

[18] Jan Hellner passed away in 2002. The last two editions of the book have been prepared by other scholars: the sixth edition by Svante Johansson and the current edition (from 2006) by Marcus Radetzki.

[19] However, it does not seem that a violation of a rule, for instance a traffic rule, per se amounts to negligence. If someone breaks a traffic rule and thereby causes damage she will normally be considered as negligent, but – as far as one can tell – there is no necessary connection between the assessment of the violation of the rule and the assessment of negligence. To put it differently, the idea of 'statutory negligence' does not seem to exist in Swedish law. The law is uncertain on this point, however.

[20] Hellner and Radetzki, *Skadeståndsrätt*, pp. 133ff. Hellner explicitly refers to Posner's work in this context. However, the reference to Learned Hand seems doubtful. It seems

modification to Posner's formulation of the formula that, in fact, turns it into something completely different.

It is not altogether clear whether Hellner means that his formulation of the *culpa* rule reflects how the courts in fact deal with the assessment of negligence, or if it is a suggestion on how the assessment *should* be carried out. Hellner writes that the first three criteria of the free assessment – the traditional Hand–Posner requirements – 'can often be found in Swedish law'.[21] These three criteria are the risk of damage, the magnitude of the probable damage and the possibility to avoid the damage. When it comes to the fourth criterion, however, Hellner's wording shifts from descriptive to normative: 'In addition [to the three aforementioned criteria] one should add a fourth factor: the acting party's possibility [or perhaps: ability] to recognise the risk of damage.'[22] These four criteria are weighed against each other in an overall assessment to evaluate whether the defendant should have acted in another way.

Even if Hellner himself is somewhat ambiguous on the issue as to whether his proposed negligence standard is descriptive or normative (or both), it is clear that as a descriptive claim it has considerable merit when it comes to understanding the Court's judgment in NJA 1981, p. 683. This decision is probably inspired by Hellner's account of the interpretation of the *culpa* rule, but focusses only on the first three criteria. As such it might seem that this decision, with its principled approach, establishes the Posner–Hand interpretation of negligence in Swedish law. This would be an exaggeration, however.

First, there is the obvious difficulty of determining to what extent this decision warrants general conclusions. Second, influential scholars have argued that the objective approach of the Hand formula is untenable and that more subjective standards should be preferred or

that more and more scholars agree that Posner's interpretation of the Hand formula does not reflect Hand's own view, as it was expressed in his other decisions. For an analysis of this see S. G. Gilles, 'On Determining Negligence: Hand Formula Balancing, the Reasonable Person Standard, and the Jury' (2001) 54 *Vanderbilt Law Review* 813; and R. W. Wright, 'Hand, Posner, and the Myth of the "Hand Formula"'(2003) 4 *Theoretical Inquiries in Law* 145.

21 This is a free translation. In Swedish: 'Även i svensk rätt kan man finna att kraven på aktsamhet ofta sker genom en sammanställning av tre faktorer: risken för skada, den sannolika skadans storlek och möjligheterna att förekomma skadan': Hellner and Radetzki, *Skadeståndsrätt*, p. 134.

22 In Swedish: 'Till dessa bör man lägga en fjärde faktor: den handlandes möjlighet att inse risken för skada'; *ibid.*

at least used to supplement it.[23] Third, in the many decisions involving negligence judgments after the case from 1981 there are few traces of the strict application of the Hand–Posner formula. It can be noticed that the more mathematical interpretation of the Hand formula often found in economic literature, where all three criteria are translated into some monetary standard, will rarely if ever be found in Swedish tort decisions. On the other hand, the Hand formula's basic idea that negligence can be established through the balancing of interests is a common theme in the courts.[24]

2 *The golfer*

In NJA 1993, p. 149 the defendant D had played golf at a course partly adjacent to a parking lot. The defendant's first shot was unsuccessful and ended up on the fringes of the golf course. His second shot was also a bad hit, flew out of bounds and hit a car at the parking lot next to the course. The car was slightly damaged. The owner of the car sought compensation in tort law for the property damage, under the argument that D's shot was negligent. As a factor in the negligence assessment the plaintiff argued that golf balls are dangerous projectiles and that D should have been more careful since his first shot had failed, taking into regard also the fact that people had been in the vicinity when he hit his second shot. As for the second shot itself, it seems fairly clear that it could not be considered as a reckless or even unusual shot for a golfer. A possibly important factor discernible between the lines in the case is that the golfer was covered by liability insurance.

The Supreme Court stated that when someone causes damage to another or another's property in the exercise of a sport, it is of importance to the assessment of negligence whether the victim was involved in

[23] See Agell, 'Kantstenar, plåtbitar, hästboxar och dylikt', pp. 1ff. Also Hellner opens up for this with his fourth additional criterion, emphasising the importance of the defendant's insight. It seems that there is also growing dissatisfaction with the economic interpretation of the Hand formula in Anglo-American tort theory; see for a recent example B. C. Zipursky, 'Sleight of Hand' (2006–2007) 48 *William and Mary Law Review* 1999. This development in legal scholarship should be of interest also for Swedish tort theory, since the Hand formula has been quite uncritically adopted into Swedish law without much debate or analysis.

[24] An earlier case, NJA 1958, p. 461, illustrates how the Supreme Court in some situations holds that the interests behind the action influence the assessment so that the defendant was not considered negligent even though his actions entailed clear risks of personal injuries.

the sport herself or if she was an 'outsider', for instance a spectator. If the victim was a participant in a game, it can sometimes be argued that she has accepted a risk of damage. Such concerns cannot be given the same relevance when the victim was not a participant in the sport. Nor can the fact that the person who caused the damage followed the rules of the sport be given the same weight as if the victim had been a participant, except in the case when the rules of the sport have been developed to protect a third party. When a person involved in a sport causes an injury or damage to someone outside the sport it is therefore the 'normal *culpa* norm' that applies.

In its decision the Court points out that golf is 'partly a dangerous game', because if a golf ball hits a person or an object serious damage may arise. Since the game of golf involves dangerous elements the player must adjust her game accordingly. In this case the Court found that D should have chosen another shot than the one he did, since the first shot had already gone wrong; he should have taken the risk of damaging the car in the parking lot into account when he took his second shot. He could have chosen another path, even if it had cost him an extra shot.

In a dissenting opinion, Chief Justice Munch (presently the president of the Supreme Court) held that a golfer who plays the game according to the rules, and in the way it is supposed to be played, should generally be able to count on the fact that he will not be liable for damages resulting from the game. Among commentators the decision has been considered harsh against the golfer.[25]

The golfer case is interesting since it illustrates how a negligence judgment takes account of norms – in this case the norms of the sport – in its assessment. It may also be seen as an illustration of how the courts may be affected by instrumental concerns in the assessment of fault. In this case the golfer was covered by liability insurance and it seems to me likely that this had some kind of influence on the evaluation of his conduct. As argued by the minority, the golfer had played the game as it is intended to be played and the two bad shots would be considered, at least by most players, as something that just happens every once in a while. Had the criteria in the decision of 1981 been applied without bias, it seems unlikely that the play could be seen as negligent. But the

[25] See J. Rebane and M. Schultz, 'Fore! Om skadestånd vid golf och annan idrott' in *Idrottsjuridiska föreningens årsbok 2002* (Farsta: SISU Idrottsböcker, 2002), p. 252, available online at www.juridicum.su.se/user/masc/fore.pdf. (The section that discusses this case has the heading 'Måste jag putta hela vägen till green?' ('Must I putt all the way to the green?'), p. 259.)

consequence if the golfer had not been considered negligent would be that the cost of the damage would have fallen outside the coverage of any insurance. With a flexible application of the negligence concept the court ensured that the damage was covered by liability insurance. Maybe this case can be seen as an illustration of how the courts sometimes bend the concepts of tort law so that the costs of damages fall under insurance to the highest possible extent.

III Fault liability in legislation

A Statutory tort rules 1850–1972

In the old medieval Swedish province legislation (*landskapslagarna*) the closest equivalent to modern rules of liability was the *bot*, a penalty that in general was paid partly to the State (or some other public entity) and partly to the victim. The penalty system was used also in the law reform of 1734, but in this reform some rules similar to those of a modern tort law were also included. However, it was only in the mid nineteenth century that the penalty system was abolished and the rules on liability became independent of the penalty rules.

In the nineteenth century an ambitious suggestion for a general statute on civil law was presented.[26] In a suggested amendment to the Code of Commerce, Chapter 15, s. 5, it was stipulated that 'a damage that someone has suffered due to another one's negligence should be paid, even in cases which are not especially regulated'.[27] This is noteworthy since this is probably the first proposal for the introduction of a general '*culpa* rule' in Swedish legislation. The proposal was never enacted. Instead it was a chapter in the Criminal Act of 1864 that became the first collection of general rules on tort liability.

Chapter 6 of the Criminal Act was, when taken literally, only applicable to damages caused by way of criminal actions (and omissions), but to some extent it opened the way for negligence liability, since the main liability rule also explicitly mentioned that damages caused through a crime of negligence entailed liability. Also included in the chapter were rules on contributory fault of the victim and on joint liability in cases

[26] See, for the following, V. Lundstedt, *Grundlinjer i skadeståndsrätten. Förra delen: Culparegeln* (Uppsala: Norblad, 1935), p. 30.

[27] This is a modern translation. In Swedish the proposal had the following wording: 'skada, som någon lidit genom annans vållande, skall gäldas, även i de fall som ej i lagen utsatte äro'.

of multiple tortfeasors.[28] The Criminal Act was later replaced by a more comprehensive Criminal Code (*Brottsbalken*), but the chapter on damages continued to serve as the main source for tort law principles up until the introduction of the Tort Liability Act from 1972.

B The rise of the Swedish (Nordic) model: legislative work from 1950 to 1972

The start of the development of what has become known as the Swedish or Nordic model of tort law can be set to 1950.[29] At a meeting between representatives of the Justice Departments of Denmark, Norway and Sweden in 1946 it was decided to carry out further investigations on how the Nordic countries could deepen their legislative co-operation.[30] Tort law was one subject that was considered suitable for future investigations on possibly harmonised legislation. The task of putting together concrete suggestions was thereafter delegated to different persons from the three countries. As for Sweden, the assignment was given to Ivar Strahl, professor of private law.

1 Strahl

In 1950 Ivar Strahl put forward his 'Principle introduction' (*Principinledning*) as a Swedish Government Official Report (*Statens Offentliga Utredningar*; *SOU*).[31] It is noteworthy that Strahl's investigation was published as an official report, because it is in many regards a very radical and provocative suggestion.[32] Strahl's proposal did not immediately lead to legislation but his ideas have had a profound influence on

[28] See J. Hellner, *Lagstiftning inom förmögenhetsrätten* (Stockholm: Norstedt, 1990), p. 43.

[29] For some general accounts of the Swedish or Nordic approach to tort law in English, see J. Hellner, 'Compensation for Personal Injury: The Swedish Alternative'(1986) 34 *American Journal of Comparative Law* 613; Hellner, 'Compensation for Personal Injuries in Sweden'; C. Oldertz, 'Security Insurance, Patient Insurance, and Pharmaceutical Insurance in Sweden' (1986) 34 *American Journal of Comparative Law* 635. Some reflections on the Swedish alternative from a policy point of view are given by G. Calabresi, 'Policy Goals of the "Swedish Alternative"' (1986) 34 *American Journal of Comparative Law* 657.

[30] See for the following the historical exposé in Proposition 1972:5, pp. 50ff.

[31] *SOU* 1950:16. Complete title: 'Förberedande utredning angående lagstiftning på skadeståndsrättens område' ('Preliminary investigation regarding legislation in the area of tort law').

[32] Similar reports were also put forward by the special investigators in Denmark and Norway.

Swedish legal culture in general and on the law of compensation for accidents in particular.[33]

Strahl's proposal focussed on personal injuries but addressed also the law on property damages. When it came to personal injuries he proposed a radical shift of focus from tort liability to insurance solutions. Strahl's view was that the point of departure for future development should be the function of compensation for the victim, regardless of whether such compensation is paid by the tortfeasor, an insurance company or the State. With this view tort law becomes but one piece of the bigger puzzle of allocation of costs for compensation for personal injuries. In more concrete terms this means that personal injury compensation, to a significant degree in Strahl's view, should fall under insurance solutions, which may be either public or private, albeit a private insurance solution could be made mandatory.

In Strahl's view on compensation for personal injuries there was thus not much room for traditional negligence liability: from the victim's perspective, at least as far as compensation in money is concerned, it makes no difference whether she was injured by a negligent person or by a non-negligent person. Therefore the costs of compensation should be allocated in a way that minimises the risk that the victim be left uncompensated. In short, Strahl suggested that personal injury compensation in general should be covered by insurance solutions in all situations.

Strahl's proposal was modern in many other respects as well. His suggestion opened up the possibility of a liability for public bodies, it proposed a far-reaching employer liability and it included the first seed of today's rules on mitigation of damages. Strahl realised that his proposals were too radical to be implemented *tout court*, in the form of a comprehensive tort statute. He therefore recommended that the legislative work should be carried out in steps and that the work on law reform ought to begin where the need for reform was greatest.

2 Law reform proposals, 1951–1971

Strahl's proposal became widely discussed, for instance at the nineteenth Nordic Lawyers' Meeting in 1951. The discussion lead quickly to two new legislation proposals regarding compensation for victims of traffic accidents (*SOU* 1957:36) and liability for public bodies (*SOU* 1958:43) Another result of the discussion and the awakened interest in tort reform was the appointment of a special committee – the Tort Law Committee

[33] See Hellner and Radetzki, *Skadeståndsrätt*, p. 49.

(*Skadeståndskommittén*), which was given the mandate to come up with more concrete suggestions for tort legislation.[34]

The Committee consisted of three persons: retired Chief Justice Gösta Wallin, Professor Jan Hellner and attorney Per-Axel Weslin. Secretary to the Committee was Associate Judge of Appeal Ulf K. Nordensson. At first the mandate given to the Committee was to make suggestions for legislation on parents' and children's liability, and on employer/employee liability. This mandate was thereafter widened so that the Committee was asked to come up with a proposal for general civil law legislation on tort liability, to be introduced when the Criminal Code was supposed to succeed the older Criminal Act.

The Tort Law Committee presented several proposals for legislation, dealing with issues such as liability for parents and children (*SOU* 1963:33) and employer and employee liability (*SOU* 1964:31), and mitigation of damages (*SOU* 1971:83). During this period an official report on 'nuclear liability' was also presented, proposing strict liability for the nuclear industry (*SOU* 1966:29). The Committee worked in close contact with similar committees in the other Nordic countries, where similar committees had been set up. The proposals and investigations of the Danish, Finnish and Norwegian committees were very similar to those proposed by the Swedish one.

3 The Government Bill

The activity that was manifested in this series of official reports culminated in 1972 with the 'proposition' (the Government Bill) on a new Tort Liability Act (1972:5). By then legislation had already been introduced in some specific areas, but general tort law had up until then not been a subject for legislation. The Government Bill behind the Tort Liability Act is an important source of information in Swedish tort law, used, for instance, for interpretation of the statute.[35]

[34] See E. Nilsson, U. K. Nordensson, C. Oldertz and E. Strömbäck, 'Personskaderättens utveckling: Ersättning på grund av individiuell skadeståndsrätt eller kollektiv försäkring' in C. E. Sturkell, *Patient- och läkemedelsförsäkringen vid ett vägskäl, Vänbok till Carl E. Sturkell* (Stockholm: Försäkrings AB Skandia, 1996), p. 3.

[35] It should perhaps be noted here that it is common for Swedish lawyers to turn to the preparatory works as a source of law, especially in situations where statutory rules are ambiguous. The method employed by Swedish lawyers thus attaches much greater importance to sources such as the Government Bill than other jurisdictions. An example might illustrate this. In 1999 the Swedish Supreme Court found that a police officer whose face had been spat into was not entitled to compensation for the violation of integrity that the offence involved. A couple of years after this decision amendments to the

The work with the Government Bill was carried out by a special task force in the Justice Department, especially assigned to the project owing to its complicated and extensive nature. The task force was made up by the then Director, thereafter Director General of Legal Affairs, Ulf K. Nordensson; Professor Bertil Bengtsson; and Associate Judge of Appeals Erland Strömbäck.[36] In the Government Bill the head of the Justice Department stressed the importance of the *culpa* norm in Swedish tort law. The *culpa* norm, the head of the Department noted, is the basic norm in Swedish tort law. The emphasis on the *culpa* rule is interesting in light of the fact that the Tort Liability Act opens up so many exceptions to the regime of traditional fault liability.

C *The Tort Liability Act*

1 General remarks

As already mentioned, the most important legislation on general tort law today is the Tort Liability Act from 1972, which takes up some basic criteria for tort liability, although many basic requirements were left outside. A short history of the statute provides an illuminating view of the process.

The Tort Liability Act is a framework statute. Against this background it is interesting to note that the legislator included not just one rule on negligence but, in fact, at least five. Before the specific rules are presented a general overview of the Act might be useful. The Tort Liability Act consists of six chapters. The first chapter provides that the Act applies to situations of damages if there is no special legislation and there are no contractual damages rules that cover the situation.

Tort Liability Act were made, which for instance opened up the possibility for relatives of victims killed by the tortfeasor to receive compensation. In the Government Bill the issue of compensation for police officers who had been spat at was taken up. It was there stated that compensation for personal integrity should be awarded in these circumstances, but this statement was not followed by any suggestions for new legislation. Another couple of years later a similar case was tried by the Supreme Court. The situation was then that the Court had, just a couple of years earlier, found that spitting in someone's face was not an action compensatable under the rule on violation of integrity in the Tort Liability Act, and that this rule had not changed in substance since the previous decision. The only change between the decisions, to simplify, was the statement in the preparatory work. The majority of the Supreme Court found in a plenary decision that the police officer who had been spat upon should be awarded damages for violation of personal integrity.

36 See Nilsson, Nordensson, Oldertz and Strömbäck, 'Personskaderättens utveckling', p. 4.

2 The basic rule

The second chapter of the Tort Liability Act starts with what can only be described as the most important general rule on liability in Swedish law, the general '*culpa* rule'. According to this rule a person is liable for another's personal injury or property damage if the injury or damage was caused 'intentionally or negligently'. This rule thus only covers liability for personal injury and property damage. Outside of this rule, therefore, fall the two other categories of damage according to the general categorisation: pure economic loss and the rather recently established damage category of *kränkning*, violation of personal integrity.

3 Pure economic loss

Pure economic loss is compensatable if it is caused through criminal behaviour according to Chapter 2, s. 2 of the Tort Liability Act. This rule is not supposed to be interpreted *e contrario*: the section does not mean that pure economic loss can never be compensatable in the *absence* of a criminal offence.[37] In some situations where compensation can be awarded also for non-criminal behaviour the standard of negligence can be said to work as a starting point for an assessment of liability.

4 *Kränkning*

A violation of the personal integrity, which is notably not considered as a personal injury in the structure of the Swedish Tort Liability Act,[38] is compensatable if it is a result of crime of a particular kind, according to Chapter 2, s. 3 of the Tort Liability Act. This kind of compensation has traditionally been possible only in cases where the activity (or omission)

[37] It was thus not the legislator's intention, according to the preparatory works, that this rule should exclude pure economic loss resulting from non-criminal behaviour. However, in the practice of the courts the rule has nevertheless been interpreted in just this way, so that pure economic loss generally will only be compensated where the defendant's action was criminal (for instance fraudulent). Some clear exceptions to this reluctant attitude towards compensation for pure economic loss in non-criminal cases are negligent misrepresentation (cf. NJA 1987, p. 692), *culpa in contrahendo* (cf. NJA 1990, p. 745; and the treatment in J. Munukka, *Kontraktuell lojalitetsplikt* (Stockholm: Jure Förlag, 2007), pp. 432 ff.) and – only recently acknowledged – inducement to breach of contract (see NJA 2005, p. 608). In these situations the issue of liability will often revolve around the notion of negligence, albeit that there are often some sort of additional criteria for liability (such as justifiable reliance; NJA 1987, p. 692).

[38] A clear distinction between personal injury and *kränkning* was drawn by the Supreme Court in a recent decision from 7 June 2007 (T4961–05). This is discussed in M. Schultz, 'Kritim mot kränkningsbegreppet' (2007) *Svensk Juristtidning* 10.

complained of falls under a particular liability rule, such as the one just mentioned in the Tort Liability Act. An exception has recently been made in situations of violations of rights under the European Convention on Human Rights.[39] Except for the case of human rights violations one can still presume that compensation for violation of personal integrity will generally only be awarded when the defendant acted criminally. In these cases the issue of negligence will thus only come into play if the crime in question is a crime of negligence.

5 Children and mentally disturbed tortfeasors

The second chapter of the Tort Liability Act takes up two other negligence rules, with a more narrow scope. In the fourth section there is a special negligence rule regarding children. According to s. 4 children are liable under ss. 1–3 (of the second chapter in the Act) to the extent that it is reasonable with regard to their age and development, the nature of the act, existing liability insurance, and economic as well as other factors. In the fifth section there is a very similar rule regarding mentally disturbed persons, which says that if someone causes damage while in a state of mental disturbance he is liable under ss. 1–3 (of the second chapter in the Act) to the extent that it is reasonable with regard to his state of mind, the nature of the act, existing liability insurance and economic as well as other factors. These two rules concerning children and mentally disturbed persons thus refer to the previous rules in the second chapter of the Tort Liability Act and are therefore not on the face of it exclusively negligence rules. However, the special liability criteria set out for both children and mentally disturbed tortfeasors have a special effect in combination with the basic negligence rule. For instance, if a child causes a personal injury, she will be liable if she acted negligently under the basic rule in Chapter 2, s. 1, but the assessment of her negligence will be made in accordance with the specific criteria set out in s. 4.

One can here note that there exist what can best be described as some unwritten rules regarding the negligence evaluation when it comes to children. For instance, even very small children fall under the rule if taken literally. There is thus no age limitation for tortious liability in the Act. The main reason for this is not that the legislator thought that the cost of damages at the end of the day should be carried by the children, but to leave open the possibility of using a liability insurance that covered

[39] NJA 2005, p. 462.

the act of the child.[40] Furthermore, it is normally assumed that very small children can *never* be negligent.[41]

Another aspect of children's liability is that the assessment of negligence when it comes to children is thought to be made more objectively than usual.[42] This is then contrasted with the assessment of negligence that is supposed to be made under the general *culpa* rule, which is often assumed to be made with regard to both subjective and objective criteria.

The rule for mentally disturbed tortfeasors resembles the rule on children's liability.

6 Employer and employee liability

In the third chapter of the Tort Liability Act the general rule on employer liability is stated in s. 1. According to this rule an employer is responsible for damage caused by her employee while the employee is 'in service' (*i tjänst*). However, this rule also presupposes fault: an employer is only liable for damages negligently caused by her employees. Employer liability is thus not a strict liability in Swedish law.

In some situations the employee will not be considered negligent, because of lack of competence or mental development. In these circumstances the employer will be able to escape liability under the rule on employer liability. In such situations, however, the courts sometimes fall back on the general *culpa* rule in Chapter 2, s. 1, and hold the employer liable for her own fault as an employer. This approach is sometimes referred to as the principle of *culpa in eligendo, vel instruendo, vel inspeciendo*. It is thus a variation on the general *culpa* rule, but applied in situations where an employer was negligent in appointing an employee (perhaps the employee was young and incompetent), in instructing the employee or in inspecting the work carried out.

When it comes to employer liability the fault principle can therefore still be considered as a basic responsibility norm. The same cannot be said for the employee's own liability. There is a rule on employee liability in Chapter 4, s. 1 that holds that an employee is only liable for damages caused at work in extraordinary circumstances.

7 The liability public bodies

The general rule on liability public bodies is provided in Chapter 3, s. 2. This rule also revolves around a notion of fault, albeit differently

[40] See Proposition 1972:5, p. 164.

[41] See NJA 1977, p. 186. Cf. Bengtsson and Strömbäck, *Skadeståndslagen*, p. 66.

[42] See Proposition 1972:5, p. 164. Cf. *ibid.*

formulated than in the rules in Chapter 2. Liability for public bodies arises when damage is caused through the exercise of public authority, if the action (or omission) that caused the damage was negligent (in this rule formulated as *fel eller försummelse*, which can be translated as 'wrongs or negligence'). The rule applies also in cases of pure economic loss and is in this respect more far-reaching than private liability. An important restriction is the requirement of 'the exercise of public authority' (*myndighetsutövning*).

There are several restrictions and supplements to this rule in the third chapter of the Act, which are not of interest here.[43]

IV Exceptions from fault liability

A Introduction to the Nordic model

Many injuries and property damages will never be tried under the general rules of fault liability. The shift from the general *culpa* rule to different insurance solutions is in fact considered as a foundational development of the Swedish welfare state in general. It is not an exaggeration to say that the introduction of overarching compensation mechanisms was a core constituent in the construction of the Swedish welfare state. This development often goes under the name of the Swedish, or the Nordic, model.

The Nordic model of tort law (with emphasis on personal injury law) can be characterised in different ways. From a policy point of view, the most fundamental and almost banal idea is probably that *personal injury should always be compensated*.[44] To achieve this goal it has generally been agreed that the cost of personal injury compensation is in general best carried by collective entities. To a lesser degree this also goes for property damages. The legal system has provided rules that promote the bearing by collective entities of costs resulting from personal injuries.

A more detailed picture of the Nordic model will reveal a complex interplay between social insurance and other kinds of collective compensation schemes as well as personal insurance, and – to a lesser extent – tort law. The Nordic model is not the same as the New Zealand approach to

[43] For instance there are restrictions when it comes to liability for the highest courts and a special rule on liability for erroneous information (which has never been tried by the Supreme Court).

[44] For some general accounts of the Swedish or Nordic approach to tort law, see references above, n. 29.

personal injuries; the idea was never that the taxpayer should cover all costs of personal injury. In fact one of the basic ideas was that the costs instead should be covered by insurance paid for by the party responsible for activities that were thought to be particularly risky (and thus not by the taxpayer).

In a narrow sense the Nordic model is sometimes used as a collective term for four important compensation schemes, covering traffic accidents, patient injuries, pharmaceutical injuries and work-related injuries.[45] These different insurance systems are crucial to an understanding of fault liability in Swedish law, since they all entail that fault liability be pushed aside in their respective areas. In a more extensive sense one can see the Nordic model as encompassing not only these comprehensive compensation schemes but a general outlook on the relationship between personal injury compensation and insurance. Some examples of this will be given below.

1 The traffic insurance scheme

Traffic injuries were the subject of special legislation already in 1916[46] and have long been covered by a no fault-compensation scheme.[47] In Sweden compensation for a victim of a traffic accident will now often be dealt with under the specific rules in the Motor Traffic Damage Act (in Swedish *Trafikskadelagen*).[48] The Motor Traffic Damage Act was the product of a proposal by the Traffic Injury Committee.[49] The Traffic Injury Committee was headed by Ulf K. Nordensson, who thereafter became a Chief Justice at the Supreme Court; Erland Strömbäck held the post of secretary to the Committee.[50]

The Act contains rules regarding claims for personal injuries as well as property damage, but provides no rules regarding the category of pure

[45] Hellner, 'Compensation for Personal Injuries in Sweden', 249. An interesting and more overarching account of Swedish tort law in an international perspective can be found in B. W. Dufwa, 'Development of International Tort Law till the Beginning of the 1990s from a Scandinavian Point of View' (2001) 41 *Scandinavian Studies in Law* 87.

[46] See generally S. Friberg and B. W. Dufwa, 'The Development of Traffic Liability in Sweden' in W. Ernst (ed.), *The Development of Traffic Liability* (Cambridge: Cambridge University Press, 2010), p. 204.

[47] See Jan Hellner, *Lagstiftning inom förmögenhetsrätten* (Stockholm: Norstedts, 1990), pp. 129ff; Hellner and Radetzki, *Skadeståndsrätt*, p. 275.

[48] *Trafikskadelag* 1975:1410.

[49] *SOU* 1974:87.

[50] For some comments on this see B. W. Dufwa, 'Vår komplicerade trafikskadesrätt och framtiden' (1979) *Svensk Juristtidning* 401, esp. 415ff.

economic loss. This statute lays down the rules concerning mandatory traffic insurance and deals with issues of compensation under such insurance.[51] In theory, however, the victim could claim compensation in tort law instead, should she be able to identify a tortfeasor.[52] In such a case the claim would be dealt with under the rules of the Tort Liability Act (*Skadeståndslagen*).[53]

In the vast majority of traffic accidents compensation claims are dealt with under the scheme of traffic insurance. The motor traffic insurance is a mandatory liability no-fault insurance. It covers not only the personal injuries of 'external' victims, but also drivers and passengers.

In cases where the victim cannot identify the driver or for other reasons cannot claim compensation from a specific insurance giver, the claim will be handled by the Motor Traffic Insurers Association (Trafikförsäkringsföreningen; TFF), under the Motor Traffic Damage Act, s. 33. By law, all providers of traffic insurance are *jointly responsible* in these cases, but the claim is handled by the TFF.

There is a special dispute resolution mechanism that handles complaints about traffic insurance. If someone is dissatisfied with the decision by the insurer she may appeal the decision to the Board of Motor Traffic Injuries (Trafikskadenämnden).

2 The pharmaceutical insurance scheme

The pharmaceutical insurance scheme differs from the other insurance solutions discussed here since it does not fall under any special statute.

[51] A general presentation of the Swedish system in English is provided in a brochure by the Swedish Motor Insurers Association:

> The attention of non-Swedish readers may be drawn specifically to these elements: (1) Personal injury claims are settled in the first instance under the MTPL (motor third-party liability) insurance of the vehicle in which the person injured had either been travelling or had been in the vicinity of. (2) Compensation is paid on objective grounds. (3) The driver is also entitled to compensation, irrespective of legal liability. (4) The claim settlement process refers to two stages, first the period of medical emergency then any period of permanent disability. (5) Full compensation is paid, after a deduction for coordination benefits, for financial loss arising from the injury. (6) Non-financial damage or loss is divided into three categories – pain and suffering, disadvantage and incapacity, and costs and specific inconveniences. (7) Compensation for future loss of income is normally paid in the form of an annuity, while non-financial compensation takes the form of a lump sum payment. (8) Compensation in respect of any period of disability is established by the impartial, specially appointed *Trafikskadenämnd* (TSN (the Swedish Road Traffic Injuries Commission)).

[52] This is also explicitly noted in the Motor Traffic Damage Act, s. 18.

[53] *Skadeståndslag* 1972:207.

When the Product Liability Committee presented its proposal in 1976, it was suggested that a mandatory accident insurance should be introduced in the area of pharmaceutical injuries and that this insurance scheme should fall under a special statute (similar to the statute on patient injuries).[54] The proposal was that compensation for injuries resulting from pharmaceutical products would be directly paid from the insurance to the victim and that the insurance should be collective and, for the most part, paid by the pharmaceutical industry.

This development was, so to say, prevented by the pharmaceutical industry, which quickly set up private pharmaceutical insurance.[55] The pharmaceutical insurance from 1978 was collective in the sense that it was financed by the pharmaceutical companies together. More specifically the insurance was set up by the Pharmaceutical Association (Läkemedelsföreningen, LFF), which is an association constituting all pharmaceutical product manufacturers or importers in Sweden.

Every Swedish person is automatically covered by pharmaceutical insurance and may receive compensation if injured by a pharmaceutical product. A prerequisite is that the pharmaceutical product that caused the injury was supplied by a member of the LFF for consumption in Sweden. Sweden has a monopoly on sales of pharmaceutical products and in practice almost all drugs used in Sweden are sold by the State-owned chain of drug stores, Apoteket. All medicine and other pharmaceutical products sold by Apoteket thus fall within the scope of pharmaceutical insurance. The pharmaceutical insurance is a no-fault insurance. The victim will thus not have to establish that a pharmaceutical company or anyone else was negligent to receive compensation. The LFF purchases the insurance from traditional insurance companies in the market, which then carry out the concrete work of handling claims etc. At present, pharmaceutical insurance is provided by the international insurance company Zürich.

There is a special dispute resolution mechanism that handles complaints against pharmaceutical insurance. If someone is dissatisfied with the insurer's decision she may appeal the decision to the Board of Pharmaceutical Injuries (Läkemedelsskadenämnden).

The scope of pharmaceutical insurance is co-ordinated with patient insurance, to avoid the risk of a claim falling outside both insurance schemes.

[54] *SOU* 1976:23.

[55] The history behind pharmaceutical insurance is described in Jan Lundberg, '17 år med läkemedelsförsäkringen' in Sturkell, *Patient- och läkemedelsförsäkringen*, pp. 37ff.

3 The patient insurance scheme

In the work on the Tort Liability Act there was an ongoing discussion as to whether there was a need for special rules on patient injuries; for instance, the introduction of a strict liability regime was discussed.[56] As with pharmaceutical insurance, legislative development was interrupted by a proactive industry with the introduction of voluntary patient insurance in 1975. At first, there was no special legislation that dealt with compensation from patient insurance. The patient insurance scheme was set up in much the same way as pharmaceutical insurance. The public Swedish health providers, which at the time of the introduction of the insurance completely dominated the 'market' for health services, made an arrangement with a consortium set up by four insurance companies. According to the arrangement, the consortium insured all patients in Sweden. In the early 1990s Sweden entered the European Community and the consortium was then considered to be in violation of EC competition rules. The consortium was therefore abolished, and instead patient insurance is now provided by different insurance companies. In 1996 a statute on patient injuries compensation was decided upon: the Patient Injuries Act (*Patientskadelagen*).[57]

The patient insurance scheme is no-fault insurance, and a patient who has been injured while undergoing treatment (and in some other situations as well, for instance while participating in experimental research) can claim compensation directly from the insurer. The victim will thus not have to establish that anyone acted negligently to receive compensation. No compensation from the insurance is given when the injury was the result of adequate medical treatment – for instance, if the patient was given CPR at a hospital she can thus not claim compensation under the insurance for any fractured ribs resulting from the treatment.

Patient insurance has another function that is not that well known. Apart from providing patients with the possibility of claiming compensation directly from the insurer in cases of personal injuries, it also works as liability insurance for the health providers.[58] The Patient Injuries Act leaves the victim with the possibility of claiming compensation in tort law, instead of patient insurance compensation. The rules of tort law

[56] See U. Hellbacher, 'Försäkringslösningar inom sjukvården och en ny patientskadelag' in *ibid.*, p. 45.

[57] *Patientskadelag* 1996:799.

[58] This is discussed in M. Magnusson, 'Patientförsäkringen inför rätta' in Sturkell, *Patient- och läkemedelsförsäkringen*, pp. 219ff.

may in different situations seem preferable to the patient. In practice it is unusual, although not unheard of, for patients to choose the tort law approach.[59] There is a special dispute resolution mechanism that handles complaints against patient insurance. If someone is dissatisfied with the decision of the insurer, she may appeal the decision to the Board of Patient Injuries (Patientskadenämnden).

4 The occupational compensation scheme

Compensation for occupational injuries is regulated differently compared to the previously mentioned types of injuries. This has to do with the background of the compensation scheme. To a significant degree the current compensation solution is the product of collective agreements between the parties in the labour market.[60] However, there are aspects of the compensation system that rather belong to social insurance law.[61] In addition, the rules of tort law may play an important part if an injury falls outside the scope of the insurance solutions.

The compensation scheme for occupational injuries can thus be described as a three-tier approach.[62] Basic coverage is provided by a special social insurance that deals only with occupational injuries: the occupational injury insurance. This insurance covers all persons involved in 'gainful employment' (*förvärvsarbete*) and is paid for by payroll taxes. The occupational injury insurance was introduced in 1976 but underwent important alterations in 1992. In addition to social insurance, there are private collective insurances, the so-called safety occupational injury insurance (*trygghetsförsäkring vid arbetsskada*). As a third solution there

[59] One special situation where it is sometimes considered that adequate compensation cannot be claimed under the patient insurance scheme is when the patient has been subjected to treatment that she did not consent to, or was not given the opportunity to give an informed consent to. The lack of consent in these situations provides a difficult problem, since it is generally not considered sufficient for a claim against patient insurance (nor in tort law) if the medical procedure was justified as such. The absence of a remedy in these situations is thought problematic since there are rules in health legislation that explicitly hold that the patient must be granted the opportunity of giving an informed consent to the treatment if possible. See for one decision NJA 1990, p. 442. See for comments Anders Agell, 'The Conceptual Relationship between Medical Malpractice and the Lack of Informed Consent' in L. Westerhäll and C. Phillips (eds.), *Patient Rights* (Stockholm: Nerenus and Santérus, 1994), p. 85; E. Rynning, 'Consent to Medical Treatment: Legal Relevancy in Sweden' in *ibid.*, pp. 321ff.; and – in Swedish – E. Rynning, *Samtycke till medicinsk vård och behandling* (Uppsala: Iustus, 1994).

[60] See regarding this C. M. Roos, *Ersättningsrätt och ersättningssystem* (Stockholm: Norstedt, 1990), pp. 73ff.

[61] *Ibid.*, pp. 57ff. [62] See Hellner and Radetzki, *Skadeståndsrätt*, p. 293.

is the possibility of claiming compensation in tort law. This possibility is mostly of interest in situations where the victim was outside the 'normal' labour market.

The occupational injury insurance scheme is one of Sweden's oldest social insurance systems. The first statute on compensation for occupational injuries was enacted as early as 1901.[63] In 1916 a statute on mandatory insurance for occupational injuries was introduced and it was followed by a statute on compensation for particular diseases that were connected with occupational risks. The current legislation came into force in 1976.

Safety occupational injury insurance has been considered unique to the Scandinavian jurisdictions.[64] This type of insurance is the product of agreements between the Confederation of Swedish Enterprises (Svenskt näringsliv) and the two major union organisations, Landsorganisationen i Sverige (LO) and Privattjänstemannakartellen (PTK). Other parties in the labour market have also joined the insurance. The agreement entails that the parties in the labour market stipulate in collective agreements that the employer must take out safety insurance for her employees. The insurance type was developed in the early 1970s and reflects the social security policy concerns that carried a lot of weight at the time. The main purpose of the insurance is to provide means of compensation for the victims of occupational injuries, but it also functions as a hindrance to litigation. A victim of an occupational injury is thus not allowed to claim compensation in tort law from an employer that falls under the insurance.[65]

5 Conclusions

One important feature of these schemes is that they are all intended more or less to replace the tort system in their respective areas and that insurance is mandatory. It is thus mandatory for someone (whether a private company or a public entity) that provides medical services to pay premiums to the patient insurance scheme. The patient insurance is supplied by a private insurance company and is supposed to cover all claims for personal injuries against the service provider. It is therefore very unusual to see, for instance, malpractice claims tried in the higher courts in Sweden, since the compensation issue is normally dealt with under the special

[63] See for the following C. M. Roos, 'Arbetsskadeförsäkringen och ersättningssystemet' in *Arbetsskador och annat* (Stockholm: Nerenus and Santérus, 1994), p. 49.

[64] According to Roos, *Ersättningsrätt*, p. 57.

[65] Hellner and Radetzki, *Skadeståndsrätt*, pp. 296ff.

system set up under the Act on Patient Injuries, which mainly deals with claims for compensation through patient insurance.[66] Similar points can be made with regard to the kind of injuries that fall under the other three mentioned compensation schemes. The type of tort claims that have plagued the American courts, for instance (associated with asbestos, DES, silicone implants, Agent Orange etc.), are today by and large unheard of in the Nordic countries. From the perspective of fault liability one can note that in the areas where special compensation schemes have been set up, the practical importance of the general *culpa* rule has been reduced. In principle it is often in these cases still possible for the victim to claim compensation in tort law, instead of, say, through patient insurance. In practice this possibility is seldom used. From a comparative perspective the compensation solution for occupational injuries seems unusual but also the most typical: complete coverage for costs associated with occupational injuries is accomplished through a rather complicated series of measures in both social insurance law and private insurance law. This compensation scheme has been set up partly by the State, partly by the parties in the labour market, and illustrates the interconnection between the public law side and the private law side that are so characteristic of Swedish labour law.

B More on the Nordic model: examples of the relationship between insurance and tort law in Swedish law

In a more extensive sense one can see the Nordic model as encompassing not only the above-mentioned compensation schemes but a general outlook on the relationship between personal injury compensation and insurance. Many damages, including personal injuries, thus fall under other kinds of insurance, such as the private 'home insurance' that covers most Swedish citizens. The view that the costs of damages to the highest extent possible should be covered by insurance has also had important influence on tort legislation as well as on court practice. It has meant not only that the victim will generally have a good chance of receiving compensation, especially in the case of personal injury, but also that the

[66] The victim still has the option to claim compensation in tort law for patient injuries according to a rule in the Act, but this is seldom used since it is mostly more convenient to claim compensation from the insurance system. There is also a special procedural system that can be used when the (alleged) victim is dissatisfied with the decision by the insurance company, which is often also more beneficial to the victim than the court system since it is generally free of charge (for the victim).

person who caused the damage will, in many situations, be shielded from the risk of severe liability. In reality this therefore has important implications for the significance of the general *culpa* rule. I will give a couple of examples from the Swedish Tort Liability Act.

1 Employer and employee liability

According to the Swedish Tort Liability Act (1972:207) an employer is liable for personal injuries and property damage caused by her employees within the scope of their service (Chapter 3, s. 1). As noted above, this is not a strict liability in the true sense of the expression since liability presumes negligence, even though the negligence of the employee is reflected on the employer. A reason behind this legislation is that the employer should include the risk of liability as a cost of the business. In reality the employer will purchase insurance that covers potential liability.

As a result of this attitude the employee that caused the damage will only rarely be under an obligation to bear the cost of damages. According to the Tort Liability Act, Chapter 4, s. 1, the employee is only liable in extraordinary circumstances (which are almost never considered to be present). This latter rule thus protects the employee from liability for damages caused while at work, and it also means that an employer who has paid compensation to a victim for a harm caused by her employee will only have a right to recover these costs from the employee in extraordinary circumstances. Not even if the employee was grossly negligent will she be liable in all situations.

An interesting detail of the employer liability regime is a seldom discussed rule on the reduction of damages only applicable in cases of employer liability in the Tort Liability Act, Chapter 3, s. 6. That the rule is seldom the subject of treatment by the higher courts does not, I think, mean that it is not of practical importance. The rule states that in a situation of employer liability damages may be lowered if the obligation would be too burdensome, considering, *inter alia*, the insurance coverage of the parties. In reality it seems that the main purpose of the rule is to provide a way for the courts to be able to allocate the costs associated with the damage to an existing insurance.[67]

[67] In an informative court decision (NJA 1996, p. 118) the Supreme Court showed how the rule might be used. The situation was as follows. Employees A and B were welders and caused a major fire in a building through grossly negligent behaviour. The building burnt down. The owner of the building had insurance issued by insurance company X covering the full amount of the building, approximately 10 million Swedish krona (approximately

2 Contributory conduct of the victim in cases of personal injury

The Swedish system generally holds that social welfare concerns require compensation for personal injuries to be awarded also when a victim contributes to her own injury. Exceptions may be made in extraordinary cases, but, if the victim negligently contributed to her own injury, full compensation is generally awarded (Chapter 6, s. 1).[68]

Even in cases where the victim was injured in a traffic accident after having driven under the influence of alcohol or other substances, full compensation (from traffic insurance) will often be awarded. The concept of fault – *culpa* – thus plays a smaller role when it comes to the conduct of the victim that contributed to the damage.

3 Reduction of damages in general

The Swedish Tort Liability Act includes a rule providing the court with an open possibility of reducing the amount of damages, 'if needed', all the way to zero, if the obligation to pay damages would be unreasonably burdensome for the tortfeasor: Chapter 6, s. 2. A factor to be regarded in the assessment of reduction of damages is whether the damage is covered by insurance. If the tortfeasor has liability insurance there is generally no reason to reduce the damages, but if the tortfeasor is not protected by liability insurance and the damage falls under insurance on the victim's side there may often be reasons to reduce the damages. The Swedish rule on reduction of damages may be used, and is in fact often used, even when the tortfeasor has caused the damage through intentional criminal behaviour (for instance theft).

€1 million). The company that employed the welders, C, was covered by liability insurance issued by insurance company Y, and this insurance was good for amounts up to 2 million krona. Company X recovered 2 million krona from Y and sued A and B, as well as C, for the remaining amount of 8 million krona, partly using the argument that the behaviour had been grossly negligent. The Supreme Court stated that in these circumstances the rule in Chapter 3, s. 6 must be interpreted as a restriction on the possibility of receiving compensation in tort law, and this especially in light of the fact that the liability insurance taken by C was a standard kind of insurance. It would be unreasonably burdensome to impose liability in these situations for the amount that was not covered by normal liability insurance. The gross negligence of the employees did not change this. The decision is a good example of how the Swedish system allocates the costs of damage to insurance solutions.

68 See Hellner, 'Compensation for Personal Injuries'.

C Reflections

These are only a couple of illustrations of how the idea that costs for damages should be allocated to insurance has influenced the Swedish tort system. In addition one should also take into account the protection provided by the social insurance system, that means that most costs for medical treatment etc. will be covered by the taxpayer. There are several effects of this system. The most important is that the victim of personal injury in most situations will be able to receive compensation from insurance, which means that she does not need to find and sue a solvent tortfeasor. This is even the case when the victim herself contributed to the cause of the injury. Another important aspect of this is that private persons will often be protected from liability. All in all these factors mean that compensation under traditional fault liability will often be superseded by other solutions. As Jan Hellner notes, with regard to the Swedish model: '[F]ault is almost completely rejected both as the basis for entitlement to compensation and … as a reason for reducing an indemnity for personal injury.'[69]

D Strict liability

Swedish law has generally held a reluctant attitude towards strict liability. It has long been considered to be a main rule in Swedish tort law that strict liability generally presumes legislative support.[70] This is in contrast with, for instance, Denmark, where the attitude towards strict liability has been more open. In a way this reluctance to let the courts expand the regime of strict liability to new situations or branches might reflect a deep commitment to the *culpa* rule in Sweden: fault liability is considered such an important basic feature of tort liability that legislation is required to depart from it.

It should be noted that the important rules on liability for employers for the damages caused by their employees are not considered as strict liability in Swedish law, since these rules generally presume fault on behalf of the employee.

1 Exceptions to the main rule: strict liability without statutory support

There are exceptions to the main rule that strict liability presupposes legislative support. There are some old examples of such exceptions when

[69] *Ibid.* [70] See Hellner and Radetzki, *Skadeståndsrätt*, p. 172.

the courts found that particularly dangerous activities should come with strict liability: the most well-known cases involved military exercises.[71] In more recent times the Supreme Court has established strict liability in situations involving damages caused by defective water pipes.[72]

2 Examples of legislation with rules on strict liability

There are several statutes in which rules of strict liability are laid down. In some cases these special rules have been introduced because of international treatises, such as strict liability for nuclear plants.[73] In some cases the rules are explained by country-specific historical factors, such as the strict liability for dogs.[74] Other examples include strict liability for railway accidents, for damage caused by air traffic and for damage caused by electricity.[75] In these areas, with the possible exception of the strict liability for dog owners, the policy argument behind the strict liability regime is that the person responsible for the risky activity should take out liability insurance that covers the potential liability. Such insurance coverage is in some cases obligatory.

Strict liability also applies for environmental damage, which is of special interest. The liability rules in the Environmental Code are rather narrowly formulated, and not all damage that would, in a wider sense of the word, be called environmental damage is covered by the Environmental Code, especially the rules contained in Chapter 32.[76] The emphasis of the rules in Chapter 32 of the Environmental Code is on relationships between neighbours, and most rules herein are thus of a type that in English law would be dealt with under the heading of nuisance law.[77] In Chapter 32, s. 3, it is stated that liability under the chapter can arise for different 'disturbances', which are listed in the section. The disturbances that entitle the victim to compensation are pollution of water areas, pollution of ground-

[71] See NJA 1928, p. 316; NJA 1946, p. 734 I and II; and NJA 1946, p. 758 I and II.

[72] See NJA 1991, p. 720; NJA 1997, p. 468; and NJA 2001, p. 368.

[73] See the Nuclear Responsibility Act (*Atomansvarighetslag* 1968:45). Notes on the background to the statute are given in *SOU* 1966:29, pp. 22ff.

[74] See *lag* 1943:459, 'om tillsyn över hundar och katter', s. 6.

[75] See concerning this Hellner and Radetzki, *Skadeståndsrätt*, pp. 172ff.

[76] For instance, ecological harm that has not been caused by activities on a piece of land would not fall under the Code.

[77] Chapter 32 of the Environmental Code includes other rules as well and not only rules on the relationship between neighbours/landowners. There are also several rules on liability for damage in relation to construction work (which would hardly fall under the expression 'environmental damage' in everyday language).

water, changing of groundwater level, air pollution, land pollution, noise, vibration or other similar disturbance.

The strict liability regimes have developed at different times. Railway liability, the archetypical example of strict liability, can provide an illustration of the development. Railway liability is traditionally held to have developed in Swedish law under the same conditions as in many other jurisdictions and was the first example of a modern type of strict liability.[78] In the nineteenth century, an increasing number of accidents were caused by railway traffic, especially by sparks from the trains.[79] At first these accidents fell under the general *culpa* norm, and the victim was therefore only entitled to compensation if she could prove that the railway company or someone else had acted negligently. According to one leading authority this sometimes led the courts to desperate attempts to squeeze the activity of the railway into the category of negligence.[80] In some situations it is rather clear that the courts simply simulated *culpa* even though the activity would not qualify as negligent by traditional standards.[81] As a result of this development, a special statute on railway liability was enacted in 1886.[82] The Act of 1886 included rules on the employer's responsibility for the negligence of the employees, but it also included a rule on strict liability for accidents caused by sparks. The statute of 1886 was succeeded in 1904 and thereafter 1916 with other statutes on railway liability, which also covered – a novelty at the time – railways run by electricity. (The Act on railway liability also included a special rule on the right to compensation for accidents involving reindeer owned by Sami reindeer farmers.) The current rules are given in the general Railway Traffic Act of 1985.[83]

[78] Hellner and Radetzki, *Skadeståndsrätt*, p. 174.

[79] See regarding this K. Grönfors, *Om trafikskadeansvar* (Uppsala: Norblad, 1952), p. 23.

[80] *Ibid.* Grönfors illustrates this with the decision NT 1868, p. 348.

[81] *Ibid.*, p. 25. [82] *Ibid.*, p. 26.

[83] *Järnvägstrafiklag* 1985:192.

INDEX

Abinger, Lord, 37–38, 40–42
academics
contribution to legal change, 6–8
England, 7–8, 18–20
France, 7, 90
Germany, 7
Netherlands, 7, 9
Sweden, 7
Scotland
contribution to convergence, 70–71
contribution to development of delictual liability, 71–75
contribution to legal change, 6
Accident Compensation Act (New Zealand 1972), 56
Accident Offices Association, 54
actio de pauperie, 136
Air Navigation Act (Spain, 1960)
Chapter XIII, Arts. 120–125, 179
Chapter XIV, 179
Airedale NHS Trust v. *Bland*, 79
Alexanderson CJ, Nils, 202
Alguer, J., 175
Allgemeines Deutsches Handelsgesetzbuch 1861, §§ 422 ff., 125
ALR (Allgemeines Preußisches Landrecht)
I 6 §72, 139
II 8 § 444 ff, 117–118
Animals (Scotland) Act 1987, 82
Apoteket, 221
Appellate Committee of the House of Lords, 14–15
Appellate Jurisdiction Act (UK 1876), 64
Asquith, Cyril, Lord Asquith, 29
Asquith, Herbert, Lord Oxford, 46–48
Association of Mutual Insurance Companies, 54
Atiyah, P. S., 41
Atkin, Lord, 23–25
Ayrton, Acton, 42–43
AZF factory explosion, Toulouse, 21 September 2001, 102

Badinter, Robert, 8, 109, 112, *See also loi Badinter*
Barker v. *Corus UK Ltd*, 87
Bartonshill Coal Co. v. *Reid*, 39, 64
Baums, Theodor, 116
Bell, George Joseph, 72
Bengtsson, Bertil, 202–203, 214
Berger, Adolf, 72
Beveridge Committee (Social Insurance and Allied Services Committee), 50–52, 54, 57–58
Beveridge, William, 50–51
BGB
§ 276 II, 130
§ 831, 138
§ 832, 138
§ 833, 138, 139, 140, 141
§ 836, 138
animal liability
1908 reform, 138–140
genesis, 135–138
Birks, Peter, 79
Black, Robert, 60

Blackie, John, 69
Blieck, 94
Bolam v. *Friern Hospital Management Committee*, 16, 77
Borrell Maciá, A., 175
Borthwick, John, *Law of Libel and Slander*, 70
bot, 210
Boudier, 94, 96–98
Brazilian Criminal Code, 1830, 184
British Employers Confederation (BEC), 54, 55
British Railways Board v. *Herrington*, 23
Broun, James, *Law of Nuisance*, 70
Brydon v. *Stewart*, 39
Burnett v. *Grampian Fire and Rescue Service*, 86–87
Butterfield v. *Forrester*, 40

Callaghan, James, 57
Campbell, Lord, 15, 63
Candler v. *Crane, Christmas & Co.*, 23
Caparo Industries plc v. *Dickman*, 23
Capital and Counties plc v. *Hampshire County Council*, 87
Capitant, Henri, 96
Carbonnier, Jean, 96
Carson, Lord, 16
cas fortuit, 104
case reporting style, France, 93–94
Castán Tobeñas, José, 8, 176–178
Cellar Hatch (Kelderluik) case, 155
Chadwick, Edwin, 47, 48
Chamberlain, Joseph, 47, 48
Civil Liability of Civil Servants Act (Spain 5 April 1904)
  Art. 1, 188
Clayette case, 98
Clelland v. *Robb*, 67
Clerk Thomson, Lord, 81–82
Clyde, Lord, 77, 78
Comisión de Reformas Sociales, 190
comparative law, in Scottish courts, 75–76
compatibility doctrine, 192
Compensation Act (UK 2006), 27
Confederation of Swedish Enterprises (*Svenskt näringsliv*), 224
Conspiracy and Protection of Property Act (UK1875), 43–44
Consumer Protection Act (Spain 1984), 182–183
Cooper, Frank, *Defamation and Verbal Injury*, 70
County Council of the Parts of Lindsey, Lincolnshire v. *Marshall*, 24
Cour de cassation, 93–94
Court of Session (Scotland), 59
  and duty of care in negligence, 67–68
Crofter Handwoven Harris Tweed Co. v. *Veitch*, 66–67
culpa rule (Sweden), 201
culpa, Scotland, 60

Damages (Scotland) Act 1976, 81
damages, reporting of awards, 21
Das Obligationenrecht als Teil des heutigen römischen Rechts (Friedrich Carl von Savigny), 116–117
Dato, Eduardo, 190–191
Daube, David, 72
Dawson, J. P., 95
de Castro, F., 175
de Jong, F. J., 151
Defamation and Verbal Injury (Frank Cooper), 70
Defective Premises Act 1972, 33
Degg v. *Midland Railway Co.*, 39
Denning, Lord, 11, 15, 19–20, 23, 24, 25, 26
Devlin, Lord, 25
Diego, Felipe Clemente de, 176
Dilhorne, Viscount, 16
Diplock, Lord, 34
Directors Liability Act 1890, 27
dissenting judgment, 24
doctrine (France), 89, 95–100
doctrine of *aemulatio vicini*, 66–67
doctrine of common employment, 38–39, 44
Donoghue v. *Stevenson*, 17, 23–24, 60–61
Drion, J., 150, 151
Duman, Daniel, 41

Dumbreck v. *Robert Addie and Sons*, 2–3
Dunedin, Lord, 60, 64–65, 67, 79–80
Dutch Civil Code, 2
  CC 1838,
    article 1374, 153
    article 1401, 143–144, 146, 147
    article 1402, 143
  CC 1838, 143
  CC 1838, 148
  CC 1992
    book 6
      article 101, 158
      article 107*a*, 164
      article 162, 152, 154, 157–158
      article 2, 153
      article 248, 153
    book 7
      article 658, 164
  CC 1992, 143
  CC Napoleonic
    article 1382, 143, 144
    article 1383, 143
duty of care, 20–21
  Donoghue v. *Stevenson*, 23, 60–61
  England
    first judicial recognition of general duty, 23
    refused because of presence of statutory remedy, 60–61
  Scotland, 60–61
Dynen v. *Leach*, 39

Edinburgh Law Review, 74
Edinburgh University, Chair of Scots Law, 71–72
Eggens, J., 151
Elliot, Derek, 56
Employer's Liability (Defective Equipment) Act 1969, 27
Employers and Workmen Act 1875, 43–44
Employers' Liability Act 1880, 36, 42–48, 53, 57
England
  academics, contribution to legal change, 7–8, 18–20
  compensation for occupational injury, 36–37
    Common Law developments, 37–42
  fault liability, 14, 33–35
    judicial development, 14–27, 33–34
    statutory development, 27–33, 34–35
  judge-made law, sources of, 17–20
  judges
    appointment of, 15–17
    class and background, 41
    contribution to legal change, 3–4, 5
    discovering law, 4
    ideology, 25–27
  post-Beveridge, 57–58
  structure and style of litigation, 20–25
  workmen's compensation, 48–50
Esmein, A., 105, 107
Esser, Josef, 115, 134
European Convention on Human Rights, 216
European law, France, 89
Expropriation Act (Spain 1954), 188–189
Eyssell, A. P. Th, 146, 147, 161

Factory Act 1844, 36
Fahrlässigkeit (negligence), 130
Farwell v. *Boston and Worcester Railroad Corporation*, 38–39
fault liability, themes of enquiry, 1–2
Faure, Felix, 105
fellow-servant rule, 40, 43, 44–45
Fisher, Matthew, 72
Florijn, E. O. H. P., 145, 148
football club, liability for escaping balls, 131–132
Foyer, Jean, 109
France. *See also* French Civil Code
  academics, contribution to legal change, 7, 90
  automobile law, 3
  courts, 91–94
  industrial accidents, 103–106
  judiciary, 100–101
    creation of law by, 4, 89–90

France (*cont.*)
 la doctrine, 89, 95–100
 legislature, 91
 motor vehicle accidents, 106–107
  finding a remedy in tort, 107–110
  influence of interest groups, 111–112
  legislative intervention, 110–111
 overview, 100–101
 sources of law, 89–90
Franken, 150
Fraser, Lord, 74
French Civil Code, 90, 91
 Article 1165, 99
 Article 1382, 97, 102, 103, 107
 Article 1383, 102–103, 107
 Article 1384
  (1), 100, 103–109, 112
 Article 1384, 99
 Article 1384, 109–110
 Article 1385, 104, 108–110
 Article 1386, 103, 104
 Article 4, 92
 Article 5, 91–92, 94
 Articles 1382–1386, 91
 interpretation of, 91–93
French Code of Criminal Procedure (*Code d'Instruction Criminelle*)
 1808, art. 1, 183
 1910, art. 51, 184

General Council of the Bar, 54
Gény, François, 95–96
Germany
 academics, contribution to legal change, 7
 Accident Insurance Act (*Unfallversicherungsgesetz*) 1884, 127–128
 courts attempt to work within BGB fault liability, 129–135
 industrial accidents, 123
 judges, creation of law by, 4
 legislation, motivation for, 128–129
 Liability Act (*Reichshaftpflichtgesetz*) 1871, 123, 127
 overview, 114–115
 reference to foreign law, 118, 119, 137, 138
 strict liability for animals, 135–141
 strict liability for railway operators
  in Prussia, 115–120
  outside Prussia, 121–122
 workmen's compensation, legislators motivations, 3
Gladstone, William Ewart, 44, 46
Glegg, Arthur, *Practical Treatise on the Law of Reparation*, 70
Goff, Lord, 19
Goodhart, A. L., 20, 25
Gratama J, 146
Grizzle v. *Frost*, 40
Guegan-Lecuyer, A., 111
Guest, A. G., 19–20
Guthrie Smith, John
 Treatise on the Law of Reparation, 70
Gutteridge, Harold, 18, 29

Hailsham, Lord, 16, 24–25
Haldane Society of Socialist Lawyers, 54
Halpérin, Jean-Louis, 105
Halsbury LC, 15–16
handelsbalken, 200
Hand-formula, 204, 205, 206, 207
Hand-Posner formula, 206–207, 208
Hanworth, Lord, 29
Heath, Edward, 56
Heaven v. *Pender*, 68
Hedley Byrne & Co. Ltd v. *Heller & Partners Ltd*, 22, 34
Heemskerk, Theo, 147, 148, 152
Hellner, Jan, 7, 206–207, 213, 228
 Skadeståndsrätt, 206
historical approach to interpretation, 92
Hoechst AG v. *Commission of the European Communities*, 86
Hope, Lord, 74
House of Lords
 Appellate Committee, 14–15
 presumption of uniformity of Scots and English law, 63–64
Human Rights Act 1998, s. 4(6)(a), 84
Hume, David, 60
Hunter v. *Hanley*, 77–78

Hunting Act (Spain 1970), 181
Hutchinson v. *York, Newcastle and Berwick Railway Company*, 39

ice hockey spectator hit by puck, 132–133
ice on paths, 131
Industrial Accidents Act (Netherlands 1901 '*Ongevallenwet*'), 163, 166
Industrial Injuries Act 1946, 53
infected meat, sale of, 133–134
Instituto de Reformas Sociales, 190
Ison, Terence, 56

Jamin, C., 95
Jand'heur case, 100, 108, 111
Jestaz, P., 95
Jhering, Rudolph von, 114
Johnston v. *NEI International Combustion Ltd*, 87
Josserand, Louis, 92
Journal of Jurisprudence, 71
Juridical Review, 71, 74
jurisprudence, France, 89

Kahn-Freund, O., 18
Kantorowicz, Hermann, 2
Kappeyne van de Coppello, Joannes (Jan), 148, 149
Karlgren CJ, Hjalmar, 202
Kemp and Dougall v. *Darngavil Coal Co.*, 67–68
Kennedy v. *Glenbelle*, 74

l'école de l'exégèse, 92
l'école de la libre recherché scientifique, 92–93
Labbé, Joseph-Emile, 95, 97, 104
lagboken, 200
Lambert, Edouard, 96
land owners' obligation to disperse sand or salt on ice on paths, 131
Laski, Harold, 16
Law Commission (UK), 32
Law Hospital NHS Trust v. *Lord Advocate*, 79
Law of Delict in Scotland (D. M. Walker), 70–71, 73, 75
Law of Libel and Slander (John Borthwick), 70
Law of Nuisance (James Broun), 70
Law Reform (Contributory Negligence) Act 1945, 40
  s. 1(1), 31
Law Reform (Personal Injuries) Act 1948, 55
Law Reform Committee (UK), 8, 9, 32
Law Revision Committee (UK), 28–32, 34
Lawson, F. H., 5, 72
legislators, constraints and motivations, 2–3
Lester, V. Markham, 45, 46–47
lex Acquiliae, 121
Ley Adicional a la Orgánica del Poder Judicial 14 October 1882, Art. 50, 170
Ley de Bases (12 June 1931), 191
Ley de Bases de la Seguridad social (28 December 1963), 192
Ley de Caza (Hunting Act) 1970, 181
Ley de Expropiación Forzosa (Expropriation Act) 1954, 188–189
Ley de Responsabilidad Civil de los Funcionarios Públicos (Civil Liability of Civil Servants Act) 5 April 1904
  Art. 1, 188
Ley Fundamental (17 May 1958), 192
Ley General para la Defensa de los Consumidores y Usuarios (Consumer Protection Act) 1984, 182–183
Ley Orgánica de Protección Civil del Derecho al Honor, a la Intimidad Personal y Familiar y a la Propia Imagen (5 May 1982), 182
Ley Provisional sobre Organización del Poder Judicial (Organization of the Judicial Power Provisional Act) 18 September 1870, 169–170

Ley Régimen Jurídico de la Administración del Estado (State Administration Act) 1957, 189
Lindenbaum v. *Cohen*, 143, 147, 148, 152, 161, 167
Llewellyn-Jones, Frederick, 28
lobbying, 9
Loder J, 146
loi Badinter, 110–111
luxury animals, 140

Macdonald, Alexander, 44
Macphail, Lord, 87
Mayor of Bradford v. *Pickles*, 66–67
McFarlane v. *Tayside Health Board*, 76
McKechnie, Hector, 67, 70
McNair J, 16, 29, 77
Meijers, Eduard, 149, 150–151, 167
Micosta SA v. *Shetland Islands Council*, 80
Mining Journal, 45
ministère public, 99
Modderman, Anthony, 148–149
Molengraaff, W. L. P. A., 146
Monckton Committee, 54–55
Monckton, Sir Walter, 54
Montagu, Lord Robert, 42–43
Montés Penadés, Vicente Luis, 178–179
Morgan v. *Vale of Neath Railway Co.*, 39
Motor Traffic Damage Act (Sweden 1975), 219
  section 33, 220
Motor Traffic Insurers Association (*trafikförsäkringsföreningen*, TFF), 220
Mühler, Heinrich Gottlob, 117–118
Munch CJ, 209
Murphy v. *Brentwood District Council*, 33

Nadaud, Martin, 105
National Association for the Promotion of Social Science, 44
National Fund for Health Insurance (CNAM), 106
National Insurance (Industrial Injuries) Act 1946, 37
Netherlands. *See also* Dutch Civil Code
  academics, contribution to legal change, 7, 9
  impetus to reform tort liability, 142–144
  judges
    contribution to reform fault liability, 144–148, 154–159
    creation of law by, 4, 5
    perception of role *vis-à-vis* the legislature, 159–162
  legislative change to reform fault liability, 148–154
    importance, 162–164
    reasons for, 165–167
  overview, 167–168
  statutory insurance, 164
  Supreme Court, 144–145, 147–148
  traffic liability, 157, 164
  workmen's compensation, legislators motivations, 3
Newcastle Programme, 46
Nordensson, Ulf K., 213, 214, 219
Nordic/Swedish Model, 201–202, 211, 218–219, 224–225
  1950 proposal, 211–212
  1951–1971 proposals, 212–213
  1972 Government Bill, 213–214
  Occupational Compensation scheme, 223–224
  Patient insurance scheme, 222–223
  Pharmaceutical insurance scheme, 220–221
  Traffic insurance scheme, 219–220
note d'arrêt, 95
Nuclear Energy Act (Spain 1964), 181

Occupational compensation scheme, Nordic/Swedish Model, 223–224
Occupiers Liability Act 1957, 32, 82
occupiers' liability, 2–3, 64–65
Occupiers' Liability (Scotland) Act 1960, 81
ordonnances, 89
Ormond v. *Holland & Holland*, 39

parents' liability for damages caused by their children, 173
Paterson v. *Wallace*, 39
Patient Injuries Act (*patientskadelagen*) 1996, 222, 225
Patient Insurance scheme, Nordic/ Swedish Model, 222–223
Patrick, Lord, 78
Pearson Commission (Royal Commission on Civil Liability and Compensation for Personal Injuries), 56–57
Pearson, Lord, 56
Pérez González, B., 175
Pharmaceutical Association (*Läkemedelsföreningen*, LFF), 221
Pharmaceutical Insurance scheme, Nordic/Swedish Model, 220–221
Picard, Maurice, 109
Picazo, Díez, 174
Pitlo, A., 149
Planiol, Marcel Ferdinand, 97
In re an arbitration between Polemis and another and Furness, Withy and Company Limited, 33–34
Pollock, F., 19
Posner, Richard, 206
Potts v. *Port Carlisle Dock Co.*, 39
Practical Treatise on the Law of Reparation (Arthur Glegg), 70
Priestley v. *Fowler*, 37–38, 40–41, 42
Pringsheim, Fritz, 72
pro damnato principle, 172
Product Liability Act (Spain 1994), 183
Proposals for Reform of the Law of Obligations and the Law of Prescription (France 2005), 107
Prussian Railway Act; Preußisches Gesetz über die Eisenbahnunternehmungen 3 November 1838
  §25
    content, 119–120
    genesis, 117
    §25, 115–119
    §25, 122–123, 124

Radcliffe, Lord, 14, 16, 26
Radetzki, Marcus, *Skadeståndsrätt*, 206
Railroad Traffic Act (Sweden 1985), 230
Reform Act 1867, 43
Reform Act 1884, 46
règlements, 89
Regout, Minister, 147
Reichshaftpflichtgesetz (RHPflG, Liability Act of the Reich) 1871, 123, 127
Reid, Lord, 16, 22, 26–27
Reparation for Mental Harm (Scotland) Bill, 83
RHM Bakeries v. *Strathclyde Regional Council*, 74
Rights of Relatives to Damages (Mesothelioma) (Scotland) Act 2007, 81
Rijksverzekeringsbank (Public Insurance Bureau), 164
Ripert, Georges, 97
Road Traffic Act (Spain 24 December 1962), 180–181
Road Traffic Regulation (*Straßenverkehrsordnung*, StVO), 135
Robens Committee on Health and Safety at Work, 56
Robert Addie & Sons (Collieries) Ltd v. *Dumbreck*, 81
Robertson v. *Fleming*, 63
Robertson, Lord, 65–66
Rodger of Earlsferry, Lord, 73, 78–79, 87, 88
Rodière, René, 96
Russell-Jones, A., 54
Rylands v. *Fletcher*, 65–66, 74

Salas Carceller, Antonio, 178–179
Saleilles, Raymond, 95–96, 104–105, 113
Sankey, Lord, 24–25, 28, 30
Santos Briz, Jaime, 178
Scholten, Paul, 149, 166–167

Schulz, Fritz, 72
Schuster, Sir Claud, 28–29, 30
Scotland
  1850–1932 from *culpa* to duty of care, 61–71
  1932–1999 development of delictual liability, 71–82
  1999 onwards, 82–88
  academics
    contribution to convergence, 70–71
    contribution to development of delictual liability, 71–75
    contribution to legal change, 6
  judges
    contribution to convergence, 61–71
    contribution to development of delictual liability, 71–82
    contribution to legal change, 3–4
    patterns of recruitment, 76–78, 83–84
  overview, 59–61
  use of foreign law, 85–86
Scotland Act 1998, s. 29, 84
Scots Law Times, 71, 72
Scottish Law Review, 71
Scottish legislation, influence of national pride, 2–3
Shaw of Dunfermline, Lord, 68–69
Shaw, Lord, 64–65
Simon LC, Viscount, 66
Simonds, Lord, 26
Singer v. *Ivens*, 145–147, 161
Skadeståndslag 1972
  207 (Tort Liability Act), 198, 201, 202–203, 214, 215, 220
    section 1, 216, 217, 226, 227
    section 2, 215–218, 226, 227
    section 3, 215
    section 4, 216, 218
    section 6, 226
Skadeståndsrätt (Jan Hellner and Marcus Radetzki), 206
Smith (Maloco) v. *Littlewoods*, 75
Smith, Sir Thomas, 64, 67, 72, 73–74
Snijders, Wouter, 151
Somervell, Donald, 28
Spain
  compensation for work injuries, 189–195
  judicial contribution to legal change, 172–174
    influential individuals, 174–179
  jurisdictions, 169–170
  legislative change, 179–183
  legislative framework, 171–172
  liability of the public administration, 188–189
  overview, 195–197
  tort law in the Criminal Code, 183–188
  workmen's compensation, legislators motivations, 3
Spanish Civil Code
  article 1104, 171
  article 1902, 171, 186
  article 1903, 187, 188
  article 1968, 186
  articles 1902–1910, 171
Spanish Constitution 1978,
  Art. 18.1, 182
  Art. 20.1, 182
  Art. 41, 193
Spanish Criminal Code
  1848
    Art. 121, 185
    Art. 15, 185
  1850, 185–186
  1995, 186
Spanish Supreme Court, 169–170
  STS 14 December 1894, 189
  STS 14 May 1968, 172
  STS 17 June 1903, 191
  STS 17 March 1981, 178
  STS 31 October 1931, 172
  STS 8 April 2006, 188
Stallybrass, W. T. S., 8, 30–31
State Administration Act (Spain 1957), 189
Steyn, Lord, 76
Stormonth Darling, Lord, 68
Strahl, Ivar, 7, 211–212
Street, Harry, 56
Strömbäck, Erland, 214, 219

Sweden
  academics, contribution to legal change, 7
  civil law system, 199–200
    implications for tort law, 200–202
  fault liability
    in legislation, 1850–1972, 210–211
    in the courts, 202
  judges, creation of law by, 5–6
  strict liability, 228
    examples of legislation with rules on, 229–230
    without statutory support, 228–229
  tort law and insurance, 225
    contributory conduct of the victim in cases of personal injury, 227
    employer and employee liability, 226
    reduction of damages, 227
Swedish Criminal Act (1864), 210
Swedish Criminal Code (*brottsbalken*), 211
Swedish Environmental Code, chapter 32, 229–230
Swedish Model. *See Nordic/Swedish Model*
Swedish Supreme Court
  justices, 202–203
  NJA 1981 p. 683 (paving-stone), 204–208
  NJA 1993 p. 149 (golf player), 204, 205, 208–210
  style of decisions, 204

Teisseire, 97
teleological methodology, 92
Texto Articulado de la Seguridad Social, Decree (21 April 1966), 192–193
Thatcher, Margaret, 57
Tort Liability Act (Sweden 1972), 198, 201, 202–203, 214, 220
  basic rule (culpa rule), 215
  chapter 2
    section 1, 216, 217
    section 2, 215
    section 3, 215
    section 4, 216
  chapter 3
    section 1, 226
    section 6, 226
  chapter 3, 218
  chapter 4, section 1, 217, 226
  chapter 6
    section 1, 227
    section 2, 227
  children, 216–217
  contributory conduct of the victim in cases of personal injury, 227
  employers and employees, 217, 226
  Kränkning, 215–216
  mentally handicapped tortfeasors, 217
  public bodies, 217–218
  pure economic loss, 215
  violation of personal integrity, 215–216
Trades Union Congress (TUC), 43–44, 45, 46, 48–49, 50, 53, 54, 55
Traffic Insurance scheme, Nordic/Swedish Model, 219–220
Trafikskadelag 1975, 1410 (Motor Traffic Damage Act), 219
traités, 89
Treatise on the Law of Reparation (John Guthrie Smith), 70
Tunc, André, 8–9, 109, 110–111

Uist, Lord, 87
Unfallversicherungsgesetz (Accident Insurance Act) of 1884, 127–128
unfortunate matter of events, 155–156
Unglück, 115
Universities (Scotland) Act 1858, 70–71
unjust enrichment *(enrichissement sans cause)*, 96
Unrecht, 115

Valverde, C. Valverde, 176
Van Maanen, G. E., 144, 161
van Maarseveen, Johannes Henricus, 150
Van Rhijn committee, 166

Verein der Privat-Eisenbahnen, 125
Verkehrssicherungspflichten
  by extending duties of care, 134–135
  courts extension of, 133–134
  definitions, 130–133
Viney, G., 108, 110, 111
volenti non fit injuria, 40, 44
von Bar, Christian, 122, 133
von Bar, Ludwig, 138
von Savigny, Friedrich Carl, 116–119, 122
  Das Obligationenrecht als Teil des heutigen römischen Rechts, 116–117
Vranken, J. B. M., 159

Walker, D. M., *Law of Delict in Scotland*, 70–71, 73, 75
Wallin CJ, Gösta, 213
Watson, Alan, 2, 9
Watson, Lord, 11, 66–67, 68
Watt v. *Jamieson*, 74
Weekblad van het Recht, 148–149
Wensleydale, Lord, 64
Weslin, Per-Axel, 213
Whitty, N. R., 67
Wiggett v. *Fox*, 39
Wigmore v. *Jay*, 39
Wilson v. *Merry and Cunningham*, 39
Winfield, Percy, 8, 30–31
Workmen's Compensation Act (France 1898), 105–106
Workmen's Compensation Act 1897, 36–37, 47, 48–49, 57
Workmen's Compensation Act 1900, 49
Wright v. *Stoddard International plc*, 87
Wright, Lord, 30–31

Zimmermann, Reinhard, 115, 122
Zürich (insurance company), 221
Zutphen neighbour case, 146–147, 161

For EU product safety concerns, contact us at Calle de José Abascal, 56–1°,
28003 Madrid, Spain or eugpsr@cambridge.org.

www.ingramcontent.com/pod-product-compliance
Lightning Source LLC
LaVergne TN
LVHW052308200926
848481LV00002B/502